# Utah

Tom and Gayen Wharton
Photography by Tom Till

COMPASS AMERICAN GUIDES
An Imprint of Fodor's Travel Publications

# Utah

## Fifth Edition

Compass American Guides and colophon are trademarks of Random House, Inc.
Fodor's is a registered trademark of Random House, Inc.

**Compass American Guides, Inc., 5332 College Ave., Suite 201, Oakland, CA 94618, USA**
ISBN: 0-679-00645-1

Managing Editor: Kit Duane
Editors: Julia Dillon, Cheryl Koehler
Photography Editor: Christopher Burt
Production House: Twin Age Ltd., Hong Kong
Manufactured in China

Contributing Editors: Barry Parr, Deke Castleman
Designers: Christopher Burt, David Hurst
Map Design: Mark Stroud, Moon Street Cartography

First published in 1991 by Compass American Guides, Inc., 5332 College Ave., Suite 201, Oakland, CA 94618, USA

10 9 8 7 6 5 4 3 2 1

## ACKNOWLEDGMENTS

WE WOULD LIKE TO THANK editor Barry Parr for patiently reviewing and re-reviewing our manuscript. Not only was Barry an editor, but a friend. Tom Till's fine photographs reveal the diversity of Utah's landscapes. We also wish to thank the following individuals: Bob Donohoe, our expert reader, for invaluable advice; Gary Topping, Manuscripts Curator of the Utah State Historical Society; the society's Photograph and Map Librarian, Susan Whetstone, who helped us track down the historical photos used in the book; the late Dr. William Lee Stokes, our geology professor at the University of Utah, who graciously edited our text for accuracy; and Genevieve Atwood. Mark Goodwin of U.C. Berkeley contributed much on the subject of dinosaurs. The Utah Wilderness Association's Dick Carter, Lagoon's Peter and David Freed, the Pack Creek Ranch's Ken Sleight, Kim Burningham, John Gallivan, Monsignor Jerome Stoeffel, and modern-day mountain man Timothy Toker Many Hats all made themselves available for interviews. Rick Reese of the Utah Geographic Series, Ward Roylance, and Mel Davis and John Veranth of Wasatch Publishers were generous in granting permission to quote from their books. Joe Rutherford of the Utah Travel Council, and the staff of the Salt Lake County Convention and Visitors Bureau were also extremely helpful. Dawn House and Ralph Wheeler helped edit the chapter on the Mormon Church for accuracy. Other institutions providing invaluable help include: Utah Division of Wildlife Resources, Utah Division of Parks and Recreation, National Park Service, U.S. Forest Service, Bureau of Land Management, Utah Symphony, Utah Opera Company, Ririe-Woodbury Dance Company, Ballet West, Pioneer Memorial Theatre, Salt Lake Acting Company, Repertory Dance Theater, University of Utah, Brigham Young University, Utah State University, Weber State College, and Southern Utah State College. Tom's long-time employer, *The Salt Lake Tribune*, has given him a chance to explore Utah for the past 20 years. For this, he is extremely grateful. Finally, we would like to thank our children—Emma, Jacob, Rawl, and Bryer—for putting up with their parents' book-writing effort, which took precious time away from family activities.

The publishers would like to thank: **Tim Kelly** for his photograph on p. 150; **Stephen Trimble** for his photographs on pp. 101, 107, 111, 298, and 299; the **University of Utah Museum of Fine Arts** for photographs on p. 124 (Janus mask, 1983.001.002; Greek vase, 1990.001.001; Chinese camel, 1977.240; Maori carving, 1972.034.001) and p. 125 (Vaccaro painting, 1973.080.005.005; Fragonard painting, 1993.034.013); the **Peabody Museum at Yale University** for the mural on pp. 168-169; and Joel Sternfeld, courtesy Pace/MacGill Gallery, New York, for the photograph on page 153.

*To our parents, Max and Althea Bennett and Jack and Vi Wharton,*
*who encouraged us to write, and instilled in us their love of travel.*

# C O N T E N T S

OVERVIEW ............................8
*Overview Map of Utah* ........................7

INTRODUCTION ..................10

STORIES IN STONE:
UTAH'S GEOLOGY ........................12
The Colorado Plateau....................13
Basin and Range ..............................16
Middle Rocky Mountain Province.....19
Prehistoric Life ............................20

THE FIRST UTAHNS ....................25
The Ancestral Puebloans ..................26
The Fremont Indians.......................27
Finding Indian Sites .........................28
The Fate of the Ancient Ones...........33
The Later Tribes .............................35
Meeting Contemporary Indians ........42

THE EARLY EXPLORERS .................44
The Spanish Explorers.......................44
*Utah History Map* ...........................47
Mountain Men.................................49
Jedediah Smith .................................54
John Wesley Powell............................56

THE MORMON PIONEERS .............62
The Founding of
    the Mormon Church....................62
Persecution......................................64
Exodus to Utah ...............................65
Establishing Zion .............................69
End of Isolation...............................73
Growth of Zion ...............................81
Entrance to the Union......................86
The Mormons Today........................89

SALT LAKE CITY ...............................97
Salt Lake City, Old and New .............98
*Map of Salt Lake City*.....................102
Temple Square.......................103
Other Faiths .................................109
Exploring the City...........................110
Along the Eastern Bench ................119
The University of Utah....................119
The Salt Lake Stage ........................127
Salt Lake Music ............................130
Salt Lake Dance..............................132

THE WASATCH FRONT .................136
The Mountains ..............................136
*Map of the Wasatch Front*..................138
Provo and Utah County .................139
South of Provo...............................144
Ogden ...........................................146
Cache County ................................149

NORTHEASTERN UTAH:
MOUNTAINS & DINOSAURS ...154
*Map of Northeastern Utah* ................155
The High Uintas ............................156
Reservoir Recreation........................160
Flaming Gorge ...............................163
Brown's Park..................................165
Dinosaur National Monument........166
Towns Around the Uintas...............175
Price Area.......................................176

GREAT BASIN .................................179
The Pony Express ...........................182
*Map of West Central Utah*................183
The Railroad ..................................184
Booms and Busts ...........................188

Island Ranges, Inland Sea ...............192
Lakeside Resorts ...........................196
The Bonneville Speedway...............199
*Map of Northern Utah* .............204-205
SOUTHERN UTAH..........................206
*Map of Southwestern Utah*................208
South Toward Cedar City...............209
Cedar City...................................210
Cedar Breaks
    National Monument ..................213
Zion National Park........................215
St. George—Utah's Dixie................220
Bryce Canyon...............................224
Kodachrome Basin .......................228
Grand Staircase–Escalante
    National Monument ..................229
*Map of Southeastern Utah* .........234-235
Capitol Reef National Park.............236
*Map of Capitol Reef National Park*....237
The San Rafael Swell .....................239
Green River ..................................240
Goblin Valley ...............................241
Lake Powell .................................243
Moab..........................................246
Arches National Park.....................250
Canyonlands Country.....................256
Mountain Escapes .........................263
The Grand Circle ..........................266

SKIING UTAH: THE GREATEST
    SNOW ON EARTH ....................276
History of Skiing in Utah ...............277
*Map of Utah Ski Areas*....................278
Little Cottonwood Canyon .............281
Big Cottonwood Canyon ...............284
Park City Ski Areas........................285
Sundance......................................287

Ogden Valley Resorts......................288
Northern Utah ..............................289
Southern Utah Resorts ...................290
Cross-Country Skiing......................292
Snowmobiling...............................294
2002 Winter Olympic Games .........296
*Map of Olympic Venues*...................301
PRACTICAL INFORMATION.........302
Finding Your Way
    Around Utah Cities....................302
Climate ........................................302
About Utah Lodging ......................303
About Utah Restaurants .................304
Utah's Liquor Laws.........................304
*Map of Utah towns with lodging*
    *and restaurant listings* ...................305
Lodging and Restaurants.................306
Festivals and Events.........................322
Utah's Public Lands ........................324
Professional Sports Teams................330
General Information Resources .......331

RECOMMENDED
    READING .................................334
Description and Travel....................334
History.........................................335
Hiking, Bicycling, Skiing,
    and Climbing ............................336
River-Running................................337
Archaeology..................................337
Natural Sciences ............................338
Reference......................................338
Miscellaneous................................338
INDEX...........................................340

# Literary Extracts

The Dominguez-Escalante Journal, 1776 .................................................45
Stanley Vestal *on mountain man Jim Bridger* ........................................50
*A Rocky Mountain tale* ...........................................................................59
John Wesley Powell *on exploring the Colorado River* ...........................60
Book of Mormon ....................................................................................63
Brigham Young and Sir Richard Burton *on polygamy* ..........................76
Diary of Hosea Stout, 1844-61 .............................................................82
Philip L. Fradkin *on water in an arid land* ...........................................95
Mark Twain *on Salt Lake City* .............................................................112
Arthur Conan Doyle *brings Sherlock Holmes to Utah* .........................181
Edward Abbey *on the National Park Service* .......................................207
Alfred A. Knopf *on the National Parks* ...............................................207
Zane Grey *on riders of the purple sage* ...............................................262

# Topical Essays

Dispute between Jim Bridger and the Mormons ....................................80
Church of Jesus Christ of Latter-day Saints ......................................90-93
Lagoon: A Pioneering Amusement Park ..............................................115
Utah Museum of Fine Arts .............................................................124-125
Robert Redford's Sundance Institute ..............................................134-135
Utah's Jurassic Park ............................................................................167
Genevieve Atwood: Pioneering Geologist ...........................................201
Utah's Natural Bridges ........................................................................253
Ken Sleight: Pioneering River-Runner ...........................................273-275

# Maps

Utah Overview .......................7
Utah History .......................47
Salt Lake City .....................102
Wasatch Front ....................138
Northeastern Utah ..............155
West Central Utah ...............183
Northern Utah ..............204-205
Southwestern Utah .........................208
Southeastern Utah ..................234-235
Capitol Reef National Park ............237
Utah Ski Areas ..............................278
2002 Winter Olympic Venues ........301
Lodging and Restaurants ...............305

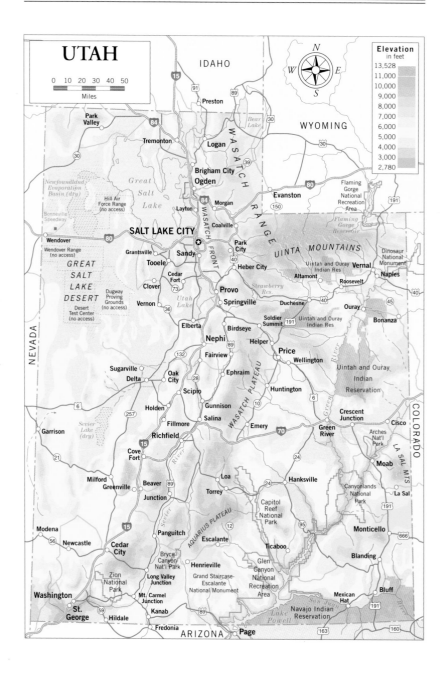

# UTAH

0  10  20  30  40  50
Miles

**Elevation**
in feet

| | |
|---|---|
| 13,528 | |
| 11,000 | |
| 10,000 | |
| 9,000 | |
| 8,000 | |
| 7,000 | |
| 6,000 | |
| 5,000 | |
| 4,000 | |
| 3,000 | |
| 2,780 | |

IDAHO

WYOMING

Preston

Park
Valley

Tremonton

Logan

*Bear
Lake*

**Brigham City**
**Ogden**

Evanston

Flaming
Gorge
National
Recreation
Area

*Newfoundland
Evaporation
Basin (dry)*

*Great
Salt
Lake*

Hill Air
Force Range
(no access)

Morgan

Layton

Coalville

*Flaming
Gorge
Reservoir*

Bonneville
Speedway

**SALT LAKE CITY**

Wendover

Wendover Range
(no access)

Park
City

UINTA  MOUNTAINS

Dinosaur
National
Monument

Grantsville

Sandy

Heber City

Uintah and Ouray
Indian Res

**Vernal**

Naples

*GREAT
SALT
LAKE
DESERT*

Tooele

Cedar
Fort

Altamont

Roosevelt

Clover

Dugway
Proving
Grounds
(no access)

*Utah
Lake*

**Provo**

Springville

*Strawberry
Res.*

Duchesne

Ouray

Desert
Test Center
(no access)

Vernon

Bonanza

Elberta

Soldier
Summit

Uintah and Ouray
Indian Res

NEVADA

Birdseye

**Nephi**

Helper

Sugarville

Fairview

**Price**

Wellington

Uintah and Ouray
Indian
Reservation

Delta

Oak
City

Ephraim

Scipio

Huntington

Holden

Gunnison

Salina

*WASATCH PLATEAU*

Crescent
Junction

Cisco

*Sevier
Lake
(dry)*

Fillmore

Emery

Green
River

Arches
Nat'l
Park

Garrison

Richfield

Moab

Cove
Fort

Milford
Greenville

Beaver

Loa

Hanksville

Canyonlands
National
Park

La Sal

*LA SAL MTS*

Junction

Torrey

Capitol
Reef
National
Park

Modena

Newcastle

Panguitch

*AQUARIUS PLATEAU*

Escalante

Monticello

Cedar
City

Ticaboo

Blanding

Bryce
Canyon
Nat'l Park

Henrieville

Glen
Canyon
National
Recreation
Area

Washington

Zion
National
Park

Long Valley
Junction

Grand Staircase-
Escalante
National Monument

Mexican
Hat

Bluff

**St.
George**

Hildale

Mt. Carmel
Junction

Kanab

*Lake
Powell*

Navajo Indian
Reservation

Fredonia

ARIZONA

Page

COLORADO

# O V E R V I E W

◆ SALT LAKE CITY *pages 97–135*

On July 24, 1847, Brigham Young arrived in the **Great Salt Lake Valley** with an advance team of 148, and that very day, they began building a settlement they called Deseret. The first town they founded, Salt Lake City, remains the centerpiece of the highly populated Wasatch Front, a 175-mile swath of land which lies at the base of the Wasatch Range and stretches from Provo north to Ogden. Both Utah's state capital and world headquarters of the Church of Latter-day Saints, Salt Lake City boasts fine museums, vibrant theaters, and sophisticated restaurants, in addition to the spectacular **Mormon Temple** and **Tabernacle** in **Temple Square**. Salt Lake City will host the 2002 Winter Olympics.

**1** WASATCH RANGE *pages 136–153*
The **Wasatch Range** draws hikers to seven wilderness areas, and in winter, skiers to world famous ski resorts. North of the city, **Provo** is home to **Brigham Young University**.

**2** NORTHEASTERN UTAH
*pages 154–178*
A favorite camping, hiking, and fishing destination, northeastern Utah is dominated by the wild and undeveloped **Uinta Mountains**, a forested range interspersed with four rivers and over 1,000 lakes. At **Flaming Gorge**, the **Green River** draws river rafters,

while the reservoir is famed for its massive trout. In stark contrast to this alpine region is the **Uinta Basin,** today a desolate landscape of red, tan, and white rock —but 145 million years ago, a lush, verdant land where dinosaurs roamed.

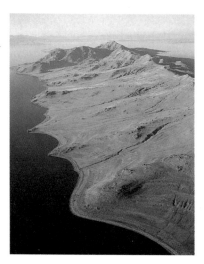

**3** GREAT BASIN  *pages 179–205*

Lying in west central Utah, stretching west toward Nevada from the Wasatch Front, the Great Basin encompasses the **Bonneville Salt Flats,** where many an automobile speed record has been set. Here too can be found the **Great Salt Lake** and its island mountains, including **Antelope Island.** The area's mining past is revealed in ghost towns with names such as Topaz, Gold Hill, and Mercur.

**4** SOUTHERN UTAH  *pages 206–275*

From the badland topography of **Cedar Breaks National Monument** to the towering 3,000-foot canyon walls of **Zion National Park,** southern Utah is nothing short of spectacular. **Bryce Canyon**—which can turn white, orange, yellow, red, or purple, depending on the time of day—is actually a series of 14 ampitheaters extending 1,000 feet down a limestone plateau. **Kodachrome Basin** is a scenic valley full of towering stone chimneys, while

**Escalante–Grand Staircase National Monument** is red-rock country, with waterfalls, small arches, and an Ancestral Puebloan ruin. In **Cathedral Valley** at **Capitol Reef National Park,** huge monolithic sandstone remnants form jutting buttes that resemble Gothic churches in the desert. Awesome **Arches National Park,** with its salmon-colored **Delicate Arch** rock formation, and **Canyonlands National Park,** with its wind-carved, sandstone needles, defy the imagination.

# INTRODUCTION
## A PIONEERING PLACE

ON THE EAST BENCH OF SALT LAKE CITY, A WEATHERED STATUE GAZES silently at the valley below. A brown haze from automobiles and industrial stacks obscures the view slightly to the west, but the blue waters of the Great Salt Lake and the mighty peaks of the Oquirrh Mountains are still visible, as they were on July 24th, 1847, when Brigham Young first looked out from this spot, ending a perilous 1,500-mile journey by declaring, "This is the right place." Could even a wise and visionary man like Young have imagined what Salt Lake City—and, for that matter, all of Utah—would become?

Those who have made Utah their home, from the ancient Indians who built magnificent cliff dwellings in the southern canyons to contemporary scientists who are mapping the DNA of the human genome, have possessed the courageous spirit of true pioneers.

This land brings out a conservative, independent streak in people: Utah's official motto is *Industry;* its state symbol is the beehive. Utahns take their work seriously.

Utah's earliest residents may not have known much about their homeland's geography and geology when they arrived, but they were quick studies. Largely by trial and error, the Native Americans, mountain men, explorers, and first settlers learned how to make a living from the land.

In the mid-19th century, newcomers from across the plains brought a distinctive, energetic spirit, which the independent mountain men, the Catholic explorer-priests, and even the Indians who preceded them might have respected. These Mormon pioneers sought the freedom to worship God in their own way, and dreamed of turning Utah into a modern-day Zion through hard work and community effort. The soldiers, miners, railroad workers, and other non-Mormon "gentiles" who came later may not have possessed the same religious beliefs, but certainly they were caught up in the pioneering spirit.

This book, to a great degree, is about all sorts of pioneers. It is based on the premise that residents and visitors cannot fully appreciate Utah's magnificent natural and cultural heritage without first understanding the spirit of the people who turned what many regarded as a wasteland into a thriving state.

Many know the story of Utah's most famous pioneer, Brigham Young, a man who knew the value of planning for the future. Young built Salt Lake City from almost nothing, laying it out in wide, square, well-organized blocks. He sent out Mormon settlers to remote corners of the unsettled West, armed with little more than faith, a willingness to work hard, and a rare courage to face the unknown. He is, by most accounts, the archetypal Utah pioneer.

But Utah's pioneering spirit did not die with Brigham Young. Witness the Greek musician, Maurice Abravanel, who came to Utah with the desire of building a world-renowned symphony, and did not retire until his vision became reality. Or consider the team of researchers and doctors at the University of Utah who, for the first time, built an artificial heart and successfully implanted it in a living human being. And remember people like Utah Jazz owner Larry Miller, who spent much of his own money to open the glittering Delta Center in the early 1990s, revitalizing the western part of Salt Lake City.

Evidence of this pioneering spirit can be seen everywhere in the Beehive State. Walk down the clean, wide streets of Salt Lake City, where dozens of new buildings rose in the 1980s, and where business executives and government leaders plot the course of the state into the 21st century. Listen to a symphony, or attend a play, opera, ballet, or modern dance company performance, and savor the enthusiasm of a community willing to support all kinds of artistic endeavors.

Then escape to the wild lands which lie in all directions from the Wasatch Front. Get a sense for the courage of explorer John Wesley Powell by taking a white-water raft trip through Cataract Canyon. Visit the site where the first transcontinental railroad was completed in 1869, to glean some feeling for the exciting day when West and East were joined for the first time. With a pack on your back, hike through one of Utah's five national parks to experience first-hand the incredibly rugged geography that the early explorers, settlers, and prospectors had to face and conquer. As you wander through the High Uintas Wilderness Area, or follow the old Pony Express Trail across the western desert, or bounce up and down in the seat of an old Jeep through an obscure southern Utah canyon, imagine yourself as a mountain man, daring Pony Express rider, or grizzled prospector. The state's wild places still allow visitors to get a sense of what our forefathers faced in this desolate but wonderful land.

# STORIES IN STONE
## UTAH'S GEOLOGY

THERE ARE MANY WAYS TO CONTEMPLATE the geological forces which have shaped Utah. Hike to the top of an alpine peak overlooking the Great Salt Lake Valley and look down on the sprawling metropolitan area. Drive across the desolate Bonneville Salt Flats, where mirages of floating mountains and disappearing lakes shimmer across the glistening, salt-encrusted surface. Listen to the roar of the rapids on a raft trip through Cataract Canyon and watch the colors and shapes of steep sandstone ledges change dramatically along the way. Then fly back over the same country and look out over the convoluted canyons, stately fins, windblown arches, and rock bridges formed by erosion. Wander down a remote, narrow canyon in Zion National Park. Examine the texture of the sandstone closely; feel the warm, red rock with your hands. Ascend an almost vertical cliff. Lie on a hard, smooth rock surface, and study the countless hues.

Nowhere in the world, perhaps, have the elements of earth, wind, and water come together with such drama. Underground forces have heaved and pushed massive plateaus and mountain ranges up more than a mile above sea level. Erosion continues to cut and gouge plateaus into spectacular pinnacles and canyons.

In most places, water, soil, or vegetation covers the rock layers that tell the earth's geological history. Things are different in Utah, which geologist William Lee Stokes called "The Bedrock State" because the rocks over much of the state are so well exposed. Only in the valleys in the western part of the state is the bedrock hidden by a cover of young sediments.

Much of Utah has a high desert climate. Little rain falls, and vegetation is sparse. As a result, rivers and streams cut directly into layers of rock, exposing them for study. Utah is one of the few states where all 13 periods of the geologic time scale are represented in the rock record. Sedimentary layers of rock from every era have yielded thousands of fossils. Even the famed Grand Canyon in Arizona exposes only seven periods of time.

A visitor to Utah can discover great varieties of each basic rock type. Rockhounds can pick up sedimentary, metamorphic, and igneous specimens. Rich and diverse mineral deposits are scattered throughout the state.

One need not be a geologist to appreciate the qualities that make Utah unique. The arrangement of its physical features has dictated the state's human settlement and economic development throughout history, and still shapes its future.

Utah is divided into three major geological provinces: the Colorado Plateau, the Basin and Range, and the Middle Rocky Mountains. The transition areas between geologic provinces are zones, some places tens of miles wide, where features of both provinces occur. Each province extends into adjacent states, and each provides its own unique recreational opportunities and monumental vistas.

## ■ THE COLORADO PLATEAU

The Colorado Plateau covers all of southeastern Utah. It also extends into adjacent areas drained by the Colorado River in Colorado, New Mexico, and Arizona. This sparsely vegetated landscape of plateaus, mesas, deep canyons, sloping foothills, imposing vertical cliffs, and barren badlands, contains some of the world's most unusual scenery. "Here," wrote William Lee Stokes, "is a kingdom of rocks, an arena where the elemental forces of time and weather meet the raw stuff of the earth with nothing to soften or hide the scars of battle."

Most rocks exposed in the Utah part of the Colorado Plateau are sedimentary rocks deposited between 40 and 250 million years ago, when the region was near sea level. Sandstones, often brightly colored, form some of the most dramatic rock outcrops.

Some of these sandstones are fossilized sand dunes, while others are ancient beaches formed when seas advanced and retreated. Vividly colored shales were deposited on mud flats while the gray shales were deposited in lakes and seas.

Fifteen or 20 million years ago, the Colorado Plateau and adjacent areas of western North America were pushed up far above sea level. Most geologists think this movement was related to the forces that cause continental drift. This increase in elevation resulted in new weather patterns, and erosion sped up. With little vegetation to soak it up, rain falling on the young plateau flowed from rivulets to gullies to rivers, carrying off sand and detritus to the ocean. The softer shales eroded fastest, leaving the more resistant sandstones as cliffs and mesas. Following the path of least resistance, the Colorado River and its tributaries in time carved southern Utah into a elaborate maze of canyons and gorges. Visitors to Arches, Zion, Capitol Reef, and Canyonlands national parks can see the impressive sandstone cliffs formed by such erosion.

Erosion has also created the extraordinary number of fins, arches, natural bridges, and reefs found on the Colorado Plateau. Water and ice pluck, cut, break, and wear down sandstone layers. Moving water carves the soft layers of rock from between harder layers. When a layer of harder rock is left standing by itself, it's

*The classic geological formation of Comb Ridge in extreme southeastern Utah.*

called a fin. A good example is the Fiery Furnace in Arches National Park. Natural bridges are formed when water works its way completely through portions of a rock fin (a narrow rock wall).

Flowing water is not the only agent of erosion. Sandstone consists of two parts: sand-sized grains of a mineral (often quartz) form a kind of framework are "bound" (often weakly) by a softer component, such as silica or calcium carbonate. Water standing in pools and potholes can dissolve those binding minerals, loosening grains which are then carried away by wind or water. When water in the cracks between rocks freezes, its expansion pushes sandstone layers apart, causing wide gaps and freeing huge slabs from canyon walls. A fin can become an arch when centuries of exposure to wind, soil moisture, and the freezing and thawing of ice open up a hole which slowly widens in the narrow rock. A sandstone spire is created when a thin wall collapses and leaves behind a solitary monolith.

Several scenic areas of the Colorado Plateau are the remnants of geological uplifts. These appear as gigantic sandstone outcroppings, with the normally horizontal rock strata being tilted almost vertically. Over time, erosion notches crack-like canyons in the upturned sandstone. Like coral reefs to sailors, these near-vertical ridges presented barriers to travel for many pioneers, who called these rock walls "reefs." The San Rafael Reef and Comb Ridge exemplify such reefs.

The mountain ranges found within the Colorado Plateau are also unusual. Geologists describe them as volcanos that never quite erupted, and call them "lacoliths." The La Sal, Abajo, and Henry mountains, as well as Navajo Mountain near Lake Powell, were formed by molten rock pushing up through and into overlying

*Rock strata millions of years in the making are exposed at the confluence of the Green and Colorado Rivers.*

strata, raising up the sedimentary strata into a dome. In many cases erosion, especially glaciation, has removed the upper layers of rock, revealing igneous inner cores. Of these ranges, only Navajo Mountain retains intact its outer shell of sedimentary rock.

On the western edge of the Colorado Plateau are eight plateaus ranging in elevation from 8,000 to 11,000 feet. These run southerly from near the center of the state, with the drainage about equally divided between the Great Basin and the Colorado River. Brian Head Ski Resort, south of Parowan, sits atop such a plateau. Nearby are Bryce Canyon National Park, Cedar Breaks National Monument, and Escalante Grand Staircase National Monument.

In fact, since all of Utah's five national parks are found on the Colorado Plateau, visiting any will help you understand the forces that form this unique and beautiful part of the world. Geological guides are sold at each park visitor center, or you can read interpretive signs along the roads.

The Colorado Plateau contains much of Utah's energy resources. Mines here, now inactive, once produced much of the United States' uranium and radium. Today, numerous Colorado Plateau fields still produce oil and gas. Nearly all of Utah's coal mines are on the Colorado Plateau, and huge reserves of coal, Utah's state rock, remain undeveloped.

## ■ BASIN AND RANGE

Western Utah is part of the Basin and Range province, a region of elongated mountain ranges separated by basins or valleys. Much of this province is part of the Great Basin, an area where water has no escape to the sea. Today, rainfall is sparse and the valleys of most of the Great Basin are no longer filled with water. Toward the end of the last ice age, about 10,000 years ago, perennial rivers fed many lakes in the basins. Utah's Lake Bonneville was the largest. This massive, freshwater inland sea dominated the landscape for at least 15,000 years, covering much of northwest Utah with shallow bays extending into Idaho and Nevada. At one time, it measured over 1,000 feet deep, 145 miles wide, and 346 long.

The pounding waves of Lake Bonneville carved out terraces and benches, many of which are preserved along the mountainsides. Rivers flowing into the lake built deltas which today stand out prominently on the mountains encircling Salt Lake City. Utah's State Capitol stands on one such delta, and the University of Utah on another. Mere remnants of giant Lake Bonneville include the Great Salt Lake, the largest saltwater lake in the Western Hemisphere, and Utah Lake, the state's largest freshwater lake, which drains into the Great Salt Lake by way of the Jordan River. Further west, part of Lake Bonneville evaporated and left behind the 44,000-acre Bonneville Salt Flats. On the east-central edge of the Great Basin lies another souvenir of Lake Bonneville: the Little Sahara Recreation Area (often called Jericho), Utah's largest sand-dune field.

The salinity of the Great Salt Lake results from its position on the floor of the Great Basin, where it receives all the dissolved minerals that would normally be carried to the sea by rivers. As lake water evaporates, minerals become more concentrated in the remaining water. Dozens of salts (in addition to ordinary table salt) saturate (and supersaturate) the Great Salt Lake. The most important products extracted from the lake by large commercial operations are magnesium, potash, and sodium chloride, or table salt.

The Great Salt Lake has several islands, some of which become peninsulas at low water levels. Antelope Island, the largest, is the site of a state park.

About the same time intrusions of magma were forming the lacolith mountains of the Colorado Plateau, intrusions of magma were also being forced toward the earth's surface in western Utah. Large volumes of magma erupted from volcanos. Some of this magma solidified below the surface to form large masses of granitic rock. Deposits of valuable minerals such as gold, silver, and copper were formed in association with these rocks. The world's largest open-pit mine, Bingham Copper Mine in the Oquirrh Range, has produced billions of dollars in ore, mostly copper, but also gold and other minerals.

Farther south, the Tushar Mountains, remnants of extinct volcanos, contain numerous mineral deposits. The Big Rock Candy Mountain, near Marysvale, was named for the distinctive multicolor pattern created by the mountain's various minerals. Iron Mountain and Iron County received their names from the ore deposits found there.

For tens of millions of years, the area that was to become the Great Basin was a broad highland. About 15 million years ago, the area began to stretch in an east-west direction. As the area stretched, it broke into long blocks trending generally north. Alternate blocks sank to form basins or valleys, while the blocks that remained high became ranges.

The Wasatch Range and most other ranges to the west in the Basin and Range province are bounded on one or both sides by faults, long fractures that reach several miles into the earth. As the earth's crust stretches, the brittle upper layer forms faults as it gets pulled apart. The faults are not entirely perpendicular, but rather slope under the basins or valleys. As the crust stretches, the valley side of the fault slides down and moves away from the range, thereby lowering the valley and lengthening its surface. As the valley drops below the level of the range, the rocks in the range are eroded by wind, water, and ice, and water carries the eroded materials into the valleys and deposits them as sand, gravel, or clay. In some valleys of western Utah, these deposits are over two miles thick.

Although the stretching of the Basin and Range overall is a slow, continuous process, the movement on individual faults can occur in dramatic slippages of several feet at a time—and large, abrupt shifts on the faults cause earthquakes. Much of the stretching of the Basin and Range province is now concentrated near the eastern and western margins.

The eastern margins of faults which trend across western Utah form a zone of frequent earthquakes—part of the Intermountain Seismic Belt. Most of the earthquakes are small, many too small to be felt, and represent minor adjustments along the numerous faults in the region. In historic time, Utah has experienced several earthquakes that have caused significant damage.

At the western base of the Wasatch Range lies Utah's most important earthquake fault, the Wasatch Fault, which has not produced a major earthquake since

*The granite of the Wasatch Range comes both polished and rough.*

the Mormon pioneers settled it 150 years ago. Geologic studies of the Wasatch Fault—not a single fault, but a zone of faults 200 miles long—have shown that a very large earthquake occurs on some fault in this zone every few hundred years. A large earthquake here would wreak havoc. Utah's population center, Salt Lake City, is built on an old lake bed (similar to Mexico City) and would jiggle like gelatin in the event of a major tremor.

Nearly all of Utah's hot springs lie in this zone of earthquake activity, sometimes on one of the active faults. These springs occur where water that has circulated deep enough into the earth to be heated rises to the surface along a fault.

## ■ THE MIDDLE ROCKY MOUNTAIN PROVINCE

The Wasatch Range dominates north-central Utah, and together with the Uinta Mountains it monopolizes the skyline of northeastern Utah. Both the Wasatch and Uintas stand within the Utah portion of the Middle Rocky Mountain Province. These mountain ranges receive much more precipitation than most of the rest of Utah. Rivers originating here supply the water for Utahns who reside in the Wasatch Front—the well-populated band west of the Wasatch Range where Salt Lake City, Provo, and Ogden lie, and where most Utahns live.

*Utah's Capitol Reef National Park.*

An assemblage of sedimentary, igneous, and metamorphic rocks, the Wasatch Range contains the oldest rocks in Utah—over three billion years old. Each major canyon along the Wasatch Front exposes a different suite of rocks. Mines in Big and Little Cottonwood Canyons and at Park City have been major producers of minerals, since the interaction of magma and rocks usually forms mineable ores.

The Uinta Mountains were pushed up to form an east-west range, perpendicular to most major ranges in the Rocky Mountains, and indeed, the continental United States. These mountains are composed primarily of old sedimentary rocks and have no important mineral deposits. Large oil and gas fields occur south of the Uinta Mountains in the Uinta Basin and north of the Uinta Mountains in an area of complex geologic structure known as the overthrust belt. In the "crossroads" region—the part of this belt where the Wasatch Range and the Uinta Mountains intersect, near Park City—the geology is extremely complex.

Another prominent geologic feature of the Uinta Basin is a rock layer called the Morrison Formation, which holds another sort of mineral treasure: fossils.

## ■ PREHISTORIC LIFE

Utah's rocks hold fossils from every geological age. Dinosaurs once roamed this area, and visitors can follow the tracks of these ancient beasts.

A boater at Lake Powell strolling on the shoreline may discover dinosaur tracks. At Dinosaur National Monument *(see pages 166–176)*, visitors view bone fossils as they appear in a quarry after being uncovered by paleontologists. Thousands of dinosaur fossils were taken from the Cleveland-Lloyd Quarry in Emery County. Utah has been called "a King Tut's tomb of fossils."

Why is Utah so full of dinosaur and other fossils? The Morrison Formation—a geologic designation for a series of strata deposited at the height of the dinosaur age—is found throughout eastern Utah. A combination of erosion and dry climate has exposed it to an extent unusual for any formation. Dinosaur National Monument, in northeastern Utah, and the Cleveland-Lloyd Dinosaur Quarry *(see page 176)*, near the town of Cleveland in central Utah, are miles apart, but both are in the Morrison Formation, and both have yielded some of the finest fossilized dinosaur skeletons found anywhere. These are the most obvious places to view actual remains. But there are sites all over Utah where amateur rockhounds and budding geologists can examine the remains of ancient worlds.

*The Dinosaur Gardens at the Utah Field House of Natural History in Vernal.*

For detailed information on Utah's fossil treasures and an overview of prehistoric history, visitors can stop by the museums in Vernal or Price, or the Utah Museum of Natural History in Salt Lake City.

The best place to actually see paleontologists extract and reassemble dinosaur bones is the quarry at Dinosaur National Monument. An ancient riverbed where the prehistoric animals were buried has been encased in a large working laboratory at the monument's visitor center. For the most part, the bones of plant-eating dinosaurs are found at the monument. Stegosaurus is common, as are several types of sauropods,

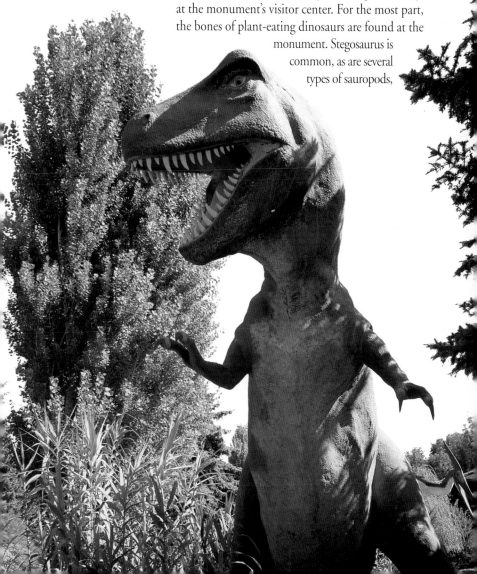

the largest animals ever to roam on land, and tiny nanosaurus, a creature no larger than a chicken.

Andrew Carnegie, the famous capitalist and philanthropist, stirred dinosaur fever throughout the world with specimens from Utah. He constructed a huge museum for the people of Pittsburgh, Pennsylvania, but could find nothing grand enough to fill it.

"Someone slapped a picture of a brontosaurus [today called apatosaurus] from the monument on his desk," once recounted the late geologist Dr. William Stokes, "and his eyes lit up. He said, 'Get me one!' Here was something finally big enough to fill up his big halls. He had a huge cast made for a 60-foot diplodocus. Carnegie had duplicates sent all over the world to the kings, potentates, and emper-

*The late Dr. William Stokes, once a leading geologist at the University of Utah.*

ors." The model outside the museum in Vernal is the last one made from this mold.

The Cleveland-Lloyd quarry is a more remote and rustic site. Relatively greater numbers of carnivorous dinosaur fossils are found there. The area was once a bog where large plant-eating dinosaurs became trapped and eventually entombed. The meat-eating allosaurus is the most common species found here. Stokesosaurus, a sauropod, was discovered here and named for Stokes.

Dinosaur National Monument and the Cleveland-Lloyd quarry are managed by different government agencies for somewhat different purposes. The fossils at the monument are uncovered but left in place. The Cleveland site, managed by the Bureau of Land Management, is an active quarry from which fossils are removed for research and study. Anyone with a proper permit may dig for fossils at the Cleveland quarry. In addition to these two locations, fossilized trilobites are common in the western desert regions of the Great Basin. Miners in Price, located in the heart of dinosaur country, have uncovered many dinosaur footprints in the coal deposits.

Petrified wood can also be found throughout the Colorado Plateau. Visitors to Escalante State Park can hike along a trail among the petrified logs of an ancient coniferous forest.

*Certain areas in northeastern Utah are rich in fossils.*

# THE FIRST UTAHNS

THE AMERICAN SOUTHWEST, AND UTAH IN PARTICULAR, contains some of the country's most spectacular traces of Native American civilization. Many of these ruins, artifacts, and rock pictures were left by the vanished Anasazi (now called Ancestral Puebloan) and Fremont cultures, while others were the work of the more recently arrived Shoshone, Ute, Navajo, and Paiute peoples. The human history of Utah, however, begins much earlier.

Paleo-Indians (as archaeologists call the first colonizers of America) were hunting and gathering throughout the area now known as Utah as early as 13,000 years again. Their stone-tipped spears, used to fell large fauna of the Ice Age, have been discovered in caves along the long-vanished shoreline of Lake Bonneville. Meat from animals like the mammoth and giant bison were probably cached in the frozen ground to sustain the Paleo-Indians, who also depended on seeds, nuts, and small rodents for food.

When the Wisconsin Glacier started to recede about 8,000 years ago, wind patterns changed. Six millennia or so later, great inland deserts were forming in the Southwest, causing many of the larger mammals to become extinct. No longer could those who had depended on big-game hunting to sustain themselves survive. Subsequent generations adapted by collecting wild seeds and nuts, and trapping game such as elk, deer, mountain sheep, antelope, rabbits, and rodents.

Around 500, corn and other crops were introduced into the North American Southwest from Mexico. With a more dependable food source, the Indians could stay in one place and produce enough corn, beans, and squash to store for the winter and for periods of drought; meanwhile, they developed effective implements for harvesting and storing, especially kiln-fired pottery and intricately woven baskets. Archaeologists classify these agricultural societies—obviously very different in many ways from the hunter/gatherer culture—as the Fremont culture and the Ancestral Puebloan culture. The Ancestral Puebloans, in general, flourished on the Colorado Plateau south of the Colorado River, while the Fremont people lived north of the Colorado River and east of the Virgin River in the Great and the Uinta Basins.

# ■ THE ANCESTRAL PUEBLOANS

The term Ancestral Puebloan has recently been adopted to replace *Anasazi*—a pejorative term used by the Navajo to refer to ancestors of the modern Pueblo people. The Pre-ancestral Puebloans, known to archaeologists as the Basketmakers, lived in pithouses, saucer-shaped dwellings half aboveground and half underground, walled and roofed with a combination of logs and mud mortar. They apparently had frequent contact with other peoples, and their dramatic cultural advancement from A.D. 700 to 1300, designated as the Pueblo Period by archaeologists, shows them to have been extremely adaptable and dynamic. Around A.D. 700, the bow and arrow made its appearance, replacing the less efficient spear and *atlatl* (wooden spear-thrower). Cotton weaving was introduced, and dogs and turkeys were domesticated.

Around 900, the Ancestral Puebloans began to build multi-story stone structures grouped around courtyards. Beneath the courtyards were underground chambers called *kiva*. The roofs were mud on top of a wooden framework, level with the surrounding plaza. A hole in the center of the roof served as entrance and smoke hole. Each kiva had a place for a fire, ventilation to keep the fire going, and a small indentation in the floor called a *sipapu*. Because modern Hopi use the same kind of room for their ceremonies, archaeologists theorize that the use and purpose of the Ancestral Puebloan kiva was similar. To the Hopi, the sipapu symbolizes the opening through which mankind entered the world. The kiva was a place for the men to come and weave and pass on their culture. Women were not allowed.

During the latter part of the Pueblo Period, dwellings were constructed in the protected alcoves of sandstone canyons. Built on cliffs high above the valley floor, most were reached by ladders or handholds and footholds chipped in the rock. Some were nestled back into large open caves in the rock walls of the canyons. Thousands of remnants of this civilization can be found throughout the Colorado Plateau in what the Utah Travel Council calls the Grand Circle. Among the sites on the Grand Circle described later in this book are Edge of the Cedars State Historic Park, Butler Wash, Grand Gulch Primitive Area, Natural Bridges and Hovenweep national monuments, Anasazi State Park, Canyonlands National Park, and Newspaper Rock.

# ■ THE FREMONT INDIANS

Much less is known about the Fremont Indians, who inhabited the region north of the Ancestral Puebloans, along the edge of the Great Basin and the Colorado Plateau. Such an extreme range of climate and geography prompted individual bands to adapt in different ways. Some lived as nomadic hunters and plant collectors. Others established villages and lived as farmers. Consequently, they have fewer communal characteristics to identify them as a common people. Among these are a particular style of basketry and leather moccasins (as opposed to the sandals of yucca fibers worn by the Ancestral Puebloans). Their pictographs, petroglyphs, and clay figurines generally have distinctive hair "boles" and necklaces. Also unique was the Fremont recipe for making pottery by mixing granular rock or sand with the wet clay.

Five distinct Fremont groups have been identified by archaeologists, each determined by geographical location and differences in styles of pottery, figurines, and projectile points: the Parowan Gap, Uintah, Sevier Fremont, San Rafael, and Great Salt Lake.

There are fewer known Fremont village sites than Ancestral Puebloan sites. One reason for this is that the pit houses of the Fremont deteriorated faster than the stone and mortar of the Ancestral Puebloans. The pit houses are hard for the layman to differentiate from the desert floor, but the granaries and rock graphics stand out clearly.

An excellent place to learn about these early settlers is Fremont Indian State Park, where Five Finger Ridge Village was uncovered when the interstate was built built through Clear Creek Canyon, about 15 miles southwest of Richfield. The state of Utah collected the artifacts together in a museum showing how the Fremont hunted for game and wild plant foods, and farmed in the canyon bottoms. Visitors can examine full-sized replicas of a pit house and granary and see the Fremont rock graphics along the Show Me Rock Art and Discovery trails.

Fremont Indian State Park superintendent Alden Hamblin often invites Indians who live in the area to give demonstrations of their traditional way of life. The park frequently sponsors special events at which guests are invited to learn an Indian dance, chip stone into an arrowhead, or make a pot in the ancient Fremont way.

Fremont Indian petroglyphs may also be viewed at Parowan Gap, 12 miles north of Parowan in Iron County, and in Nine-Mile Canyon, northwest of Price.

# ■ FINDING INDIAN SITES

There are thousands of sites containing Ancestral Puebloan and Fremont remains throughout Utah. Go to a state or federal park, such as Anasazi State Park, Fremont Indian State Park, or Hovenweep National Monument, to research the prehistoric inhabitants of the area. You might take one of the tours available in towns like Blanding, Bluff, or Moab.

Next, set off on your own to smaller areas in these parks or to several BLM sites throughout Utah.

Our family has made a hobby out of hunting for ancient Indian dwellings. Before the children could walk, they were carried through the doorways of the magnificent pueblos of Mesa Verde in Colorado and Chaco Canyon in New Mexico. They grew up listening to lectures from mom at the museums, and often fancied themselves as the half-naked Ancestral Puebloan children they saw in displays. After educating ourselves, we decided it was time to go exploring on our own. One Easter, we walked into a BLM ranger station in Monticello, looking for a backpacking trail we could take to see Indian ruins. We don't like to say where we went because, like many, we cherish our own secret places. After a few hours on the

*Hunting scenes on a prehistoric fresco in Nine-Mile Canyon.*

*This ancient reptile appears to have been drawn yesterday.*

trail, we were lost. We acknowledge the fact that we are horrible map-readers, so we always keep track of landmarks, should we have to backtrack, as we did that evening. By the time we were hiking on another trail, the sun was low in the sky. We set up our tents for the night within a mile of our car. We heard coyotes in the distance and slept under a blanket of stars. The next morning was like Christmas, Easter, and birthdays all wrapped together. Before setting off down the trail, the youngest looked back and said, "What's that?" He saw the unmistakable walls of a cliff dwelling tucked into an alcove. For the next half hour, our exclamations of delight and discovery echoed off the walls of the canyon. Here were pieces of pottery—white, red, black, some smooth, some crimped. The patterns on them were reminiscent of jigsaw puzzles. One gray piece had an unmistakeable fingerprint in black, as if it were a photograph negative. We saw fingerprints, too, in the clay mortar between the stones of the walls. A fingerprint is so personal and so immediate. What would the owner say if he saw us here? A small corn cob lay back in the sand of one of the rooms. Here were so many things we had seen behind the glass of museum displays. Here was a kind of dwelling we had seen before but

*(following pages) A cliff dwelling at Island-in-the-Sky, Canyonlands National Park.*

never on our own and never with so many pieces of pottery scattered wherever we looked. That night we set up camp far down the trail from the Ancestral Puebloan ruins—but still we found pottery. Our dreams were filled with visions of brown-skinned women sitting in front of their neatly plastered homes, grinding corn or painting geometric designs on smooth white pots.

Sit in the stillness of the canyon. Try to hear the echoes of the Ancestral Puebloans as they go about their daily chores. Women chatter as they grind corn, children chase domesticated turkeys. Young adults carefully beat the tops of rice grass, letting the seeds fall into their ornate baskets. While you try to recreate the centuries-old scene, please remember the words of modern Hopi, Navajo, Ute, Paiute, Shoshone, all who trace their ancestry to canyons such as this. You are in someone's home, resting in someone's cemetery. Treat it with respect. Ruin walls are fragile; the mortar holding them together crumbles easily. Please do not walk or lean on them. Please leave all artifacts in place. The beauty of these places is that pieces of the past can be seen. If any one artifact is taken or destroyed, the quality of the experience for hundreds of visitors to come is diminished. Touching rock graphics deposits skin oils which hasten deterioration of the pigments and rock surfaces. Besides, all prehistoric remains are protected by law by the United States government. Fines of up to $20,000 and or imprisonment may be imposed on anyone removing or destroying these cultural resources on public lands. Rewards are offered for information leading to the arrest and conviction of anyone disturbing a site.

## ■ THE FATE OF THE ANCIENT ONES

Many ask the question, what became of the Ancestral Puebloans and Fremont? Several theories have been proposed but no solid evidence has been produced to support one theory over the other. By studying tree rings, scientists have documented that a severe 20-year drought hit the Southwest where the Ancestral Puebloans and Fremont people lived. Cutting timber for fuel and building material and clearing land for agriculture may have started a cycle of erosion, ending with a loss of fields due to gullying. With a diminished capacity to grow and store enough food, social disruptions undoubtably took place. While no evidence of violence has been found in the cliff dwellings, their relative inaccessibility makes them seem like fortresses. The abandonment of the ancestral lands was gradual. Perhaps a few people at a time migrated south to more hospitable lands until no

*Ancestral Puebloan pots from the vicinity of Cedars State Park.*

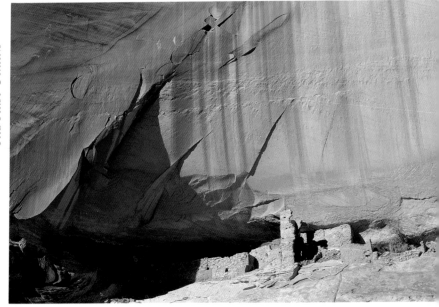

*Poncho House ruins at Chinle Wash.*

one was left. It is believed the Ancestral Puebloans migrated to the northern Rio Grande tributaries and the upper Little Colorado River drainage on the Hopi Mesa and Zuni Plateau, where active settlements were already prospering. By 1300, the pueblos were sprawling. New rooms could be easily added. Their construction was less formal than the classic cliff dwellings. Indians living in pueblos probably traded corn and pottery for the Plains Indians' meat and hides.

While anthropologists and archaeologists dig into Ancestral Puebloan and Fremont village sites, trying to solve the mystery of what happened to their old occupants, many modern Indians feel the answers can be found somewhere else. May Perry, a Shoshone, says, "If you want to find out what happened to the Fremont Indians, just ask us." Perry explains that in a recent trip through the Utah Natural History Museum the curators showed her several round stone balls. She said, "My people use these for juggling! We always have." May found many items on display at the museum that closely resembled her own household utensils. The styles of grinding stones, jewelry-making tools, and moccasins are all very similar.

Will Numkena, a Hopi, says, "The Hopi feel a strong kinship with those you call Fremont and Anasazi [Ancestral Puebloan]." The Hopi recognize many petroglyphs and pictographs as representations of their *kachinas*, or offspring of the Creator. Many of the symbols found on the rocks are common in Hopi iconography.

Perhaps with a changing climate and pressure from migrating tribes, the Fremont were assimilated into the erstwhile separate groups, like the Shoshone. Research into the Fremont Indian culture is still inconclusive.

## ■ THE LATER TRIBES

Although it is not scientifically proven that the contemporary Indians of Utah and the Southwest are direct descendants of the Fremont and Ancestral Puebloans, it is a fact that the Ute, Shoshone, Paiute, Goshute, and Navajo people inhabited Utah long beford the non-Indian explorers and settlers came along.

During a panel discussion in which representatives from the Ute, Paiute, Shoshone, Navajo, and Hopi tribes talked about their kinship with the Fremont,

*Ancestral Puebloan dwellings in Road Canyon. The Ancestral Puebloans vanished 600 years ago as mysteriously as they had appeared centuries before.*

every speaker expressed the desire to see all visitors respect the Ancestral Puebloan and Fremont cultures, and particularly their burial sites. Travis Parashonts, a Paiute, said, "Archaeologists see it as a science—Indians see it as a spiritual or emotional thing. There is a reason for everything. Our forefathers were put away with special things. When they are dug up, an imbalance is made." Clifford Duncan, a Ute from the Uinta Basin, agrees. He says, "The Indian people have roots here in this country. When people bother the remains of the ancients, it is us they are bothering. Those who tell others to leave the dwellings and rock markings alone are speaking for the Indian. They are landmarks and sacred areas. They remind the world that The People once lived there."

Modern Indians feel their ancestral heritage, geography, and religion are common bonds between all the different tribes. They see the religious symbols of the Ancestral Puebloans and Fremont as proof that the modern Indian religion grew out of the old. Will Numkena says that when he is among the symbols on the canyon walls, he is among spirits of his family.

The story of Utah's Indians, their domination and frequent betrayal at the hands of non-Indian settlers and politicians, parallels that of other tribes throughout the United States. The first Spanish explorers in the Southwest encouraged Utes to prey on Paiutes and Goshutes and bring them as slaves for trade. The settlers were generally accepted by the Indians in the beginning until the number of non-Indians increased along with their demand for more land.

Historically, Utah's Indians were hunters and gatherers, with each group moving from place to place within particular boundaries. Small bands camped near water in cooler areas in the summer and moved to warmer areas in the winter. There were many different bands belonging to each Indian tribe. The bands would come together occasionally for seasonal celebrations. Each band had its own leader, but there was no one head of the Shoshone, Hopi, Navajo or Ute. The concept of "chief" seemed to develop after the arrival of non-Indians, who were accustomed to negotiating with a spokesman for every nation. This lack of an overall leader led to many misunderstandings. A treaty signed between one group of Utes and the pioneers did not, in the Ute scheme of things, bind all Utes to its promises. At Fort Panguitch in the early days of the Walker War, a man was killed by an Indian arrow. When another group of Indians later came to the fort, they were not asked their purpose, but were murdered as enemies.

*These Northern Shoshone were photographed around the turn of the century.*

The Utes and Shoshone picked up the idea of using teepees for housing from the Plains Indians. Horses obtained from the Spanish changed the way of life of the Utes by enabling them to chase and hunt larger game, like buffalo and antelope, and to trade more easily.

The Paiute and Goshute used conical pole lodgings covered with grass or brush. The article of clothing used universally by the Indians was the rabbitskin blanket, made of long strips of skin with the fur on. A wide variety of baskets were produced by coiled and twined techniques. A pitch-covered bottle with a globular body and narrow neck was used for carrying liquids on long treks into the desert in search of wild seeds.

The first Spanish to visit the Indians in Utah were Dominguez and Escalante. They found the Laguna Utes living along the shores of Utah Lake and described them in this way:

> Their dwellings are some sheds or little wattle huts of osier (willows) out of which they have interestingly crafted baskets and other instruments of ordinary use. They are very poor as regards dress. The most becoming one they wear is a deerskin jacket and long leggings of the same. For cold seasons they wear blankets made of jackrabbit and coney rabbit furs. They employ the Yuta language but with noticeable variances in pronunciation, and even in some words. They possess good features, and most of them are fully bearded. All the sections of this sierra along the southeast, south-southwest, and west are inhabited by a great number of peoples of the same nations, language, and easy-going character as these Laguna, with whom a very populous and extensive province could be formed."

The Paiute were also farmers, growing corn, beans, and squash in the river bottoms. Every autumn the Paiute and other Indians of Utah went to gather pine nuts from the piñon pine forests, a practice adopted later by pioneer settlers.

Something else the pioneer settlers adopted was the Indians' water supply. In a dry climate like Utah's, whoever had access to the water was able to dominate all others. In many cases, Indians would go off to a seasonal hunting or gathering area and return to find their traditional water source fenced off or in some way appropriated. Varied ways were used to encourage the Indians to leave. Pioneers around Huntsville in northern Utah were digging a ditch to the South Fork of the Ogden

*(opposite) Spires in Monument Valley at Navajo Tribal Park.*

River when a band of Indians told the settlers to leave the valley or they would pollute the water. Captain Hunt told the Indians that at their first suspicious act he would burn all the water in the canyons. When they looked incredulous, he grabbed a dipperful of colorless liquid, probably alcohol, and burned it. The Indians backed down. Sometimes the Indians were left parcels of land, not always the prime parcels, and encouraged to take up the same lifestyle as their new non-Indian neighbors. Brigham Young preached that it was far cheaper to feed and clothe the Indians than to fight them. He encouraged the Mormon pioneers to hand out food, tobacco, and clothing whenever the need arose. One of the first settlers of Kanosh remembered occasionally passing out food and blankets to members of Chief Kanosh's band when the Indians occasionally showed up at her door. She also remembered employing an Indian woman to do the family's wash.

As one band of Indians was forced from its traditional land, it entered the lands of another band. This caused conflict between groups, but they often joined against the common invader. It is surprising that the Indian conflicts in Utah did not last longer than they did. It has been suggested that this is because the Indians were not warlike to begin with. According to the 1941 edition of *Utah, A Guide to the State*, "The Walker War of 1853-54 was precipitated by the occupation of Indian lands by white people, and would probably have been more serious except for the restraining influence of the Ute war chief, Sowiette. Shoshone resistance to white settlement was crushed when six hundred Indians were surrounded and killed by Federal soldiers in January,

*Chief Kanosh*

*Goulding's Trading Post, circa 1950.*

1863. The Black Hawk War of 1865-68 was waged over the same question of white pre-emption of hunting grounds, and had the same sort of ending. In 1879, the Indian agent, N. C. Meeker, and others were killed at the White River Agency in western Colorado by Ute Indians who objected to maltreatment and to having soldiers on the reservation. The outbreak was quickly subdued—largely because of Chief Ouray's peaceful attitude—and the Utes were afterward moved to reservations. There were Navajo raids into southwestern Utah in the 1860s and '70s, and trouble with Paiutes and Utes in the San Juan area in the 1880s and 1890s. Between 1861, when the Uinta Basin was set aside for Indian use by President Lincoln, and 1929, when the Kanosh reservation was established, all of the Indians within the state were settled on reservations."

The "last battle" between Indians and non-Indians in the remaining frontier of the United States took place in 1923 outside of Blanding, Utah. Chief Posey and his band had eluded a large posse by making a 15-foot jump in west Comb Wash. Posey was wounded and died of blood poisoning. His band gave itself up two days later. The event brought the tribe's plight to the nation's attention and they were later given the White Mesa Indian Reservation, 12 miles south of Bluff.

The inevitable ending to the clash between the Indian and non-Indian cultures was a virtual elimination of the Indians' way of life. The Indians were forced to stay on reservations and become ranchers and farmers. Those who chose not to live on the reservations where the conditions were never very good had to fit into a society that did not accept the Indians' culture. Most Indians adopted non-Indian clothes and homes. Perhaps worst of all was the attitude that the Indians had to abandon their religious beliefs and social customs. Children were sent away to school to learn "civilized" ways. The federal government ran a large boarding school in Brigham City. The Mormon Church sponsored an Indian Placement Program where Indian children were placed in Mormon homes to be raised and educated.

## ■ MEETING CONTEMPORARY INDIANS

As the consciousness of many Americans was raised in the 1960s in respect to the Indians' plight, Utah began to change with the rest of the country. The Intermountain Indian School was closed, and schools were built on the reservations where students could live at home and learn many of the traditional ways both from their families and schools. The challenge still remains, however, of solving how the Indian can live in the modern world and retain his cultural roots.

Besides visiting the Ancestral Puebloan and Fremont ruins in the state, visitors to Utah should get to know its modern Indians, many of whom do not live on reservations.

The White Mesa Institute in Blanding, sponsored by the College of Eastern Utah, offers educational programs for youth and adults on Southwest archaeology, modern Indian tribes, pioneer history, wildlife, and geology. The Museum of Natural History in Salt Lake City and the Canyonlands Field Institute in Moab offer similar programs.

In Cedar City in June, the local Indian community sponsors the Paiute Restoration Gathering, with a parade, dances, traditional games, native food, and a beauty pageant. Many Indians from southern Utah attend Southern Utah State University in Cedar City.

The Annual Southern Utah Folklife Festival is held in Springdale, outside of Zion National Park, every September. Southern Utah's Paiutes are included in this festival.

In Bluff, Indians from the Navajo reservation across the San Juan River occasionally have dance performances, horse races, rodeos, and other get-togethers.

Utes from Fort Duchesne, on the Uintah and Ouray Indian Reservation, hold a "Ute Indian Powwow" every summer, with tribes from all over the West in attendance. Rodeo action, craft displays, and food booths entertain the crowds. Other Indian powwows, dances and rodeos are held throughout the year. Information on dates and times is available at the headquarters of the Ute Indian Reservation in Fort Duchesne, near Roosevelt. The Uintah and Ouray Indian Reservation covers nearly one million acres scattered across the East Tavaputs Plateau. Non-members are asked to keep to the main roads on the reservation and purchase permits for most activities, such as camping, hunting, boating, or fishing.

Monument Valley, in the southeast corner of Utah, has been described as the "Eighth Wonder of the World," an enduring symbol of the West. Monument Valley is located on the Navajo Indian Reservation, which sprawls over vast areas of Utah, Arizona, and New Mexico. Like their neighbors, the Hopi, the Navajo have been able to retain much of their ancestral lands and maintain more of their old ways of life. Round mud and log hogans, the Navajo winter homes, are scattered throughout the reservation. Fine examples of Indian jewelry and blankets can be seen and purchased from stores like Hatch Trading Post, on the way to Hovenweep National Monument, and Montezuma Creek Trading Post, just east of Bluff. Once in a while a few individuals will set up a stand by the side of the road to sell their wares. Expect to pay high prices for the jewelry and blankets. These articles take a long time to produce and are priced as works of art.

In the Mystery Valley section of Monument Valley Tribal Park are several hundred Ancestral Puebloan dwellings, most of them small and unnamed. Guides are needed to locate them. The caretakers of this land, the Navajo, though unrelated to the Ancestral Puebloan, live in a similar fashion to that of their predecessors. They are isolated and clannish, depending on the land and little else to survive.

The Indians of Utah have a rich heritage. Their history is told in the markings on the rocks and in their dwelling places. It is told through the legends and traditions of those who came after—the Hopi, Ute, Paiute, Goshute, Shoshone, and Navajo. In a state that claims so many diverse natural wonders, the added dimension of a proud native people is a bonus. As those who travel Utah come to love the beauty of its canyons, mesas, mountains, and deserts, they must learn to appreciate the beliefs of the first Americans. The idea that mankind must live in harmony with the earth and protect it from harm is gaining more and more acceptance. It would be sad to see the end of the wide open spaces and the ancient caretakers of the land.

# THE EARLY EXPLORERS

UTAH IS A VAST TERRITORY JUST WAITING FOR ADVENTURERS. Freeways may criss-cross the land, the nearest town might loom just around the corner, and an airplane can fly across the entire state in less than an hour. But great expanses of alpine forest still remain wild and natural. Red-rock canyons, forbidding-looking deserts, high pristine mountains, and gleaming white salt flats stretch far into the horizon.

Take a day—or better yet, several—to explore a wild part of Utah. Find a place without roads, reservoirs, or restaurants. Imagine that you are an early adventurer seeing this country for the first time. Conjure up visions of mysterious Indian tribes camped nearby. Dream that grizzly bears and wolves roam the forests.

Perhaps then can you imagine what Utah's early explorers—Escalante, Domin-guez, Bridger, Smith, and Powell—experienced as they ventured through this fas-cinating land.

## ■ THE SPANISH EXPLORERS

Soon after Cortez conquered Mexico, Coronado pushed northward in search of the legendary Seven Cities of Cibola. The conquistador came searching for cities made of gold, but found only adobe pueblos belonging to the Hopi Indians. Catholic missionaries came to the land—now including parts of New Mexico, California, and Arizona—and established outposts at Santa Fe and all along the Pacific coast. Their purpose was to convert the Native Americans and reap whatev-er bounty they could from the vast new land. The Indians were also encouraged to capture and sell slaves.

To ensure the success of the precarious California missions, the Spanish needed a trade route from Santa Fe to the Pacific. Hopis and Apaches, tribes that stub-bornly resisted foreign incursions into their territories, inhabited the country in between. The Spanish desperately sought a northern route around them.

Father Silvestre Velez de Escalante came to Santa Fe. He talked to the visiting Ute (whom he called *Yuta*) Indians from what is now Utah. He sensed from the information they gave him that he could find a way to California, perhaps by water, by heading north.

Escalante and Father Francisco Atanasio Dominguez, the expedition's leader, set out in 1776, a month after members of the Continental Congress signed the Declaration of Independence. His superiors charged the expedition with scouting out any new Indian settlements favorable for missionary work. With a party of six explorers and a map-maker, they became probably the first Europeans to enter the uncharted regions that would later become Utah. Several Indians joined in the expedition as guides along the way.

Dominguez and Escalante did not succeed. The explorers found no northern route to California, and the Indians did not convert. The priests died in obscurity. Nonetheless, the expedition did open Utah to further exploration. The expedition's map-maker, Don Bernardo Miera y Pacheco, charted Utah's first maps. Modern travelers who read Escalante's journal and visit the rugged country of the Colorado Plateau, the Uintas, and the Wasatch Front can only marvel at the exploits of these brave men.

EARLY EXPLORERS

## THE DOMINGUEZ-ESCALANTE JOURNAL, 1776

**Sept. 25 near Utah Lake, on first learning of the Great Salt Lake from the Indians.** . . The other lake with which this one comes in contact covers many leagues, so we were informed, and its waters are harmful and extremely salty, for the Timpanois assured us that anyone who wet some part of the body with them immediately felt a lot of itching in the part moistened.

**Oct. 11:** Many times before leaving La Villa de Santa Fe we had reminded each and every one of our companions that in this journey we had no other destination than the one which God would grant us; nor did this tempt us to any worldly purpose whatsoever; and that whosoever among them tried either to trade with the infidels or to follow out his private notions by not keeping before him the sole aim of this undertaking, which has been and is God's greater glory and the spreading of the faith, had better not go in our company. On the way we time and again admonished (some) to rectify their intentions, because otherwise we would suffer hardships and misfortunes and would not achieve all that we were aiming for—as they saw in part come true under circumstances which, unless they close their eyes to the Light, they could never attribute to accident. With all this they plagued us more each day, and we were very much disheartened by seeing how in the business of heaven the one of earth was being sought first and foremost. . . .

**Oct. 14 in the vicinity of present-day Toquerville, Utah** . . . Here it is already very temperate country for, in spite of our having experienced plenty of heat yesterday, last night, and today, the river poplars were so green and leafy, the flowers and blooms which the land produces so flamboyant and without damage whatsoever, that they indicated there had been no freezing or frosting around here. We also saw growths of mesquite, which does not flourish in very cold lands. . . .

*Escalante enters Utah Valley, as portrayed by Eddington. (Utah State Historical Society)*

How different might Utah have been if the fathers had succeeded! The Utes (or *Lagunas*, as the Spanish fathers called them) on the shores of Utah Lake grew to like the missionaries so much that they begged them to return. Dominguez and Escalante promised to send missionaries but their superiors in Mexico chose not to. Almost a hundred years passed before another church, the Latter-day Saints, arrived in their land. Utah was never colonized by the Spanish even though the early explorers described it as "the most pleasing, beautiful, and fertile site in all New Spain." Colonization was left to the Mormons. If Dominguez and Escalante had succeeded, Utahns might speak Spanish as their native language and Provo would be home for Catholic priests instead of Mormon bishops.

# UTAH HISTORY

Modern towns shown in gray

0    25    50
Miles

Anasazi Culture AD 800-1300
Early Mormon Settlement Area 1850-1859
Escalante 1776
Fremont 1842-1844
Fremont 1845
Powell 1869

IDAHO

SHOSHONE

WASATCH RANGE

WYOMING

Great Salt Lake

SALT LAKE CITY

UINTA MOUNTAINS

Fremont 1845

Camp Floyd

PROVO

UINTA BASIN

GREAT SALT LAKE DESERT

Utah Lake

Escalante 1776

GOSHUTE

Fremont 1842-'44

Powell 1869

Green River

NEVADA

Sevier Lake

FILLMORE

Sevier River

WASATCH PLATEAU

UTE

COLORADO

MOAB

SOUTHERN PAIUTE

AQUARIUS PLATEAU

Powell

WATERPOCKET FOLD

CANYONLANDS

N
W    E
S

CEDAR CITY

Hole in the Rock

Colorado River

San Juan River

PARIA CANYON

NAVAJO

ARIZONA

Monsignor Jerome Stoffel, a retired Catholic pastor in Salt Lake City, appreciates the efforts of the explorers more than most. Using maps and descriptions from old journals, he researched and followed Escalante and Dominguez's route on a 1976 trek sponsored by the Utah Bicentennial Commission.

Though the expedition's original journal has never been found, Monsignor Stoffel used copies made by subsequent explorers, written in 18th-century Spanish —each slightly different from the others. No map of the route is absolutely dependable.

Like a detective working to solve a mystery, Monsignor Stoffel and his fellow historians used the journal to search for the original trail and campsites. His eyes twinkle as he relates a discovery he made in comparing the journal entries and his knowledge of the landscape at that time. "Escalante became suspicious of his Indian guides. Upon reaching a ridge, Escalante discovered a route obviously easier than the one his guide was using. 'Why,' he must have wondered, 'do they not go in that direction? Are we being led into an ambush?'

"We know there were Comanches in that part of the country," Monsignor explains. "Comanches were feared by Europeans and other Indians. It came to us as we looked at the route that Escalante's guide was probably trying to save them. The explorers possessed horses, mules, and supplies that the Comanches would do anything to get. We appreciated the wisdom of the guides, apparently more than did Escalante!"

Arriving at what is now Utah Lake, called *Timpanogos* (the Stone One) by the Indians, they learned of a larger lake to the north that the Utes said was filled with bitter water (the Great Salt Lake). There were also tantalizing tales of a river, Tizon, that flowed from the salty lake to the Pacific Ocean. With neither time nor supplies to explore this route, however, the explorers instead headed south toward Santa Fe, hoping to find Indians who would trade with them for food. The myth of a river connecting the Great Salt Lake to the Pacific Ocean persisted until the mountain man Jedediah Smith explored the lake.

It is ironic that the physical barriers to travel that exasperated Dominguez and Escalante now are popular tourist destinations. Split Mountain, where the priests crossed the Green River, guards a campground in Dinosaur National Monument. When Monsignor Stoffel tried to determine the exact point at which the fathers crossed the river, he was baffled. The river had changed too much in the past 200 years to cross at the exact location.

Escalante described a canyon near present-day Palmyra campground on the Diamond Fork River of Spanish Fork Canyon, southeast of Provo, as a place where "there were many dangerous defiles and slides, with no other trail than the one we went opening all along, and over the sierra's corrugated ruggedness which all over here made us change direction and wind about excessively at every step." Visitors to the canyon today travel on pavement to view the same rugged mountains that so vexed the Spanish fathers.

Hikers in Paria Canyon near the Utah-Arizona border carry maps and water and enjoy the spectacular red-rock scenery. In 1776, the tall, vertical walls of Paria Canyon stifled the Spanish explorers in their search for a way to ford the Colorado River. They had been warned by the Indians not to continue south to the Colorado because of the impassable sandstone terrain. They distrusted this advice. For ten days they struggled to find their way through trackless mesas, across massive gorges, suffering from hunger and thirst. Horses were killed to feed the starving party. Finally they reached the only point where, for 50 miles upstream and 150 miles downstream, a horse could reach the water. The river was wide and deep here. "We found nothing but insuperable obstacles for getting to the ford without retracing much terrain," wrote Escalante. The fathers called their camp in Paria Canyon *Salispuedes* ("Get Out if You Can"). The Crossing of the Fathers, as it is now called, where the explorers forded the Colorado is now submerged under Lake Powell. Escalante described the climb out of the canyon as having "extremely difficult stretches and most dangerous ledges." They made the arduous climb and camped that night above the present-day swimming beach at Wahweap, on Lake Powell.

## ■ MOUNTAIN MEN

Fashionable citizens no longer wear tall hats manufactured from beaver pelts. Mountain men, who forged a path through the wilderness in search of beaver, otter, and other furry creatures, are no longer needed to supply the wants of 20th-century fashion. Gore-Tex jackets, hiking boots with Vibram soles and backpacks constructed of nylon have long replaced buckskins and moccasins. But the spirit of men like Jedediah Smith, Jim Bridger, Miles Goodyear, and Peter Skene Ogden lives on in the hearts of people like Timothy Toker Many Hats, a modern-day trapper born 150 years too late.

# JIM BRIDGER, 1804-81

Jim had a marked linguistic gift and, wandering over the West as he did for so long, had picked up Spanish and frontier French, besides nearly a dozen Indian tongues, including those of the Snake, Bannock, Crow, Flathead, Nez Perce, Ute, and Pend Oreille, with a smattering of others. He was so adept in the use of the sign language that he habitually accompanied his remarks with slight unconscious corroborative gestures. He was a crack shot and an expert trapper—none better—while his courage and good judgement were acknowledged by all who knew him.

Jim also excelled at trailing. He could read and recognize signs made by any critter on four legs or on two, readily determining the sex, age, gait, and often the purpose of any animal whose trail he picked up. He could at once identify the tribe of any Indian whose moccasin tracks crossed his trail, and was so familiar with his own horse and those of his companions that he could usually recognize the tracks of any horse in the *caballada*. He could estimate accurately by the warmth of the ashes of a dead campfire how long it had been since those who had built it had departed. If a track were in sand, he could tell by the amount of sand that had crumbled into it how long before it had been made. In grass he could tell whether or not the tracks had been made before or after dewfall, before or after a shower. Even at night, by dismounting and feeling the ground with his hands, he could usually make out the trail with his hands.

—Stanley Vestal, *Jim Bridger, Mountain Man,* 1946

*Trappers spend an evening around the fire. (Special Collections, Utah State University)*

"I guess we never died off," says Many Hats, who frequently lives in a teepee, still traps, and does his best to keep the tradition of the mountain man alive. "I don't believe in reincarnation, but I've seen a few guys who must have come back."

Fort Buenaventura State Park in Ogden, where Many Hats works part-time, regularly joins with other state parks and black-powder muzzle-loading organizations to sponsor mountain-man rendezvous throughout Utah. At rendezvous, visitors walk from one teepee to the next, watching men or women in buckskins or furs work on Indian beadwork or stir up Dutch-oven meals. There are skilled gunsmiths, tanners, leatherworkers, and hat makers. The cracking black-powder muskets echo in the distance while Indian drums and chanting beckon visitors toward a dancing circle. And mountain men and women like Timothy Toker Many Hats begin to feel like the trappers and traders of the old American West.

"Actually, the whole fur trading era was a fad," says T. T. Many Hats. "The men who got involved in it at the beginning got very rich. They would pay $17.50 for an English long rifle. They would then go to an Indian, who would say, 'Yes, I would like a thunderstick.' Then they would say to the Indian, 'Oh, very expensive. You must bring in beaver pelts and pile them this high. . .' So, these Indians were paying almost $2,000 in furs for a rifle that only cost $17.50. But, for the Indians, it was worth it."

The old fur-trading business provided employment to loners, colorful characters, and adventurers. Some lived and trapped together in small groups. Others were independent types who saw other humans only at rendezvous to exchange goods and news. Many had Indian wives and families. All mountain men soon learned to live with the land or perish. Often, the Indians taught the trappers how to survive in the mountains. Indian crafts are still taught at the rendezvous.

T. T. Many Hats is one of the few modern mountain men who can say he got his start in the old way. He was born in Canada. His mother was French. His father was a hunter, trapper, gold prospector, and an American citizen. A Blackfoot Indian guardian helped to raise him, teaching him about the Blackfoot religion in the process.

The mountain-man rendezvouz has its roots in the early days of fur trapping in the West. John Jacob Astor, who established a fur company at the mouth of the Columbia River in Oregon, sent the first non-Indian trappers to northern Utah in 1811. Twelve years later, General William H. Ashley led a party sent by the British-owned Hudson's Bay Company to Cache Valley, near present-day Logan. Jim Bridger, a member of that party, is believed to be the first non-Indian to see the Great Salt Lake.

General Ashley quickly realized the country did not lend itself to established methods of trapping, which used rivers to transport goods and furs. He ambitiously organized a system of pack trains and an annual rendezvous at designated spots. The rendevouz became the most important link with the outside world for many trappers, a chance to stock up on civilized goods, and the premier social event of their long, lonely year.

General Ashley took buffalo hide boats down the Green River through Flaming Gorge searching for a western passage to the Pacific. Instead, he found the Colorado Plateau and a maze of red rock canyons. "The river," he wrote, "is bounded by lofty mountains heaped together in the greatest disorder, exhibiting a surface as barren as can be imagined." Giving up his journey, he purchased horses from the Ute Indians for the return trip, and circled around the Uinta Mountains on his way to a rendezvous at Henry's Fork.

Ashley soon announced that he had seen enough of the mountains, sold his fur-trading interests, and departed to greener pastures. But the tradition of the rendezvous lived on, and still lives on. Most of the men and women who attend rendezvous today do so as a brief escape from the modern world, to barter, trade, share ideas, and exchange stories. They come to dance and rejoin their family, other mountain men and women. The meetings are seldom as uproarious as in times past; after all, there are more opportunities these days to party.

*Old miner's cabin near Ophir*

It is at night, when most of the tourists have gone, that the feeling of the past returns like the flames of the campfire. Tales are told of the first mountain men, and legends grow larger. Many of their deeds died along with the trappers and their families. "There were so many people that were in the mountain man era who didn't write down what they did," explains T.T. Many Hats. "Some went out and trapped for a few years. Some went out and just got killed."

Many left their names on Utah's map. The city of Ogden honors the memory of Peter Skene Ogden. Provo bears the name of Etienne Provot. The trapper custom of hiding or "caching" their furs until rendezvous time gave Cache County its name.

Other trappers left their marks without their names. Miles Goodyear erected the first fort in the Wasatch Mountains. A replica of it can be seen at Fort Buenaventura in Ogden. In 1837, Philip Thompson and David Craig constructed Fort Davy Crockett in Brown's Hole, south of where the Flaming Gorge Dam was later built. It was renamed Fort Misery by the trappers who frequented it, who called it "the meanest fort in the West."

## ■ JEDEDIAH SMITH

Perhaps the most remarkable of all the mountain men was Jedediah Smith.

"He was a very enthusiastic man," says T.T. Many Hats. "He'd be very excited and enthusiastic about his ideas and he'd convince a large group of men to go with him. Then they'd all meet with disaster. He was just beautiful for living through disasters."

These disasters, chronicled in a very literate and colorful journal kept by Smith and later discovered and published, turned Jedediah into a legend. The mountain man possessed a reputation for being different. Unlike most men of his day, he disdained the use of tobacco, did not drink liquor, never swore, and stayed away from loose women. If he had a flaw, it was his recklessness with both his life and the lives of others.

Smith opened South Pass to the great route of Western migration. He traveled the length of Utah from north to south before any other non-Indian. He used the maps and journals of Spanish explorers to blaze the trail between California and the rest of America. Crossing the Great Basin, he proved once and for all that the legendary Buenaventura River linking the Great Salt Lake to the ocean did not exist. He was the first non-Indian to cross the Sierra Nevada and follow the California and Oregon coasts to the Columbia River.

Smith returned in 1826 from an expedition to California, where he had been imprisoned by the Spanish, battled snow in the Sierras, and became separated from his men.

Jedediah and his companions, Silas Gobel and Robert Evans, left most of the group in California and set out in May for Utah. On June 20, they entered Utah just north of present-day Great Basin National Park in Nevada. After turning north through the Snake Valley, the bogs of Salt Marsh Lake trapped them. One of their six horses became hopelessly mired in the mud. They killed it and saved the meat.

Smith described the Great Salt Lake Desert as "a country completely barren and destitute of game. We frequently traveled without water, sometimes for two days over sandy deserts where there was no sign of vegetation. When we found water in some of the rocky hills, we generally found some Indians who appeared the most miserable of the human race, having nothing to subsist on (nor any clothing) except grass-seed, grasshopper, etc. With our best exertion, we pushed forward walking as we had been for a long time over the soft sand. That kind of traveling is very tiresome to men in good health who can eat when they choose and drink as often as they desire. To us, worn down with hunger and fatigue and burning with thirst increased by the blazing sands, it was almost insupportable."

During the day, the men buried themselves in the sand to escape the heat. At night, they pushed on through what is now the Dugway Proving Grounds (a government bombing range and nerve-gas testing area because of its isolation and desolation). The men ate the horses and mules as the animals died along the way.

On June 25, Robert Evans could go no further. Smith left him under a small juniper tree and headed for the distant mountains in search of water. He found it three miles away at the foot of the Stansbury Mountains, on the edge of Skull Valley. The men plunged into the water and drank their fill. Jedediah took five quarts back to Evans, who was barely alive. Evans drank every drop and asked for more. The three rested for a day and moved on.

Two days later, they saw the Great Salt Lake.

"Those who may chance to read this at a distance from the scene may perhaps be surprised that the sight of this lake surrounded by the wilderness of more than 2,000 miles diameter excited in me these feelings known to a traveler who after long and perilous journeying comes again in view of his home," wrote Smith. "But so it was with me for I had traveled so much in the vicinity of the Salt Lake that it had become my home in the wilderness."

In two days' time, Smith, Gobel, and Evans reached the rendezvous on the south shore of Bear Lake, a rendezvous that is still held annually. Because they had been thought to be dead, their presence caused a commotion. Ashley fired a cannon, the first wheeled vehicle to cross South Pass, to salute the returning heroes.

Unfortunately, a few years later, Smith's luck ran out. He was killed by Comanches on the Santa Fe Trail.

## ■ JOHN WESLEY POWELL

"On the right, the rocks are broken and ragged, and the water fills the channel from cliff to cliff," wrote John Wesley Powell, the first man to explore the Green and Colorado rivers in 1869. Every new river runner who floats through Cataract, Westwater, Desolation, and other Utah canyons sees the same wild river and feels the same excitement. "Now the river turns abruptly around a point to the right and the waters plunge swiftly down among great rocks. . . . I stand up on the deck of my boat to seek a way among the wave-beaten rocks. All untried as we are with such waters, the moments are filled with intense anxiety. Soon our boats reach the swift current; and a stroke or two, now on this side, now on that, and we thread the narrow passage with exhilarating velocity, mounting the high waves, whose foaming crests dash over us, and plunging into the troughs, until we reach the quiet water below. Then comes a feeling of great relief. Our first rapid is run."

Boatmen may take dozens of trips down the same stretch of river in a summer, but each time is different because the rivers are ever-changing. Sometimes they are low, with new boulders looming above the rapids. In high-water years, the rivers become raging torrents, whipping the rafts downriver with frightening speed. The Flaming Gorge and Glen Canyon dams have altered the Colorado and Green rivers of Powell's day, but these waterways inevitably surge and swell in wet years and wither in dry ones.

Thousands of adventurers try the Green and Colorado each year. In the evening, at the water's edge in the remote wilderness, the reflections of Powell written long ago, softly echo from the canyon walls.

"As the twilight deepens," he wrote, "the rocks grow dark and somber; the threatening roar of the water is loud and constant and I lie awake with the thought of the morrow and the canyons to come, interrupted now and then by characteristics of the scenery that attract my attention."

*John Wesley Powell conversing with an Indian who was probably one of his guides.*
*(Utah State Historical Society)*

In the morning, as the rafts full of people dart past rocks and brown water, the rafters' thoughts are similar to Powell's: "Today we have an exciting ride. The river rolls down the canyon at a wonderful rate and, with no rocks in the way, we make almost railroad speed. Here and there the water rushes into a narrow gorge; the rocks on the side roll it into the center in great waves, and the boats go leaping and bounding over these like things of life, reminding me of the scenes witnessed in Middle Park—herds of startled deer bounding through forest beset with fallen timber."

It is all but impossible to run a Utah river and not hear of the exploits of John Wesley Powell at some time during the trip. Guides often read from the early explorer's journal around the campfire and tell of the one-armed man who ran the river sitting in an armchair, lashed onto the bow deck of a flatboat.

Powell named most of the rapids and many of the physical features of the canyons shaped by the Colorado and Green rivers. Names like Disaster Falls, 'Bin Hurt, Brown Betty, and 10 Cent most likely recall the experiences of the first men down the river. Most river runners know and appreciate the Major's knowledge of the rivers, but few realize the impact that Powell had in bringing the West into the 20th century.

Though Powell advanced to the rank of lieutenant colonel in the Civil War, it was the title of major that stuck with him. He lost his right forearm in the Battle of Shiloh. After the North won the war, he secured a college professorship of geology and natural history from Illinois State Normal University without benefit of a college degree. He was, in essence, a self-taught man.

After two years of field work, he became convinced that he could explore the canyons of the Colorado and

*James Baker (1818-1898) was the quintessential mountain man. He drank and gambled, trapped with Jim Bridger, and married an Indian princess named Flying Dawn. (Utah State Historical Society)*

its tributary, the Green, even though it would be impossible to replenish supplies for more than 500 miles of the river's length. He used his own money, secured private contributions, solicited money from several colleges and friends, and secured free railroad passes for his men and supplies. The Smithsonian Institute loaned scientific instruments to the expedition. The brave men of his crew received no pay and little glory for their work.

The journey into the last great unknown and unmapped country of the continental United States began at Green River Station, Wyoming, and passed through places like Flaming Gorge, Echo Park, Desolation Canyon, and Cataract Canyon.

By the time Powell left the Colorado, at the mouth of Utah's Virgin River, he was making plans for a second trip. On this adventure, he stopped along the way to study the Indians living in the territory surrounding the Colorado River. He

## ROCKY MOUNTAIN TALE

As is generally known, the Great Salt Lake, though fed by the Bear, Jordan, and possibly other rivers, has no outlet, and it was a common belief that the great lake had a subterranean outlet, otherwise the vast quantity of water poured into it by the two considerable rivers would cause it to overflow its banks. Down in southern Colorado there was, at the time I am writing of, and it may yet be there, a good sized lake that had neither inlet nor outlet, so far as surface indications showed, and it was the general belief that the lake was kept supplied by a subterranean inlet.

According to one, a certain man ventured out on the Utah lake in a small boat. The boat was caught in a whirlpool and, then some distance from the shore, sucked beneath the surface. Clinging to the sides of the boat, with desperation born of despair, the man found himself plunging almost straight downward, with water roaring over and all around him. Suddenly the boat, riding on an even keel, shot forward through a wonderful tunnel-like cavern, the roof and walls covered with vari-colored stalactites, presenting a scene surpassing description. Just how long he floated in the underground channel the man could not tell, but an end came to his trip eventually when he found his boat shooting upward, with its occupant holding on for dear life. As perhaps the reader has guessed, the boat and its owner reached the surface of the Colorado lake, but little the worse for the underground voyage, and the great mystery of the outlet and inlet of the two lakes had been solved.

—Edited by Levette Davidson and Forrester Blake,
*Rocky Mountain Tales,* 1892

also took notes on the area's geology.

The chief topographer of Powell's expedition, A. H. Thompson, discovered and named the last major river added to the United States map while on the expedition. He called it "Escalante" in honor of the Spanish fathers who explored the region in 1776.

Together with photographer John Hillers, in 1871, Powell studied the Ute and Paiute Indian tribes at a time when their way of life was beginning to disappear. He was appointed special commissioner to the Indians in Utah and eastern Nevada in 1873 to help establish the tribes on reservations. He told his superiors that the Indians, numbering only 5,500 in the territory, were on the verge of extinction. His suggestions for reservation sites were adopted, but unfortunately, his vision of a reservation as a school of industry, where instructors taught trades, skills,

---

## JOHN WESLEY POWELL,
## *DIARY OF COLORADO RIVER EXPLORATIONS, 1869*

### Describing Grandview Point in what is now Canyonlands National Park

What a world of grandeur is spread before us! Below is the canyon through which the Colorado runs. We can trace its route for miles, and at points catch glimpses of the river. From the northwest comes the Green in a narrow winding gorge. From the northeast comes the Grand, through a canyon that seems bottomless from where we stand. Away to the west are lines of cliff and ledges of rock—not such ledges as the reader may have seen where the quarryman splits his blocks, but ledges from which the gods might quarry mountains that, rolled out on the plain below, would stand a lofty range; and not such cliffs as the reader may have seen where the swallow builds its nest, but cliffs where the soaring eagle is lost to view ere he reaches the summit. . . . Wherever we look there is but a wilderness of rocks—deep gorges where the rivers are lost below cliffs and towers and pinnacles, and ten thousand strangely carved forms in every direction, and beyond them mountains blending with the clouds.

Now we return to camp. While eating supper we very naturally speak of better fare, as musty bread and spoiled bacon are not palatable. Soon I see Hawkins down by the boat, taking up the sextant—rather a strange proceeding for him—and I question him concerning it. He replies that he is trying to find the latitude and longitude of the nearest pie.

and English to help the Indians prosper in the modern world, was not. America was not ready to accept responsibility for Indian welfare. The Indians were simply herded onto the reservations and largely ignored. Powell later joined the Smithsonian Institute, where he continued his work with the Indians as director of the Bureau of Ethnology.

Powell's travels and studies of Indian philosophy taught him that mankind needs to keep in balance with the land. His geological training helped him realize that the Colorado Plateau and River, and its tributaries, are part of an equilibrium of precipitation, evaporation, and erosion. He preached that civilization must fit within the system or run out of water.

His travels led to suggestions on ways the lands of the West should be managed. Systems that worked in the water-rich East did not apply to the arid West, where the right to own water had to go along with the deed to the land. Engineers needed to create reservoirs so that precious water could be managed for recreation, agriculture, and flood prevention. He called for the preservation of forests, land-use studies, and the setting aside of public land for the use of all citizens.

When Powell became the second director of the United States Geologic Survey, in 1881, he went to work establishing both an irrigation survey for the West and a department of science to help the government make intelligent decisions about its future handling of the environment and the Indians. Many of his ideas failed to be implemented until after his death in 1902. His part in the development of environmental conservation came to fruition with the withdrawal of public lands for the public good, the harnessing of the Colorado River, a bureau of forestry, and a federal department or agency for the encouragement of science.

To get a feel for John Wesley Powell's exploits visit the **John Wesley Powell River Running Museum** in Green River. A multi-media show also examines the history of river running in the state. Exhibits include the Utah River Runners Hall of Fame and several of the earliest boats used by rafters. For an even more first-hand look, try taking a spring "ghost boat" trip down the Yampa or Green rivers with Holiday River Expeditions of Salt Lake. Some of the rafts used are replicas of the originals. Plus, river historians offer guided walks and campfire discussions on Powell and other adventurers. *885 E. Main, Green River; 435-564-3427.*

As a river runner floats down the mighty Colorado into the canyons and over rapids named by John Wesley Powell, he lives the legacy of the man whose bravery and vision helped preserve this part of the country for all Americans.

# THE MORMON PIONEERS

To UNDERSTAND THE MANY NUANCES of Utah's culture without knowing anything about the Mormon pioneers would be as likely as visiting Italy with no knowledge of Roman Catholicism.

Travelers in Utah cannot fail to sense the presence and heritage of the Mormon Church. Its influence is evident in the gleaming white temples found in cities like Manti and St. George. It is preserved at historical sites and museums. It is woven into the fabric of the state's politics, cultural activities, and laws. Many names on the state's road map—Brigham City, Moroni, Nephi, Lehi, and Heber City—reflect Utah's Mormon origins. The Mormons play, and will continue to play, a tremendous and often misunderstood role. This is their story.

## ■ THE FOUNDING OF THE MORMON CHURCH

Persecution either destroys or unifies a people. Seventeen years of persecution gave the Mormons the strength and religious faith to leave the civilized world east of the Missouri River and cross the Great Plains and Rocky Mountains in order to practice their faith. Under adverse conditions they took a dry and inhospitable wilderness avoided by the rest of the immigrants and made it "blossom like a rose."

The history of the Mormon Church begins with Joseph Smith. As a young man in the early 1800s, Smith questioned the many Christian religions competing for converts in the eastern United States. Mormons believe that when Smith prayed for an answer as to which church to join, God and Jesus told him that they had chosen him to institute the true religion. Later, an angel named Moroni appeared and showed Smith where he could uncover some gold plates containing the history of Ephriam and Manasseh, two of the ten tribes of Israel that had fled Jerusalem before it was destroyed by the Babylonians.

The plates told of their escape to the Western Hemisphere, where they established a new civilization. Eventually they divided into two warring camps, the Nephites and the Lamanites. The plates recorded the ultimate victory of the Lamanites, from whom the Mormons believe American Indians are descended. Moroni was himself one of the characters in this history, being the last surviving member of the Nephites and the one who buried the gold plates.

Besides showing Joseph Smith the location of the gold plates, Moroni also gave him some stone spectacles with which to translate the plates from an ancient language into English. When he was finished with his translation, the angel Moroni took the plates back. Smith later produced witnesses who claimed to have seen the gold plates.

## THE BOOK OF MORMON

### Does the Bible Contain All of God's Word?

**2 Nephi 29:6-9:** Thou fool, that shall say: A Bible, we have got a Bible, and we need no more Bible. Have ye obtained a Bible save it were the Jews?

Know ye not that there are more nations than one? Know ye not that I, the Lord your God, have created all men, and that I remember those who are upon the isles of the sea; and that I rule in the heavens above and in the earth beneath; and I bring forth my word unto the children of men, yea, even upon all the nations of the earth?

Wherefore murmur ye, because that ye shall receive more of my word? Know ye not that the testimony of two nations is a witness unto you that I am God, that I remember one nation like unto another? Wherefore, I speak the same words unto one nation like unto another. And when the two nations shall run together the testimony of the two nations shall run together also.

And I do this that I may prove unto many that I am the same yesterday, today, and forever; and that I speak forth my words according to mine own pleasure. And because that I have spoken one word ye need not suppose that I cannot speak another; for my work is not yet finished; neither shall it be until the end of man, neither from that time henceforth and forever.

### The Plates

**Mosiah 8:9-11:** And for a testimony that the things that they had said are true they have brought twenty-four plates which are filled with engravings, and they are of pure gold.

And behold, also, they have brought breastplates, which are large, and they are of brass and of copper, and are perfectly sound.

And again, they have brought swords, the hilts thereof have perished, and the blades thereof were cankered with rust; and there is no one in the land that is able to interpret the language or the engravings that are on the plates. Therefore I said unto thee: Canst thou translate?

—*The Book of Mormon*

In the spring of 1830, Joseph Smith published the *Book of Mormon* and founded the Church of Jesus Christ of Latter-day Saints (LDS) in Fayette, New York. Members of the LDS faith hold the Book of Mormon to be divinely inspired. They called themselves Latter-day Saints in reference to a prophecy by Paul in the New Testament that the true believers in the last days of the world would be called saints. Smith was believed to be bringing about these last, or *latter,* days by restoring the Gospel to the world. Contemporary visitors to Salt Lake City find the angel Moroni depicted in gold atop the Mormon Temple, blowing his horn to announce the restoration of the Gospel of Jesus Christ. (The popular term *Mormon,* incidentally, comes from the name of a Nephite general who wrote the Book of Mormon contained on the gold plates.)

## ■ PERSECUTION

Persecution of the Mormons began almost immediately. Members of the new church called themselves the "chosen of God." They were active missionaries and quietly practiced polygamy. Their zeal and fervor were not appreciated by other citizen or religious leaders. It wasn't long before Smith and his followers were forced to move from New York to Kirkland, Ohio, and Independence, Missouri.

Tensions between Mormons and non-Mormons were inflamed further by the depression of 1837, when many banks all over the United States collapsed, sending their depositors into a panic, and heightening suspicions against newcomers, or those who appeared to be different. Joseph Smith owned several banks, which undoubtedly inflamed the resentment. In short, the Mormans were again expelled from their new homes.

After leaving Ohio and Missouri, the Mormons founded the city of Nauvoo, Illinois, which became home for 20,000 inhabitants, making it the second largest city in that state. Smith and the city council were permitted by the state to raise a militia, levy taxes, and make laws, thus provoking concern in the surrounding non-Mormon communities. The first municipal university in the United States was built in Nauvoo. The city's prosperity, however, brought jealousy. The Mormons soon irritated both political parties in Illinois by voting for neither one.

The Illinois Legislature considered repeal of Nauvoo's charter. Again and again, mobs descended on outlying Mormon farms, killing and mutilating Mormons, and burning their houses and crops. Joseph Smith decided it was time to move again and sent scouts to look for a suitable place. Meanwhile, on May 17, 1844, he declared his candidacy for president of the United States. His stated intention was to spread "the dominion of the Kingdom of God" throughout the country. If this didn't work, he was prepared to head west.

Smith's political ambitions were cut short when he and his brother were arrested when members of the Mormon city council smashed a printing press which they believed was being used to print anti-church libel. Joseph and his brother Hyrum were taken to await trial in a jail in Carthage, the county seat 15 miles to the east. On the night of June 27th, 1844, a mob stormed the jail and killed Joseph and his brother.

*In this rare portrait of Joseph Smith, circa 1838, he stands behind his brother Hyrum. No photograph of Smith is known to exist. (From* History of the Mormons, *1852)*

## ■ EXODUS TO UTAH

Brigham Young became the second leader of the LDS Church. He had grown up near Joseph Smith's New York home and was baptized into the church in 1832. At the time of Smith's death, Young was president of the ruling body of the church, the Council of the Twelve. Since that time, the leader of the Council of the Twelve has assumed church presidency upon the death of an existing president.

Descriptions of Brigham Young vary with writers' views of Mormonism. Some describe him in glowing terms, others with suspicion and contempt. At the time of the exodus to Iowa, he was a thick-chested man of middle age. In *Giants of the Old West*, Frederick R. Bechdolt wrote that the first impression one received from him was of heavy strength: "There was no fineness in his lines. Throughout, there was a certain homely indomitability. His face was large and fair; the blue eyes keen. A brown beard ringed his strong jaw; his upper lip was shaven, revealing the coarse, firm mouth. He would have passed for a well-to-do farmer or a British drover. He was, by trade, a carpenter. By destiny he had become leader of a people."

After Smith's death, the Mormons continued to have problems with their non-Mormon neighbors. Looting, arson, and riot repeatedly tore through the town and surrounding countryside. Fearing for their safety, Young sent scouts to search for sites for possible resettlement. Maps of explorers and mountain men were studied.

Late in 1845, the state of Illinois repealed Nauvoo's city charter and the violence increased. Young sent an advance party to the plains of Iowa, which arrived in February of 1846. The exodus of the Mormons from Nauvoo took several months.

In Council Bluffs, Iowa, the Mormons were asked by U.S. Army Captain James Allen to supply 500 men to help the United States in the Mexican War. Church leaders had a right to be bitter about the lack of support the United States government had given them in the past. Instead, this was seen as an opportunity to prove their patriotism and earn some needed cash. The Mormon Battalion departed in July for a 2,000-mile march to California. They saw no military action but were in the San Francisco area when gold was discovered. It is said San Francisco's first lawsuit was between the LDS church and battalion leader Sam Brannan, who stayed in California to become the state's first millionaire. The LDS Church wanted its share of it. Sam kept the money.

Winter quarters for the remaining church members were established near the site of present-day Omaha, Nebraska. Many Mormons died during the severe winter of 1846. Young decided that there could be no lasting peace until his people found a place where they could live unmolested by the outside world. He felt that if the Church could remain isolated for at least 10 years, it would become strong and able to survive. Young used maps made by explorers of the West, like John C. Frémont, to find a place where the Mormons might be left undisturbed. When Sam Brannan urged him to go on to California, Young said, "Brannan, if there is a place on earth that nobody else wants, that's the place I am hunting for."

Brigham Young found such a place. Two early Mormon pioneers, George Washington Brimhall and Gilbert Belnap, described the Great Salt Lake Valley as "a vast desert whose dry and parched soil seemed to bid defiance to the husbandryman." On July 24, 1847, Young led an advance party of 143 men, three women, and two children to the mouth of Emigration Canyon overlooking the Great Salt Lake Valley. The Mormon leader, sick with mountain fever, raised himself from his wagon bed and announced that they had found what they were looking for. That same afternoon, the pioneers began diverting streams for irrigation, plowing and planting, even before starting construction of their homes. Thus began the transformation of Utah.

The Mormons named the territory they settled the State of Deseret. The word Deseret comes from the *Book of Mormon* and means "honeybee." Thus, the bee and hive have become symbols of the state, signifying industry and community. Both are depicted on the Utah state flag. The emphasis by Young on these qualities made the new territory prosper.

MORMON PIONEERS

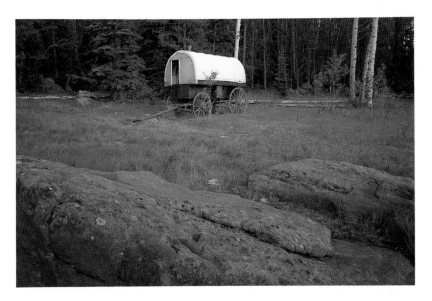

*A renovated pioneer wagon, reminiscent of the ones used by the first Mormon immigrants.*

## ■ ESTABLISHING ZION

Brigham Young proved to be a master planner with a vision for what the future Mormon "Zion" should look like. Mormon history records that he was instrumental in attracting 100,000 people to Utah, founding more than 200 cities, towns and villages, and establishing many schools and factories. To this day, the state has benefited from his far-sighted planning.

The settlers faced innumerable hardships. In the spring of 1848, a late frost hurt much of the beans, corn, and wheat. Then came a cloud of crickets, "by the thousands of tons." The pioneers fruitlessly tried to beat them off the crops, but were rescued finally by hungry sea gulls who flew in to gobble up the crickets. This "miracle of the gulls" is a cherished part of Mormon folklore, and the seagull is the state bird. The state flower, the sego lily, also helped the pioneers survive their first year. Its nourishing, edible bulb was eaten when there was little else.

MORMON PIONEERS

*(above) Brigham Young's original boundaries for the State of Deseret. (Utah State Historical Society)*

*(opposite) These witnesses testified to the existence of the Book of Mormon when Joseph Smith first began to translate it from the "reformed Egyptian." (LDS Archives)*

Church leaders initially divided up the land among all married males. Each received one city lot and one country lot, and was required either to work the land or lose the right to own it. The early settlers lived in Salt Lake City both for protection and companionship.

The early Mormons held property in common. They were also required to give 10 percent of their income for the good of the Church, a practice called tithing that dates to Biblical times. An extensive welfare system was established, whereby large storehouses were built to house excess crops that were passed out to members in accordance to their needs. The arrangement proved so successful that it still exists in much the same form today.

Polygamy remained one of the main tenets of the Latter-day Saints' faith. Church members believed that the only way to achieve the highest reward in heaven was to have more than one wife. In some cases, women entered into purely contractual marriages, providing themselves and their children with a means of financial support.

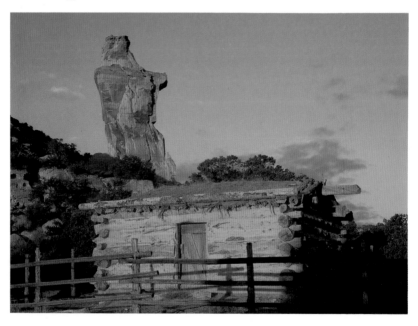

*Swasey Cabin near San Rafael Swell is typical of the sod-roof structures of the early pioneers.*

All Mormon men were (and are) expected to serve as missionaries for a period of time, usually two years. Deseret was to be the gathering place for all Latter-day Saints. A Perpetual Emigration Fund Company was established in 1849, with voluntary donations given to help converts travel to the Salt Lake Valley. Those taking advantage of these funds were expected to pay back the amount they had borrowed as soon as possible so that others could come. In the early years, missionaries to Scandinavia and Europe sent tens of thousands of immigrants to Utah. When organized funding became insufficient to help the flood of converts, Brigham Young came up with a unique solution.

"We cannot purchase wagons and teams as in years past," he told the faithful. "I am consequently thrown back on my old plan and that is to make handcarts and let the emigrants foot it. They can come just as quick, if not quicker, and much cheaper—can start earlier and escape the prevailing sickness which annually lays so many of our brethren in the dust."

Three thousand immigrants pulled handcarts across the United States to join the Latter-day Saints in Utah. There were surprisingly few fatalities. Only the two largest parties, the Willie and Martin companies, suffered disaster. They had left the East too late in the year and then were hit with unusually early winter storms. Brigham Young sent rescuers to the companies stuck on the Wyoming plains. Mormon leader George D. Grant was one of the first Mormons to reach the stranded handcart company. According to William Smart in *Old Utah Trails*, Grant found "between five and six hundred men, women and children, worn down by drawing handcarts through snow and mud; fainting by the wayside; falling, chilled by the cold, their feet bleeding and some of them bare to the snow and frost. The sight is almost too much for the stoutest of us."

As the crippled company was brought into the Great Salt Lake Valley, Brigham Young cut short the church meeting and sent the Saints to ready their homes for the new immigrants. "Prayer is good," he told the faithful, "but when baked potatoes and pudding and milk are needed, prayer will not supply their place."

As the Mormon population grew, so did its "capital" between the Wasatch Mountains and the Great Salt Lake. Civil engineering projects initiated by Young and the Mormon pioneers still impress modern visitors to Salt Lake City. The broad, tree-lined streets are laid out in a grid-like pattern, and clear water runs down the gutters today—just as it did a hundred years ago. All street numbers start from the corner of South Temple and Main Street, and radiate out from the

*Salt Lake City founder and upholder of the Mormon faith, Brigham Young. (Utah State Historical Society*

temple, making it easier to find one's way around in Salt Lake City than in other large cities lacking such urban planning.

Brigham Young built Temple Square in the heart of Salt Lake City. The temple itself, which took 40 years to build, was constructed of granite quarried in Little Cottonwood Canyon, some 20 miles away. Because sacraments like marriage had to be performed in the temple to make them eternal, Mormons were for many years obliged to make pilgrimages to the Salt Lake City temple until other temples could be built.

Another major feature of Temple Square is the famed Mormon Tabernacle, designed by bridge-builders William Folsom and Henry Grow. An egg-shaped dome set above a series of stone buttresses, the Tabernacle is a remarkable building, especially when one considers the primitive conditions under which it was constructed. Because nails were scarce, wooden pins and rawhide were used in construction. The Tabernacle is now home to the world-famous Mormon Tabernacle Choir.

Young's city home was located just east of Temple Square, where it still stands today. It is called the Beehive House because of the sculpted beehive on its roof. Here, Young entertained visitors and passing dignitaries. One of Brigham's 27 wives lived with her children in the Beehive House; more of his families lived next door in the Lion House. Another family lived on the outskirts of the city in his farm home. A store was part of the Beehive House, where all of his wives and children had accounts.

With more than four million visitors a year, Temple Square today is Utah's most popular tourist attraction.

## ■ END OF ISOLATION

The Great Salt Lake Valley's isolation had been advantageous for the church leaders of the young State of Deseret, but isolation could not last forever. In fact, Salt Lake City was becoming an important stop-over on the trail linking the East and West coasts.

The outside world first intruded in 1849 when throngs of miners en route to the gold fields of California stopped in the valley to buy supplies for their journey. Mark Twain passed through during the Comstock silver boom of the 1860s. He recorded in *Roughing It* the sentiments shared by many immigrants during this early period: "The high prices charged for trifles were eloquent of high freights and bewildering distances of freightages. In the east, in those days, the smallest moneyed denomination was a penny and it represented the smallest purchasable

quantity of any commodity. But, in Salt Lake there did not seem to be any money in circulation smaller than a quarter, or any smaller quantity purchasable of any commodity than twenty-five cents' worth."

In 1850, the legislature of the State of Deseret sent a delegate to Congress to petition for statehood. Instead, Congress passed a proposal by Henry Clay to admit California as a state, and New Mexico and Utah as territories. Utah Territory embraced the present states of Nevada and Utah, and its capital was Fillmore. The Mormon name of "Deseret" was repulsive to Congress because of its religious connotations. Congress instead named it after the Ute Indians, but the Mormons persisted in calling it the "State of Deseret."

Tensions during this period of American history were rampant. There were rumblings that the South was about to secede from the Union. Compounding this crisis was the Mormons insistence on governing themselves in a manner much different from the rest of the United States.

Utah Territory was unusual in that Mormon religious leaders also wielded political power. The Mormons resented the federal government's attempts to install its own representatives in the territory. And polygamy was deemed an assault on morality. The Republican National Convention platform of 1856 labeled polygamy and slavery "the twin relics of barbarism." Authorities in Washington were eager to focus public attention on something other than the constant strife over slavery. Given the political climate of the time, it was perhaps a surprise only to the Mormons when President Buchanan revoked Brigham Young's governorship and sent an army detachment commanded by Colonel Albert Sydney Johnston— a man who would later distinguish himself as a commander for the South in the Civil War—to the Great Salt Lake Valley to put down any insurrection which might arise.

This persecution was familiar to the Mormons who, although intent on staying in Utah, were nonetheless prepared to flee the Great Salt Lake Valley and to fight the United States government. The populace was willing to burn the city if the army threatened occupation. When interviewed by Captain Van Vliet for a response to President Buchanan on September 8, 1857, Brigham Young replied boldly: "We shall do the best we can; and I will tell you, as the Lord lives, we shall come off conquerors. . . . We have three years' provisions on hand, which we will cache, and then take to the mountains and bid defiance to all the powers of the government."

*The Mormon Temple and nearby Tabernacle are the most sacred places for members of the Church of Jesus Christ of Latter-day Saints.*

## BRIGHAM YOUNG AND SIR RICHARD BURTON ON POLYGAMY

In the full eloquence of his later years Brigham once told his congregation: "Ladies who come into my office very frequently say, 'I wonder if it would hurt his feelings if I were to ask him how many wives he has?' Let me say to all creation that I would as lief they should ask me that question as any other; but I would rather see them anxious to learn about the Gospel. Having wives is a secondary consideration; it is within the pale of duty, and, consequently, it is all right. But to preach the Gospel, save the children of men, build up the kingdom of God, produce righteousness in the midst of the people; govern and control ourselves and our families and all we have influence over; make us of one heart and one mind. . . is our business, no matter how many wives a man has got, that makes no difference here or there. I want to say, and I wish to publish it, that I would as soon be asked how many wives a man has got, that makes no difference here or there. I would as soon be asked how many wives I have got as any other question, just as soon; but I would rather see something else in their minds, instead of all the time thinking, 'How many wives have you;' or 'I wonder whom he slept with last night.' I can tell those who are curious on this point. I slept with all that slept, and we slept on one universal bed—the bosom of our mother earth, and we slept together. 'Did you have anybody in bed with you?' 'Yes.' 'Who was it?' It was my wife, it was not your wife, nor your daughter nor sister, unless she was my wife and that too legally. I can say that to all creation, and every honest man can say the same; but it is not all who are professed Christians who can say it."

❖ ❖ ❖

*R*efused admittance to the Church, [in 1860 Captain Richard] Burton defended his sincerity. He had, he said, traveled from the Old World to the New simply to become part of a people "sensible enough to permit polygamy." Persuasive though his visitor's argument was, Brigham would not relent. Instead he firmly changed the subject. Had his visitor, in his African explorations, covered the same ground as Dr. David Livingston, the Scottish missionary? Burton replied that he had traveled ten degrees north of Zambezi and the Victoria Falls. One of the Apostles present, Albert Carrington, rose to locate Burton's route on a wall map but moved his finger too near the equator. Brigham called to Carrington, "A little lower down." Carrington obeyed, dropping his finger lower on the map. This was accurate and Burton was impressed. "There are many educated men in England," he wrote, "who could not have corrected the mistake as well." With this the interview was terminated, and

Burton left without the license to practice polygamy, which he had hoped to acquire.

Burton remained almost a month in Salt Lake City and continued to study polygamy as an outsider. He had arrived favorably disposed toward the doctrine. What he saw at firsthand did not disappoint him. "To the unprejudiced traveller," he wrote, "it appears that polygamy is the rule where population is required, and where the great social evil has not had time to develop itself. In Paris or London the institution would, like slavery, die a natural death; in Arabia and in the wilds of the Rocky Mountains it maintains a strong hold upon the affections of mankind. . . . The other motive for polygamy in Utah is economy. Servants are rare and costly; it is cheaper and more comfortable to marry them."

*This idealized portrait of a pioneer family contrasts sharply with the harsh conditions faced by original settlers. (Utah State Historical Society)*

Of course, admitted Burton, the Mormons had, with plural marriage, reduced romance and love "into a calm and unimpassioned domestic attachment." The monogamous company of two encouraged tenderness; the polygamous company of three made it rather a crowd. Still, perhaps this was not too bad. "Womanhood is not petted and spoiled as in the Eastern States; the inevitable cyclical revolution, indeed, has rather placed her below par, where, however, I believe her to be happier than when set upon an uncomfortable and unnatural eminence."

Before leaving Utah for California, Panama, and England, Burton came to this conclusion: "The Mormon household has been described by its enemies as a hell of hatred, envy, and malice— a den of murder and suicide. The same has been said of the Moslem harem. Both, I believe, suffer from the assertions of prejudice or ignorance. The temper of the new is so far superior to that of the old country, that, incredible as the statement may appear, rival wives do dwell together in amity; and do quote the proverb 'the more the merrier.' . . . They know that nine tenths of the miseries of the poor in large cities arise from early and imprudent marriages, and they would rather be the fiftieth 'sealing' of Dives than the toilsome single wife of Lazarus."

❖  ❖  ❖

## HORACE GREELEY ON BRIGHAM YOUNG

At two o'clock in the afternoon of July 13, 1859, Horace Greeley sat down across from Brigham Young. . . . Greeley began to pose his questions, and Brigham replied with pleasing frankness. "He spoke readily," Greeley told his readers, "not always with grammatical accuracy, but with no appearance of hesitation or reserve, and with no apparent desire to conceal anything, nor did he repel any of my questions as impertinent. He was very plainly dressed in thin summer clothing, and with no air of sanctimony or fanaticism. In appearance, he is a portly, frank, good-natured, rather thick-set man of fifty-five, seeming to enjoy life, and to be in no particular hurry to get to heaven."

—Irving Wallace, *The Twenty-Seventh Wife*, 1961

The Mormons' early attempts at guerrilla warfare were impressive. They first burned all the available forage between South Pass and Fort Bridger, Wyoming, cutting off the advance army supply trains and burning them. Swinging behind the main column of the Utah Expedition, they burned several more supply trains. Fewer than 50 shots were fired, and no one was killed, but the troops were forced to spend the winter near Fort Bridger, 300 miles short of their objective.

While the Mormons were under siege and with U.S. troops marching on Utah, the infamous Mountain Meadow Massacre occurred. In the fall of 1857, a wagon train of 140 immigrants from Arkansas and Missouri (a state where Mormons had been severely persecuted) passed through Salt Lake City. The wagon train was rich with livestock and had picked up a few defecting Mormons. Rumors flew that the Arkansans had poisoned springs and even poisoned beef which they had given the Indians. Some said that members of the wagon train had boasted about plans to attack the Mormons. For these reasons, the wagon train was marked for attack. A group of men under President Issac Haight and Bishop John D. Lee disguised themselves as Indians and convinced several hundred Paiute Indians to join them in attacking the immigrants. When the direct attack failed and the Indians would not finish the job, the Mormons took off their disguises and offered a flag of truce and a chance for the men, women, and children to put down their arms and walk away from the wagons. The frightened immigrants complied. The men under Haight and Lee then fell upon the unarmed party and within five minutes the entire group, except for a number of children believed too young to talk, was massacred. All participants swore themselves to secrecy but the story leaked out and evidence was discovered by a wagon train which happened upon the site. Haight was excommunicated. It wasn't until 1874, however, that John D. Lee was caught, convicted and taken to Mountain Meadow, where he was shot. (Lee's Ferry on the Colorado River was operated by Lee during his period of hiding.) A newly dedicated monument marks the site.

While Johnston's army was camped for the winter near Fort Bridger, the political mood in Washington changed. Captain Van Vliet had reached Washington with Brigham Young's message. A scandal concerning army contracts was exposed. Because millions of dollars were being spent with questionable results, the press started calling the whole affair "Buchanan's Blunder." Through an intermediary, Colonel Thomas L. Kane, Brigham Young agreed to admit the army into the territory as long as it neither molested the people nor settled there permanently. Johnston assured the Mormons they would not be disturbed. He marched his men through Salt Lake Valley and on to the west side of Utah Lake in Cedar Valley, where he established Camp Floyd near the present-day hamlet of Fairfield.

The camp followers of Johnston's army soon transplanted themselves to Great Salt Lake City, bringing with them tendencies toward alcohol, theft, and violence. The capital's main thoroughfare became known as Whiskey Street. Yet at the same time, farmers could now sell surplus foodstuffs and livestock to the army at high prices, and cheap manufactured good were available in Utah for the first time.

Although Johnston's army left at the outbreak of the Civil War in 1861, government pressure on the Mormons did not end. In 1862, the Mormons drew up their third constitution for a "State of Deseret," and elected Brigham Young as governor. The federal government viewed this as an act of rebellion and passed a new law aimed at preventing polygamy. They sent Colonel Patrick Edward Connor to Utah with 300 volunteers from California and Nevada. He vowed to "subdue the obstreperous Mormons though all Hell yawned." Connor marched his men into the Great Salt Lake Valley, building Fort Douglas on a bench overlooking the city. Many of the original sandstone buildings at Fort Douglas remain today, as well as a small museum tracing the history both of Fort Douglas and the U.S. Army in the Beehive State.

The Mormons may have caused Connor and his men no trouble, but the influence of the army certainly troubled the Latter-day Saints. Connor set out to undermine the totalitarianism of the Mormon Church. He encouraged his men to

## TWO ACCOUNTS OF A DISPUTE BETWEEN JIM BRIDGER AND MORMONS, 1853

Bridger's description of usurpation of his fort as described by his friend Captain William L. Marcy:

At length. . . his prosperity excited the cupidity of the Mormons, and they intimated to him that his presence in such close proximity to their settlements was not agreeable, and advised him to pull up stakes and leave forthwith; and upon his questioning the legality or justice of this arbitrary summons, they came to his place with an army of 'avenging angels' and forced him to make his escape to the woods in order to save his life. He remained secreted for several days, and through the assistance of his Indian wife was enabled to elude the search of the Danites and make his way to Fort Laramie, leaving all his cattle and other property in possession of the Mormons.

Bridger's letter to his Senator, G.B. Butler, gives the story in his own words:

I was robbed and threatened with death by the Mormons, by the direction of Brigham Young, of all my merchandise, livestock, in fact everything I possessed, amounting to more than $100,000 worth, the buildings in the fort partially destroyed by fire, and I barely escaped with my life.

prospect for minerals, a practice frowned upon by the Church. He organized the first mining district in the Territory in 1863 and wrote its mining code. He never personally benefited from his efforts, yet he earned the title "the father of Utah mining." Silver was found in nearby Park City; copper in the Oquirrh Mountains west of Salt Lake. Mining thrived, so more "outsiders" poured into Utah, diluting the once homogeneous culture.

The Pony Express, and especially the transcontinental telegraph and railroad systems, signalled the end of Utah's isolation. Church leaders who had worked hard to ingrain in their society the idea of cooperation and communal life now worried that gentile (non-Mormon) traders would come to economically enslave the Mormons, who were expected to maintain their spiritual goals before achieving financial reward. On the other hand, the improvements in communication and transport allowed church leaders better contact with members scattered throughout their large territory.

## ■ GROWTH OF ZION

The new railroad facilitated the expansion of Utah's mining industry. Boomtowns sprang up along the Wasatch and Oquirrh mountains. The coal-rich areas of Carbon and Emery counties was exploited. Cattle and sheep ranching prospered. But Mormons were exhorted to trade with Mormon merchants rather than with gentiles.

Brigham Young envisioned his new society as completely self-sufficient socially, religiously, and economically. He frowned upon the export of his people's money, goods, and crops in payment for merchandise. Pioneer lore details experiments undertaken to fulfill the Church president's wishes. Mulberry trees, for example, were imported along with silkworms to produce silk for ladies' fine garments. Perhaps the best-known experiment was the establishment of a cotton mission in sunny St. George. Cotton and silk were produced there, but abandoned with the advent of the railroad.

Drawing on examples of existing cooperative tanneries and mills, the Mormons formed Zion's Cooperative Mercantile Institution (ZCMI) in 1868. This department store (now owned by the May Company) still operates in Salt Lake City today.

Mormon leaders believed that only by extensive settlement could Deseret remain in Church hands. There was to be no room for outsiders in the promised

# ON THE MORMON FRONTIER—THE DIARY OF HOSEA STOUT, 1844-61

*(as it appears in the original)*

**Tuesday 28th 1851 January.** This morning quite a company went out with the Band to meet the governor B. Young & others who were gone to Weber County Davis & the settlements North to preach visit & Organize the County of Davis.

The went to congratulate him on the news of his appointment of Gov. by the President of the U.S. They returned about and were recieved here by the firing of artillery and the shouts of a large concourse of citizens and a display of fire works at Messrs Kinkead & Levingston's Store. The whole scene was joyful peaceable and quiet. The Gov when he was escorted home delivered a short address to the people assembled.

I spent the day at home and around the Council house Weather fine clear & warm

**Monday July 5th 1852.** This morning the citizens of this city were awakened by the roar of artillery at break of day followed by a Serenade by two Bands of music to hail the birth day of our national liberty and at half past seven I went to the Tabernacle to meet the Committee of arraingements preparitory to forming the Gov escort after which according to a previous invitation from his excellency the Gov I repaired to his house at half past 8 o'clock to join his suit to be escorted to the Tabernacle where the ceremonis of our celebration would commence

When the escort arrived The 31 veterans, then the "Mormon Battalion" The escorted pay and Gov forming betwen them while the Minute company of Horse were in the rear the escort proceeded with proper cerimonies to the Tabernacle under the continual roar of cannon. After which the meeting was opened by prayer and the order of the celebration commenced which consisted of alternate speaches, songs, airs, toasts & c.

I read the Declaration of Independence, immediately after the opening prayer.

Had a short adjournment for dinner. The day past off well and all seemed to enjoy themselves well. About four the assembly dispersed. Had some legal business for Thomas Moor to attend to about dark. So well was Mr Lely satisfied with the compromising manifested that he gave me 5 dollars in the presence of Br Moor although I was Moor's attorney vs him

**Thursday 15 June 1854.** Mr Elisha Ryan with some seven Shoshone Indians arrived here, There is several lodges of shoshonee's been encamped here sevral days. In the after noon we had a regular talk with Ryan, as chief, and his braves He aid he was sent by the Head Chief to learn what our intentions were. Whether we intened to take their land & if so whether peaceably or not. What was the feelings of the

General Government & also Governor Young and the mormons, towards them. That they did not want their timber cut or have houses built on their land nor have settlements established. That if we did not and were friendly all was well for they desired to live in peace with all men but at the same time they would not allow any infringement on their lands.

That they had given Green River to him the said Ryan and those mountaineers who had married shoshonee wives. They complained bitterly about the general government neglecting them in never making a treaty with them and not sending men to trade for their skins and furs &c Ryan said he had been robbed of his last bottom dollar (refering to the suit against him last year) That he considered this land his own and no one had a right to keep a ferry here but himself and those who had married shoshonee wives. He said he [had] nothing against the mormons as a people but had againts those individuals who robbed him last year, and many such things spake he.

—*On the Mormon Frontier: The Diary of Hosea Stout, 1844-1861*
(Hosea Stout was a lawyer and an officer in the Nauvoo Legion)

*The furniture in this pioneer cabin was laboriously hauled West by covered wagon. (Utah State Historical Society)*

land of Zion. Mormon pioneers spread to all corners of the territory and into lands now part of Nevada, Idaho, Arizona, Wyoming, Colorado, New Mexico, and California.

As new immigrants arrived, they were organized into groups and assigned land for development into self-sufficient communities. Many were dispatched to settle remote parts of Deseret, guided by experienced settlers, who were often called upon to leave the farms that they had established earlier. These moves often tested the faith of Church members who had spent long, hard hours working to make their land prosper, only to be asked to leave and begin someplace else. Much of Utah is dry and must be irrigated in order to cultivate. Only faith in their leaders and the Mormon belief that good works on earth promised salvation induced these pioneers to start over again.

Settler Parley P. Pratt described the feelings of many: "My family and myself, in common with many of the camp, suffered much for food. I had ploughed and subdued land to the amount of near 40 acres and had cultivated the same in grain and vegetables. In this labor every woman and child in my family. . . had joined to help me. . . . Myself and some of them were compelled to go with bare feet for several months, reserving our Indian moccasins for extra occasions. We toiled hard and lived on a few greens and on thistle and other roots. We had sometimes a little flour and some cheese, and sometimes we were able to procure from neighbors a little sour skimmed milk or buttermilk." But he would write his brother in England, "All is quiet—stillness. No elections, no police reports, no murders, no wars, in our little world. . . . It is the dream of the poets actually fulfilled."

Even occasional threats from sometimes hostile Indians seemed minor compared with threats the Mormons had received from their old neighbors in Illinois.

One of the most inspirational stories about the pioneers' faith and perseverance in the settlement of Utah was the Hole-In-The-Rock expedition. Two hundred and fifty men, women, and children took 82 wagons and hundreds of head of livestock to colonize the most remote corner of the state. The most difficult part of the journey was the descent down a narrow, 2,000-foot cliff, where they crossed the Colorado River. The pioneers had to cut their path through solid rock, from ledge to ledge, a disheartening, week-long task. "While they were doing it, Mons Larson and his 23-year-old wife, Olivia, reached the top of the mesa in a blizzard," wrote William B. Smart in *Old Utah Trails*. "On the climb up, Olivia had carried a two-and-one-half-year-old under one arm and a one-and-one-half-year-old child under the other, just as she had carried them down the Hole. The children's feet had been frost-bitten in the bitter cold, and the parents spent most of the night doctoring them. The next day, February 21, lying in the wagon seat while her husband struggled to pitch a tent against the raging blizzard, Olivia delivered her third child, a healthy boy."

Today, boaters on Lake Powell can look up at the route the pioneers took down the Hole-In-The-Rock. Four-wheel-drive enthusiasts can peer down into the crevice after driving to the spot from Escalante over Bureau of Land Management property. Dance Hall Rock, where the brave company relaxed and danced before their difficult journey, can be seen along the way.

*A passage had to be cut through solid rock so that the wagons of the Hole-in-the-Rock expedition could proceed. (Utah State Historical Society)*

MORMON PIONEERS

■ ENTRANCE TO THE UNION

By 1868, Congress had taken sizeable chunks of land away from the Territory of Utah, paring it to its present shape.

When Ulysses S. Grant became president in 1869, the issue of polygamy was eliciting increasing criticism of the Mormons. In 1882, Congress passed the Ed-

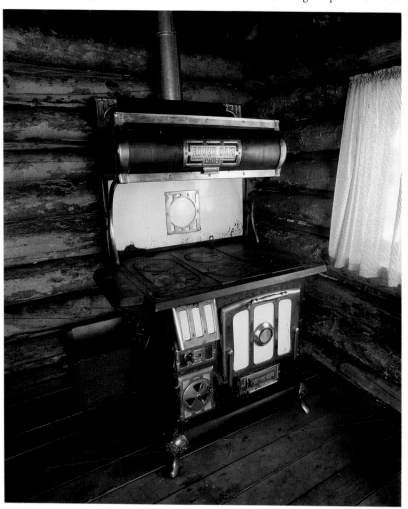

*Pioneer cabin stove.*

munds Bill, allowing the federal government to fine and imprison polygamists. Many polygamists hid their plural wives and children when federal marshals came to town. Mormons were not allowed to vote or hold office in the territory. By the end of 1885, hundreds of Mormons were pouring into the Mexican state of Chihuahua to escape persecution. The Mexican government had outlawed polygamy also but did not actively prosecute. Anti-Mormons formed the Liberal Party. Its voice for many years was the *Salt Lake Tribune*. The Mormon Church owned, and continues to own and operate, *The Deseret News*. The competition between the two worlds of thought in Utah still exists.

In 1877, with controversy whirling around him, Brigham Young died in the Lion House. Many wondered if Mormonism would die with him. The succeeding church president, John Taylor, died in hiding in 1887. That same year, the Edmunds-Tucker Act dealt another severe blow to the Mormons by disincorporating the LDS Church, confiscating all of its property, abolishing female suffrage and the Perpetual Emigration Fund, mandating a federally appointed government for Utah, and requiring an oath that they were not polygamists before they could vote, hold elective office, or serve on juries.

In September of 1890, the new Church president, Wilford Woodruff, published a manifesto in *The Deseret News* describing some revelations in which the Lord had directed him to ask his followers to cease practicing polygamy. "The Lord showed me by vision and revelation exactly what would take place if we did not stop this practice," he wrote. "If we had not stopped throughout the land of Zion, confusion would have come upon the whole Church, and we should have been compelled to stop the practice. Now, the question is, whether it should be stopped in this manner, or in the way the Lord has manifested to us, and leave our Prophets and Apostles and fathers free men, and the temples in the hands of the people, so that the dead may be redeemed. . . . The Lord has decreed the establishment of Zion. He has decreed that the Devil should not thwart it. If you can understand that, that is the key to it."

This significant change made life easier for the Mormons. After publicly abandoning the practice of polygamy, they were allowed to vote and hold public office. They formed the People's Party. In a gesture of reconciliation in 1889, the Mormon People's Party offered four places on their Salt Lake City ticket to prominent gentiles. As a result of the infusion of gentiles into politics, the Territorial Legislature established public schools in 1890, further separating church and state. A year

later, to offer proof of their desire to keep religious leaders from governing, the LDS leaders asked members to join the Democratic and Republican parties instead. The Church, however, continues to wield power in Utah's politics to this day.

A seventh constitutional convention met in Salt Lake City in 1895 in hope of getting Utah Territory admitted to the Union. Those attending gave women the right to vote and officially outlawed polygamy, though polygamous marriages already in existence were allowed to continue. On January 4, 1896, President Cleveland proclaimed Utah the 45th state in the Union.

## ■ THE MORMONS TODAY

At one time, being Utahn meant being Mormon. This is no longer the case; the isolationism of the past is gone. The Mormon Church's influence is everywhere in Utah, but other creeds are found, as well. Mormons are in the majority in most rural communities and many suburban neighborhoods. The religious population of the urban areas is much more diverse (though still 50 percent Mormon).

State politics is influenced by the conservative opinions of the Church. Most Mormons tend to vote Republican, though there have been and are many Democratic officials, including governors and congressmen. Most candidates are sensitive to Mormon thought and avoid being labeled as "liberal."

The Mormon church owns KSL Radio and Television, as well as the state's third largest newspaper, *The Deseret News*. Mormon viewpoints are expressed therein, along with differing opinions. The Church also owns radio and television stations in other parts of the country. Deseret Book is an LDS-owned bookstore where Mormon as well as non-Mormon publications are sold.

The Mormon Church maintains many landholdings in Utah and around the world. In downtown Salt Lake City, 35 acres, including Temple Square and part of what was once Main Street, are owned by the Church, since it was the first landowner. The city has benefited from this in many ways. For instance, the land where Salt Lake County's convention center, The Salt Palace, sits, is loaned to the city for $1 a year. (These and other Church businesses do not have non-profit status, and are handled separately from the religious affairs of the Church.)

The heart of the Church has always been Temple Square, and although the Tabernacle Choir will contine to broadcast from the Tabernacle, a new 21,000 seat Conference Center has just been constructed north of Temple Square. In 1999,

*Utah became a state on January 4, 1896, after decades of conflict with the federal government over polygamy. (Heritage Prints, photo courtesy of Rell Francis)*

# THE CHURCH OF JESUS CHRIST OF LATTER-DAY SAINTS: A BRIEF OVERVIEW

## ◆ BEGINNINGS

If given the word "Mormon" during a free-association test, most Americans would probably respond "polygamy." This is unfortunate, because the Mormon faith, with over five million adherents worldwide, offers a rich body of original religious thought and springs from one of our nation's most fascinating histories. In fact, polygamy—which has been banned by the church since 1890—has played a very minor role in the overall development of the church since its inception by Latter-day Saints prophet Joseph Smith.

In Jan Shipp's *Mormonism*, the author defines the first episode in Mormon history as beginning with Joseph Smith's "First Vision" at the age of 14. The young Joseph Smith, confused about which church he ought to join, prayed that the truth would be revealed to him. One spring morning in 1820, he entered a grove of trees near Palmyra, New York, in a state of despair. There he had a vision lifted him from his depressed state. Joseph Fielding Smith's *Essentials in Church History* details the prophet's own description as follows:

"'It no sooner appeared than I found myself delivered from the enemy which held me bound. When the light rested upon me I saw two personages, whose brightness and glory defy all description, standing above me in the air. One of them spake unto me, calling me by name, and said, pointing to the other—'This is my beloved Son, hear him!'

"My object in going to inquire of the Lord was to know which of all the sects was right, that I might know which to join. No sooner, therefore, did I get possession of myself, so as to be able to speak, than I asked the personages who stood before me in the light, which of all the sects was right—and which I should join. I was answered that I must join none of them, for they were all wrong; and the personage who addressed me said that all their creeds were an abomination in his sight; that those professors were all corrupt; that they draw near to me with their lips, but their hearts are far from me; they teach for doctrines the commandments of men, having a form of godliness but they deny the power thereof. He again forbade me to join with any of them. . ."

According to Shipp, Joseph Smith had a second vision on the night of September 22, 1823:

"This time it was a vision of an angel who identified himself as Moroni, 'a messenger sent from the presence of God to tell of records written on gold plates which, along with two special stones called the Urim and Thummim, were buried in a hill not far from the Smith family farm. From Moroni the young man learned that the possession and use of these stones were what constituted 'seers' in ancient or former times, and that God had prepared them for the purpose of translating the book that was engraved in Reformed Egyptian characters on the gold plates."

Smith made four annual visits to the site where the plates were buried (where he would also converse with the angel Moroni) but was not able to obtain the plates until September 22, 1827.

The Mormons believe that through Joseph Smith, the true church was restored. He is considered to be the authentic successor of the priesthood which began with Adam but for centuries had been interrupted by the establishment of the Roman Empire. Certain priestly powers (the "Aaronic priesthood") were restored when John the Baptist laid hands on Smith; further priestly powers (the "Melchizedek priesthood") were restored by the laying on of hands by the Apostles Peter, James, and John. Joseph Smith's later visitations by the Apostles Peter, James, John, and the angel Moroni, supplied details pertaining to the lost history of the Americas. In *The Mormon Corporate Empire*, John Heinerman and Anson Shupe provide a summary of this history,

"In about 600 B.C. a band of inspired Hebrews had left Jerusalem shortly before the Babylonian army overran the city. These Hebrew refugees sailed west across the Atlantic and founded a mighty civilization in both the North and South American continents, where Jesus Christ manifested himself several times again to supplement His Middle Eastern visitations. Moroni, the last prophet of one warring Jewish faction called the Nephites and son of Mormon, the Nephites final historian, led Joseph Smith to ancient gold plates on which the account of these events was written. Fourteen centuries earlier, Moroni had hidden the plates beneath a large rock on a hillside near Smith's house after the Lamanites (who became the root stock from which American Indians sprang) wiped out the Nephites. The Lamanites' advanced civilization then deteriorated into barbarism. Smith was appointed to translate the golden texts, creating from them a third biblical testament, the *Book of Mormon*, which would establish the legitimacy of the new Zion in North America and complete the books of the Bible."

In 1830, after a few years of arduous work by Smith, the translator, and his appointed scribe, Oliver Cowdery, *The Book of Mormon* was published.

The name "Mormon" comes from the name of a Prophet in *The Book of Mormon*

—a second witness to Jesus Christ. The King James Version of the Bible, *The Doctrine and Covenants*, and *The Pearl of Great Price*, are fundamental to the faith, as well.

The growing band of Mormons suffered continuous persecution in New York. In search of a place where the new Zion might be based, Smith led the group to Kirtland, Ohio and then on to various counties in Missouri. They finally settled in Nauvoo (Commerce), Illinois. Heinerman and Shupe note that at each stop, "they were pursued by angry mobs, denounced by the local newspapers and clergy, and spied on by suspicious politicians." It was not long after Joseph Smith and his brother, Hyrum, were murdered in a jail in Carthage, Illinois (they were being held for suppressing the *Nauvoo Expositor*—an anti-Mormon paper), that the Mormons, faced with renewed persecution, fled to Iowa. There, four temporary settlements were established. Shipp writes that "The Pioneer Company" left the settlement at Winter Quarters, Iowa "to search for a permanent settlement site." On July 22-24, the pioneers reached the Great Salt Lake Valley and, four days later, a site was selected for the Temple.

### ◆ MORMON CUSTOMS

The first thing that strikes the inquirer about the Mormon faith is its adherents' deep, abiding commitment to family—the second is their emphasis on order. David O. McKay, President of The Church of Latter-day Saints in the late sixties, once stated that, "There is no success that can compensate for failure in your own home."

The Mormon love of family and adherence to what is recognized by them to be the natural order of things is reflected in such church customs as baptisms and sealings.

There are two baptisms for the remission of sins: one for those who are repenting and another for the deceased. Children are not baptized until the age of eight. The Mormons believe that children come into the world innocent—each child is thought of as being a child of God—and are not able to choose clearly between good and evil, right and wrong, until around this age. The baptisms of the living take place in a baptismal font in the chapel.

The baptisms of the dead take place in the Temple's font. A Mormon is encouraged to trace his or her genealogy as far back as possible and to submit the name of non-member relatives to headquarters in Salt Lake City. They are then baptized vicariously; Mormons claim that all individuals are free moral agents. They hold that even the spirit of the dead has the choice to accept or not to accept the teachings of the church. (The spirits of all persons come from the spirit world and at death return until the time of the Resurrection.) Good human agency, for them, is a matter of presenting humans with the correct principles and letting them govern themselves.

Sealings are defined, in Bruce R. McConkie's *Mormon Doctrine* as, "ordinances performed in the Temple whereby husbands and wives are sealed together in the marriage union for time and eternity, and whereby children are sealed eternally to parents. . ." McConkie informs the reader that sealings for the dead are available on a proxy basis, too.

There are approximately 85 Temples worldwide. Services are held in the chapel on Sunday but ordinances such as baptisms for the dead and sealings are performed at the Temple.

Another striking feature of Mormonism is that the Temple is not open to everyone. Admission to the Temple requires what is called a "Temple recommend," that is, a certificate issued by the church. Some of the qualifications which must be met in order to enter the Temple are as follows: Upholding the Testimony of Jesus Christ, sustaining general authorities of the church, paying full tithe, honesty in all business dealings, being morally clean (this includes being free of sexual sin), and abstaining from drugs, alcohol, coffee, tea, and tobacco. One must also wear his or her "Temple garment," that is, special underclothing worn daily by all who are worthy to wear them. Temple garments are symbolic of the promise to Father in Heaven.

A prominent feature of the Mormon religion is its extensive missionary program. Typically, Mormon men are sent (anywhere in the world) on a two-year mission when they reach nineteen years of age. Women who are not married at the age of twenty-one are eligible for an eighteen-month mission. Each missionary is guided by an older church member of the same sex. The places the missionaries are sent are not decided at random but are, rather, individually chosen by the church authorities in Salt Lake City. During the mission, missionaries must obey a set of strict rules pertaining to moral purity. They are not permitted to swim, date, attend parties, and the like, or they will be sent home—something akin to receiving a dishonorable discharge from the military. Conversely, the completion of one's mission is regarded as a great honor.

What of holidays? The Mormons celebrate most traditional holidays. Christmas is celebrated on December 25th, although the Mormons do not believe that Jesus Christ was born on that day. Traditional holiday lore is downplayed in favor of the original religious essence of the holidays, however, the appearance of Santa Claus and the Easter Bunny is generally tolerated for the sake of the young children. Pioneer Day—a day replete with huge festivities—takes place annually on July 24th, in honor of the settlers entering Salt Lake City.

—Holly Cratty

MORMON PIONEERS

some five million people visited Temple Square to see the headquarters of the LDS Church. Authorities estimate that two-thirds of this number are not Church members.

The Church of the Latter-day Saints, likewise, is no longer confined to Utah. As of 1999, 60,200 Mormon missionaries resided in 113 different countries, while the number of foreign converts runs into the hundreds of thousands. The Church has an ambitious program of building new temples throughout the world, so Mormons no longer have to come to Salt Lake City for sacraments.

Today, mainly young men between the ages of 18 and 20 are expected to spend two years as missionaries. Young women have been allowed to become missionaries, too, and their numbers are growing. Married couples are volunteering more and more to do mission work. Women and married couples may serve from one to one-and-a-half years.

Mormon boys are expected to start saving for their missions early, as it is primarily the family's responsibility to finance the mission. Money spent supporting a missionary is not tax deductible. The missionaries are given intense language training if necessary, and sent out in pairs. Several sets of missionaries may work in the same area. They must adhere to strict moral guidelines while in the field. Dating, and even holding hands, is not allowed. Many a Mormon woman, however, will wait for her missionary and keep in touch by mail and telephone while his two-year commitment is fulfilled.

Visitors to Utah often notice the abundance of children in the state. The Church's teaching that children are blessings and that family life is essential has helped give the state the youngest population in the nation.

The Church teaches that alcoholic beverages, caffeine, and tobacco are harmful to the body, and discourages their use by Mormons. This has resulted in a state population statistically healthier than the rest of the country, as well as some unusual liquor laws. The state has slowly been working on changing these laws, however, to attract more tourists.

Though punishable by law and excommunication, the practice of polygamy still exists in a few isolated places. It is not actively prosecuted in Utah. Several fundamentalist groups have broken from the established Church over the polygamy issue, and also over the idea of communal property.

With its emphasis on family life and clean living, the Mormon Church has enabled a prosperous and vital state to evolve. As it holds on to these values into the future, Utah will remain a great and beautiful place to live.

## WATER IN AN ARID LAND

No group of people in the West since the coming of the whites has been more aware of the importance of water, more cohesive and diligent in searching, capturing, and distributing it, or more suitably adapted to preserving and perpetuating a water-dependent culture in an arid land than the Mormons, those members of the Church of Jesus Christ of Latter-day Saints who make up the vast bulk of Utah's population. Like the Indians, the Mormons have their own distinctive relationship to the waters of the Colorado River system. The Mormons have shared in it greatly, the Indians minimally. Unlike the disparate, transient whites that make up most of the West's population, these two groups (not really minorities since they dominate and rule their own lands to a great extent) possess separate identities and unique institutions that have survived despite constant encroachments from the outside world. To wander

through their separate nations is to feel like a stranger in one's own land.

The Mormons wasted no time in establishing their own special relationship to water that was later to be emulated throughout the West. . . .

From the start it was the Mormons conquering the desert, ceaselessly seeking prosperity and progress in an inhospitable locale—what was to become the second driest state. There was no private ownership of water. The church controlled its distribution and made the decisions on where and how to capture it. The family was the basic social unit, and farming, not mining, was the preferred occupation.

*Sunset over Utah Lake, Utah Lake State Park.*

With the coming of the energy shortages in the early 1970s, all these basic Mormon tenets would be challenged during the mad scramble for Utah's mineral wealth. But until then, in the small Mormon towns scattered like frontier outposts throughout the Colorado River basin in the remote eastern and southern portions of Utah, it would still be an almost completely closed, agrarian society, one which viewed the goings-on in the metropolitan area of Salt Lake City as being somewhat akin to those of ancient Babylon. . . .

Farming had been the traditionally approved Mormon occupation in Utah; search for and production of minerals was historically discouraged. Water followed socio-religious preferences, with 90 percent of it diverted to agriculture. But in the last ten to fifteen years, mineral production—particularly if it was energy-related—has gained an accepted, even preferred, status in the Beehive State. Employment was a principal reason. No longer did agriculture supply jobs in sufficient numbers, so water was to be directed more and more toward municipal and industrial use. Agriculture would remain stable, but energy uses of water would expand, or so it was hoped. A 1967 policy statement of the Utah Board of Water Resources, reiterated in 1975, was revealing: "The Board considers the use of water for the irrigation of new lands to be relatively less advantageous to the State under conditions now existing than some possible alternative uses." Energy, for instance. The state's large reserves of coal, oil, oil shale, tar sands, and uranium were located in the Colorado River basin, precisely in those remote regions where the population was dropping most alarmingly and that basic Mormon unit, the family, was disintegrating. The problem was to get the water there, back to its basin of origin, since most of it was already committed to urban areas west of the divide. . . .

That there was any controversy in the 1970s, or even a difference of opinion on something so basic as the use of water, was a rarity in monolithic Utah and a testimony to how tight things were getting. Again, the Indians were central to the differences, but there were other elements— environmentalists, Uinta Valley residents, agricultural and energy interests.

—Philip L. Fradkin, *A River No More,* 1981

# S A L T   L A K E   C I T Y

■ HIGHLIGHTS                              *page*

Temple Square                              103
Mormon Tabernacle                          105
Cathedral of the Madeleine                 110
South Temple Mansions                      110
Trolley Square                             113
Liberty Park                               113
Lagoon                                     114
Utah Museum of Fine Arts                   121
Performing Arts                            126
Sundance Institute                         133

SALT LAKE CITY IS THE HEART OF A METROPOLITAN AREA of more than a million people spread through the Salt Lake Valley. For over a hundred years, people from Wyoming, Idaho, Nevada, Utah, and parts of Montana and Colorado have traveled to Salt Lake City to shop, work, worship, make transport connections, and simply enjoy themselves. It has served as a hub of the Intermountain West ever since the Mormons founded it in 1847. Wrote one of the writers of the 1941 Work Project Administration's *Utah: A Guide to the State:*

> *F*rom the time of its settlement, an air of the incredible has attended Salt Lake City. . . . Travelers have forever been coming to see for themselves 'the New Jerusalem,' the 'Utah Zion,' the 'City of the Saints.' In all but a handful of the books written on Utah and the Mormons during the first 30 years of the city's existence, the Mormon capital was Utah, a way of thinking not yet entirely disposed of.

Naturally, many a citizen of the more sparsely populated southern and eastern portions of Utah have grumbled that Salt Lake City residents think the state ends at the city's southern boundary. It is, of course, the state's capital. Utah's major television and radio stations, and two of its three major newspapers, operate in the city. It is also the world headquarters for the Mormon Church, whose annual spring and fall conferences draw thousands into the city from all over the world, and whose Temple Square is easily Utah's top tourist attraction. Salt Lake City is the state's cultural center: people flock into the valley to enjoy the Utah Symphony, Pioneer Theatre Company, Ballet West, the Utah Opera Company, the Ririe-Woodbury Dance Company, the Salt Lake Acting Company, the Repertory Dance Theatre, and the Mormon Tabernacle Choir. The state's three most popular professional sports teams—the Utah Jazz of the National Basketball Association, the Starzz of the Women's National Basketball League, and the Salt Lake Buzz of the Pacific Coast League—play in the valley. The largest state university, the venerable University of Utah, sits on the east bench of the city. (Its arch rival both in athletics and academics, the 28,000-student Mormon-owned Brigham Young University, is located less than 50 miles south in Provo.) The huge Salt Palace convention complex, the Delta Center sports arena, a large and continually expanding international airport, Utah's largest shopping centers, and its most important federal, state, and local government offices are found in Salt Lake City. Eleven major ski areas are located within a 90-mile drive of the airport.

## ■ SALT LAKE CITY, OLD AND NEW

Modern-day Salt Lake City still reflects the vision of Brigham Young, the Mormon prophet who brought the small band of 143 men, three women, two children, 70 wagons, one boat, one cannon, 93 horses, 52 mules, 66 oxen, and 19 cows into the Salt Lake Valley on July 24, 1847.

Visitors to Salt Lake City can see the result of his early urban vision: first-timers usually comment on the width of the streets. After brief exploration, they marvel at the ease with which addresses are found. Most streets run north-south and east-west, and are numbered according to their direction and distance from the southeastern corner of Temple Square. Thus, the first street to the south of Temple Square is First South. Ninth East is nine blocks east of that corner. Nearly every Utah city is laid out in much the same manner.

When the U.S. government sent Captain Howard Stansbury to survey the Great Salt Lake in 1849, the city was already developing into an important urban area.

"A city has been laid out upon a magnificent scale, being nearly four miles in length and three in breadth," wrote Captain Stansbury. "Through the city itself flows an unfailing stream of pure, sweet water, which by an ingenious mode of irrigation, is made to traverse each side of every street, spreading life, verdure and beauty over what was heretofore a barren waste."

Though officially a part of the United States, for many years Salt Lake City operated largely as a kind of theocracy under Brigham Young. Greater cultural and religious diversity arrived in later years, starting with the California gold rush of 1849, when many non-Mormons (referred to as "gentiles" by the Latter-day Saints) passed through the area. During the Civil War, soldiers were stationed in the city. The joining of the transcontinental railroad 80 miles to the north in 1869, and the promise of silver, gold, and lead in the nearby mountains, brought more gentiles.

At times, the clash between the Mormons and non-Mormons became intense. In fact, many of the rivalries between the factions exist today, though they are certainly less evident than in the 1890s.

"The split between Mormon and non-Mormon communities was evident in the use of land in Salt Lake City," wrote Ted Wilson in his Utah Geographic Series book *The Wasatch Front.* "The Mormons dominated the north end of the city with Temple Square, Brigham Young's homes and offices, retail facilities and other buildings. Non-Mormon business leaders, including Samuel Newhouse, Albert

SALT LAKE CITY

*Modern-day Salt Lake City reaches skyward.*

Fisher, and the Auerbach family, built more than a dozen major buildings at the south end of the city's business district as a counter-weight to the Mormon influence at the north end. The area became the nucleus for the Auerbach Department Store, the Newhouse Hotel, the New Grand Hotel, the Salt Lake Stock Exchange (especially in mining stocks) and the Commercial Club, founded in 1902 to attract outside business to Utah."

Salt Lake City's present character began to take shape at that time. Buildings like the State Capitol and the Gothic Cathedral of the Madeline were completed. Residents of the new neighborhoods—the Avenues, Capitol Hill, Liberty Park, and Sugarhouse—rode trolley cars into the city. During the Great Depression, buses gradually replaced the trolleys and construction slowed.

Like many urban areas across the country, Salt Lake City seemed threatened in the 1960s when new malls and shopping centers opened in the suburbs, and the city retail district began to decline. That's when the Salt Palace, a downtown convention complex, keyed an urban renewal effort designed to bring people back into the heart of the city. The Mormon Church invested $40 million to develop a downtown shopping mall, the ZCMI Center, named for Zion's Cooperative Mercantile Institution, which claims to be the oldest department store in the United States. (ZCMI was sold to the May Company in 1999, but retains its name.) Shortly thereafter, the Crossroads Mall was built directly across the street from the ZCMI Center, effectively concentrating most of the retail trade on both sides of Main Street between South Temple and First South. A city-wide beautification project was completed at about the same time.

The concentration of businesses on the north end of town did cause problems with the old "non-Mormon" district to the south. Famous old department stores like Auerbachs and the Paris Company went out of business. The Newhouse Hotel was razed. Now, the city fathers have begun to revitalize this area, first by completely restoring the Gothic-style City-County Building and then by constructing a combination of open spaces and new office buildings in the southern portion of downtown. Many of the city's older buildings located just south of the Salt Palace were tagged for redevelopment as part of a restaurant-entertainment district. The Peery Hotel Complex, containing two restaurants and an elegantly restored luxury hotel, is a good example of what can be done when older buildings are rehabilitated into useful, modern structures.

As the metropolitan area grows a new light rail system called TRAX has created efficient travel from the downtown Delta Center through Salt Lake Valley. To the

*A view of the City and County Building in downtown Salt Lake with the Wasatch Range looming in the background (photo by Stephen Trimble)*

SALT LAKE CITY

## CENTRAL
## SALT LAKE CITY

0     .5     1 mi

0     .5     1     1.5 km

Wasatch National Forest

Beck St

Victory Rd

To Ogden

Children's Museum of Utah

Wall St

Center St

East Capitol Blvd

City Creek Canyon Rd

City Creek

18th Ave

Northcrest Ave

Chandler

600 North St
500 North St
400 North St
300 North St
200 North
North Temple

Memory Grove Park

13th Ave
12th Ave
11th Ave
10th Ave
9th Ave
8th Ave
7th Ave
6th Ave
5th Ave
4th Ave
3rd Ave
2nd Ave
1st Ave

11th Ave
Virginia St

Pioneer Memorial Museum

State Capitol

Utah Heritage Foundation
Utah Travel Council

Tabernacle
Temple Square

Union Pacific Depot
Assembly Hall
Abravanel Hall

Mormon Temple
Kearns Mansion

Delta Center
Salt Lake Art Center
Family History Library

Brigham Young Mon
Hansen Planetarium
Cathedral of the Madeleine

South Temple
100 South

Capitol Theatre
200 South

Visitors Bureau
Gallivan Utah Center
300 South

To SLC International Airport
Utah State History Museum

Peery Hall Complex
Exchange Place Hist Dist
400 South

SALT LAKE CITY

University of Utah

Pioneer Park

City & County Building
500 South

500 South

Rice Stadium

Mt. Olivet Cemetery

600 West
500 West
400 West
300 West
200 West
West Temple
Main St
State St
200 East
300 East
400 East
500 East
600 East
700 East
800 East
900 East
1000 East
1100 East
1200 East
1300 East

600 South
700 South
800 South
900 South

Trolley Square
Trolley Corners

McClelland St

1000
Herbert Ave
Liberty Park

Kelsey Ave
1300 South

Princeton Ave
Yale Ave
Laird Ave

To Provo

Cleveland Ave
Kensington Ave
Harris Ave
1500
1700 South

Cleveland Ave

6th East

Emerson Ave
Logan Ave

Harrison Ave
Roosevelt Ave
Bryan Ave

1400 East

700 West

Wilson Ave
Downington Ave
Coatsville Ave

1000 East

A B C D E F G H
1 2 3 4 5

south in Jordan is the new Jordan Commons, an entertainment and restaurant complex. The new South Towne Exposition Center will draw conventions and concerts to Sandy.

Despite their modern veneer, Salt Lakers still keep a warm spot in their hearts for the past. The state's biggest event is the **Days of '47** celebration, commemorating the day (July 24, 1847) when Mormon pioneers first entered the Salt Lake Valley. Every July 24, one of the largest parades in the United States marches through downtown Salt Lake, preceded by horse and children's parades, and drawing hundreds of thousands.

## ■ TEMPLE SQUARE  *map page 102, D-2*

In much the same way that Trafalgar, Red, and St. Peter's squares reflect the personalities and histories of their respective cities, so is Temple Square the focal point of Salt Lake City.

Drawing close to four million visitors a year, the 10-acre stone-walled complex of gardens, statuary, and historic buildings fashioned in the last half of the nineteenth century by Brigham Young and the Mormon pioneers is Utah's premier tourist attraction. Over 1,100 volunteer guides, hosts, and hostesses—350 of whom speak one or more languages other than English, and some of whom use sign language—explain the history of Temple Square and the origins of Mormonism. The largest crowds come during the Christmas season, when some 300,000 twinkling lights draped on trees, bushes, and buildings turn Temple Square into a holiday treasure. A life-sized nativity scene, concerts, Christmas movies, and slide shows add to the festive atmosphere.

### ◆ SALT LAKE TEMPLE

The majestic focal point of the square, the Salt Lake Temple is a cathedral-like building with six spires that took 40 years to complete. Designed by architect Truman O. Angell, this is the most famous of 85 such structures maintained throughout the world by the Latter-day Saints. Don't expect to be admitted to the temple when you visit; entry is restricted to Latter-day Saints with passes, or written "recommends," from their bishops. (One of the two large visitors centers displays an exhibit giving non-Mormons a vicarious tour of the temple.) Mormon temples are not used for Sunday worship services, which take place instead in thousands of local churches. Temples are used on weekdays for marriages, baptisms, and other sacred ordinances.

According to author Quig Nelson in Temple Square: The Crown Jewel of the Mormons, the walls of the Temple are made of granite blocks, hewed to fit tightly together. At the base, the walls are nine feet thick and taper to six feet at the top. The granite was quarried in Little Cottonwood Canyon about 23 miles from the Temple site. Until 1873, teams of oxen pulled the wagons loaded with the gargantuan blocks of granite from the quarry to the construction site. After 1873, the granite was shipped via a new railroad.

Perhaps the most distinctive feature of the temple is a 12-foot, $5^{1}/_{2}$-inch-tall statue of the **Angel Moroni**, which stands on the middle spire on the east side of the structure. Mormons believe Moroni to be the last prophet of the Western Hemisphere, who finished compiling the writings of other ancient prophets in the Americas. Prior to his death, Moroni buried the plates on a hill. Upon resurrection, he returned to the earth, appeared to Mormon founder Joseph Smith, and showed him where the records were buried. The statue was constructed of

*Non-Mormons may view the temple only from the outside.*
*Mormons need a pass or a "recommends" from their bishop to enter the temple.*

*The Mormon Temple in Salt Lake City took 40 years to complete. (Utah State Historical Society)*

hammered copper covered with glistening gold leaf. Nielsen writes that architects utilized a unique suspension system to keep the statue sturdy but flexible. Leverage action in the system allows the statue—which has stood on its spire for 85 years —to withstand wind storms of up to 90 miles per hour. With the exception of the Temple, all other buildings on Temple Square are open to the public.

## ◆ MORMON TABERNACLE

Next to the Temple, the most famous building on the square is the Mormon Tabernacle, an egg-shaped, silver-domed building completed in 1867. The building is 250 feet long, 150 feet wide, and 80 feet high. It sits on 44 cut sandstone buttresses.

"The roof is a great bridgework of timbers, with the wooden arches, beams and supports latticed and pinned together with wooden pegs and rawhide thongs," writes Nielsen. "Very few bolts or nails were used and what were available were homemade."

The Tabernacle was completed in 1867. When a balcony was added three years later, the seating capacity was increased from 4,500 to about 6,500. The original roof, which was replaced by metal in 1900 and aluminum in 1947, was covered with 400,000 wood shingles.

Noted for its fine acoustics, the Tabernacle served as the cultural center of Salt Lake City for over a century. Many Utah Symphony patrons remember sitting through concerts on the hard, wooden seats until the orchestra moved in 1979 to the new Symphony Hall less than a block away. The building still houses the world-renowned **Mormon Tabernacle Choir,** a 320-voice ensemble known for its weekly network radio and television broadcasts, top-selling records (five gold albums), and worldwide concert tours. When the choir is in town, the public can attend rehearsals at 8:00 P.M. each Thursday, and the Sunday CBS Radio broadcast at 9:30 A.M. (doors close at 9:15 A.M.). The choir also performs in the 2,000 seat Conference Center north of Temple Square.

The choir formed a few weeks after the arrival of the pioneers and sang in a quaint bowery constructed of adobe blocks, with poles supporting a roof of leaves and branches to hold back the warm August sun. Choir members are volunteers between 30 and 60 years of age and are limited to 20 years of service. *For performance schedules and tickets call 801-240-3221.*

The giant 10,857-pipe **Tabernacle Organ** was originally designed by an English carpenter named Joseph Ridges, and constructed before the coming of the railroad. Ridges had suitable lumber for the wooden pipes transported 300 miles by ox team from the southern part of the territory. Wind to operate the organ was furnished by four men pumping bellows. The organ was rebuilt by Niels Johnson in 1885, and again, several times in the present century: in 1901 by the Kimball Organ Company, in 1915 by the Austin Organ Company, in 1945 by the Aeolian-skiner Organ Company of Boston, and in 1948 by G. Donald Harrison. Its present configuration consists of eight divisions, played from five manuals and a pedal board, with 191 ranks, totaling 10,857 pipes. That is a far different instrument than the 32-rank, 1,600-pipe, 25-note pedal board and two 56-note manuals first designed by Ridges. After a cleaning of the pipes and installation of a new console to the organ in 1988, the president and tonal director of Schoenstein and Co. of San Francisco, Jack Bethards, wrote in The American Organist that the organ has a signature sound: "By this I mean an organ that is instantly recognizable, one with individual character. Creating a unique sound while staying well within the bounds of good taste and tradition is the work of genius. Achieving these things in an eclectic instrument is a miracle."

*The organ in the Mormon Tabernacle boasts 10,857 pipes. Here it is played to accompany the world-renowned Mormon Tabernacle Choir. (photo by Stephen Trimble)*

## ◆ OTHER TEMPLE SQUARE ATTRACTIONS

### Assembly Hall

The four-gabled Assembly Hall seats about 1,200. It was completed in 1880 using left-over granite from the Temple construction. It now dominates the southwestern portion of Temple Square. Free concerts are presented every Friday and Saturday in this building, which is also used for funerals, lectures, musical programs, and summer-time non-denominational services.

### Temple Square Visitor Centers

Temple Square's two visitor centers—one located on the north side of the square and the other on the south—house exhibits relating the history, beliefs, and programs of the 6.5-million-member Mormon Church. The focal point of the north visitors center is a large white marble statue of Jesus Christ, a reproduction of "The Christus," created in the nineteenth century by Danish master Bertel Thorvaldsen, whose original graces the Church of Our Lady in Copenhagen, Denmark. Other displays in the centers include giant murals and paintings on the life of Christ, automated dioramas, and a variety of audio-visual presentations. *801-240-2534.*

### Nauvoo Bell

The 782-pound bronze bell, cast in England, once hung in the Nauvoo Temple in Illinois before the Mormons were forced to leave. The bell can be seen and heard at Temple Square.

*The Lion House was home for Brigham Young's wives and children.*

### Seagull Monument

The monument honors the birds that Mormons believe were sent from God to eat a massive infestation of crickets which threatened to destroy crops planted by the pioneers. It is also found inside the Square. Admission to Temple Square (and to all activities held there) is free.

### Conference Center

Part of the roof of the newly-constructed Conference Center is landscaped with trees and native plants. The Tabernacle Choir performs here as well.

### The Mormon Family History Library

Better known as the church genealogical library, this is the largest library of its kind in the world. Visitors come from all over the world to search out their family roots. There is no charge. Finding one's ancestors is important to the Mormons, who hold a "baptism of the dead" for people not baptized in the LDS church before its founding. Many of the records are stored in tunnels carved into the granite near the mouth of Little Cottonwood Canyon. *35 N. West Temple; 801-240-3702.*

### Museum of Church History and Art

The museum contains pioneer artifacts, a large collection of Southwest Indian artifacts, and works of art; paintings, sculpture, and photographs by artists from early through modern times, illustrating the history of the Latter Day Saints in Utah, as well as early Utah history. *45 N. West Temple; 801-240-3310.*

### Latter-day Saints Office Building

Mormon Church headquarters are in a 28-story office tower with the city's highest observation deck. *50 E. North Temple.*

### Beehive and Lion Houses

Visitors can tour Brigham Young's primary residence, the Beehive House, built in 1854. The beehive, a symbol representing industry, appears as a decorative motif throughout the house. *Corner of South Temple and State; 801-240-2671.*

A stone lion guards the entrance to the Lion House next door. The house was once a sort of apartment complex for Young's wives and children, but it now serves as a social center with a cafeteria called The Pantry in its basement. *63 E. South Temple; 801-363-5466.*

## ■ OTHER FAITHS

It would be too much to say that non-Mormons always get along or got along with the dominant Mormons in Salt Lake City. People who move from other parts of the United States into Utah often complain that government and culture in the state are dominated by the LDS Church. Still, Catholics, Methodists, Buddhists, Baptists, Greek Orthodox, Jews, and most major Christian denominations can be found in Salt Lake City. Many thrive on their minority status. Although Mormons do dominate state and local elected offices, Dee Dee Corradini, the first woman to be the city's mayor, was a non-Mormon.

Early Mormon pioneers and the Catholic Church interacted cautiously, and only when necessary. Bernice Maher Mooney, in her book *The Story of the Cathedral of the Madeleine,* discusses the association between Lawrence Scanlon, first Catholic bishop of Salt Lake City, and high Mormon officials: "The reciprocal effort at peaceful association continued throughout the territory. In 1879, Apostle Erastus Snow, leader of the Latter-day Saints at St. George, invited Bishop Scanlon to offer High Mass in the Mormon Tabernacle there. The bishop did so on September 25, 1879. The Tabernacle Choir, conducted by John M. MacFarlane who had become friends with Bishop Scanlon, obtained the music for the Kyrie, Gloria and Credo and practiced diligently for some weeks."

The spirit of cooperation between the Mormons and the Catholics continues to this day. Many prominent Mormons contributed to the $6.5 million drive to restore the interior of the historic and architecturally significant **Cathedral of the Madeleine.** Utah's Catholic population (which has grown from 90 in 1873, when Bishop Scanlon first arrived from Ireland, to 98,880) regards the cathedral as the heart of its diocese. Bishop Scanlon purchased the cathedral property, at 331 E. South Temple, for $37,000 in 1890. The exterior of the building was finished in 1909, but the ornate interior was not completed until 1926. The cathedral possesses some of the most beautiful stained-glass windows in North America, created in 1906 by Zettler Studios of Munich, Germany. *331 E. South Temple, just east of Temple Square; 801-328-8941.*

**St. Mark's Episcopal Cathedral,** at 100 South Street, was constructed in 1871 and is Utah's oldest non-Mormon church. The red sandstone exterior of the **First Presbyterian Church** at East South Temple and C Street makes it stand out as one of the most impressive structures on South Temple.

## ■ EXPLORING THE CITY

### ◆ SOUTH TEMPLE MANSIONS *map page 102, D-4*

Some of the most impressive mansions in the state can be viewed when walking or driving along South Temple. These include the **Enos A. Wall Mansion,** which now serves as the headquarters for the LDS Business College, and the **Kearns Mansion** at 603 East South Temple, constructed by Thomas Kearns, an early mining baron who founded the state's largest daily newspaper, *The Salt Lake Tribune.* Kearns' heirs do not own, but continue to manage the newspaper, but his elegant 28-room residence now serves as the official residence of Utah's governor.

The morning *Tribune* and the *Deseret News*, which publishes on weekday evenings and weekend mornings, are long-time rivals, as evidenced by a debate the two had during a local election in the late 1800s. Writes Ted Wilson in his Utah Geographic Series book *The Wasatch Front:*

> The Peoples party represented the Mormon faction and Gentiles flocked to the liberal party," "*The Deseret News,* owned and operated by the Mormon Church, became the feisty advocate of the People's party, while *The Salt Lake Tribune* held forth for the non-Mormons. The fight occasionally got tough. In 1876, the *Tribune* labeled the People's party ticket for city offices 'a Priesthood city ticket' made up of #'1 President of the Church, 1 Apostle, 2 Bishops, 3 Bishop's Councilors, 2 sons-in-law of Brigham Young, and Brigham's private secretary.'

◆ UTAH STATE CAPITOL
*map page 102, C-2/3*

The ornately decorated Capitol overlooks Salt Lake City from a hill atop State Street. Constructed of granite and capped by a copper dome, the building was completed in 1915 at a cost of $2,739,529. Housing the state legislature, governor's office, and Supreme Court, the building is certainly worth exploring. Don't miss the basement displays of Utah's history and industry. *350 N. Main; 801-538-3000.*

*A row of historic mansions lines South Temple Street. (photo by Stephen Trimble)*

## MARK TWAIN'S SALT LAKE CITY

Next day we strolled about everywhere through the broad, straight, level streets, and enjoyed the pleasant strangeness of a city of fifteen thousand inhabitants with no loafers perceptible in it; and no visible drunkards or noisy people; a limpid stream rippling and dancing through every street in place of a filthy gutter; block after block of trim dwellings, built of "frame" and sunburned brick—a great thriving orchard and garden behind every one of them, apparently—branches from the street stream winding and sparkling among the garden beds and fruit trees—and a grand general air of neatness, repair, thrift, and comfort, around and about and over the whole. And everywhere were workshops, factories, and all manner of industries; and intent faces and busy hands were to be seen wherever one looked; and in one's ears was the ceaseless clink of hammers, the buzz of trade and the contented hum of drums and fly-wheels.

Salt Lake City was healthy—an extremely healthy city. They declared that there was only one physician in the place and he was arrested every week regularly and held to answer under the vagrant act for having "no visible means of support." They always give you a good substantial article of truth in Salt Lake, and good measure and good weight, too. Very often, if you wished to weigh one of their airiest little commonplace statements you would want the hay scales.

❖   ❖   ❖

It is a luscious country for thrilling evening stories about assassinations of intractable Gentiles. I cannot easily conceive of anything more cosy than the night in Salt Lake which we spent in a Gentile den, smoking pipes and listening to tales of how Burton galloped in among the pleading and defenseless "Morisites" and shot them down, men and women, like so many dogs. And how Bill Hickman, a Destroying Angel, shot Drown and Arnold dead for bringing suit against him for a debt. And how Porter Rockwell did this and that dreadful thing. And how heedless people often come to Utah and make remarks about Brigham, or polygamy, or some other sacred matter, and the very next morning at daylight such parties are sure to be found lying up some back alley, contentedly waiting for the hearse.

—Mark Twain, *Roughing It*, 1872

♦ OTHER ATTRACTIONS

**Council Hall** *map page 102, C/D-2/3*
This historical building once served as city and territorial government offices. It was moved to the hilltop in 1960, where it now serves as the home of the **Utah Travel Council.** *utah.com. Located just south of the Capitol; 801-538-1030 or 800-200-1160.*

**Salt Lake Convention and Visitors Bureau**
*map page 102, D/E-2*
This is another good place to pick up tourist information and current details about cultural activities. *visitsaltlake.com. Located in the Salt Palace convention complex, 100 S. West Temple; 801-521-2822.*

**The Pioneer Memorial Museum**
*map page 102, C-2*
Here you will find one of the West's most complete collections of authentic 19th-century pioneer memorabilia. Collections of dolls, Brigham Young's personal effects, paintings, pioneer fashions, a carriage house, and a children's playroom provide glimpses of early life in Salt Lake City. The Daughters of the Utah Pioneers, who operate the facility, are diligently seeking stories and histories concerning the people who settled Utah. *300 North Main, southwest of the Capitol; 801-538-1050.*

**Hansen Planetarium** *map page 102, D-2/3*
Located near the historic Eagle Gate entrance to Capitol Hill, the planetarium, is a favorite of science buffs. Housed in what was once the Salt Lake City Library, the planetarium, with its laser shows, live stage plays, spectacular star shows, and science museum, is among the most innovative facilities of its kind anywhere. Learn how to use telescopes to view the evening sky. *15 S. State Street; 801-538-2104*

**Children's Museum of Utah**
*map page 102, B-2*
It calls itself the "Doing Place". Kids can fly a plane, stage a puppet show, explore the Old West, see a flash flood, or shop in a grocery store. Parents are invited, too! *childmuseum.org. Located in the old Wasatch Baths building at 840 North 300 West; 801-328-3383.*

**Salt Lake Art Center** *map page 102, D-2*
The two-level gallery features traveling art displays and a small collection of locally significant pieces. *Located near the Salt Palace convention complex at 20 S. West Temple; 801-328-4201.*

**Utah State Historical Society Museum**
*map page 102, E-1*
The 1910 **Rio Grande Depot** is the home of the Utah State Historical Society Museum and research library. The library provides a fascinating glimpse into the past for those with time to spend rummaging through old books and magazines. The Historical Society's bookstore has perhaps the most complete selection in the state of publications dealing with all Utah subjects. If a book has been published about Utah, chances are you can buy it there. (Try the Rio Grande Mexican restaurant on the northern end of the building.) *300 South Rio Grande Street; 801-533-5755.*

**Shopping**

Many Salt Lake City shopping trips begin at the May Company's **Zion Cooperative Mercantile Institution** (ZCMI), which was founded by Brigham Young in 1868 while Macy's was still a specialty stop. Shoppers can find major department stores like Nordstrom and Mervyn's in the **Crossroads Mall** west of ZCMI on Main Street. Historic **Trolley Square** provides the most interesting shopping atmosphere. This upscale complex of high fashion items, restaurants, and movie theaters once housed the city's trolley systems and is patterned after places like San Francisco's Ghirardelli Square. Take time to explore the winding brick hallways and one-of-kind antiques found in this charming center. *550 South 700 East*

◆ PARKS AND NATURAL AREAS

**Liberty Park** *map page 102, F/G-3/4*

One of the oldest recreation areas in Salt Lake City, this is the city's answer to New York's Central Park. The venerable green space, four blocks long and two blocks wide, has served as a gathering place since Isaac Chase built a mill there in 1852. Free flour from the mill saved many families during the two-year famine of 1856-1857. The millstones and irons used at the mill—which still stands at Liberty Park—were brought across the plains by ox-team. A small amusement park, a modern children's playground, and landscaped gardens stand between the mill and Chase's yellow adobe brick home, which was constructed in 1853. For the most part, though, Liberty Park serves as a quiet, shaded retreat. Just spending a fall afternoon walking through the manicured grounds or paddling a canoe on the pond delivers one from the hassles of the big city. Many Salt Lakers learned to play tennis in the large public complex on the west end of the park, and to swim in the nearby pool. The park is the site of community fairs, horseshoe contests, and road races.

Stroll through the shaded grounds of the **Tracy Aviary** to watch golden and bald eagles, flamingos, peacocks, golden pheasants from China, and hundreds of other unusual birds. In the summer, the aviary hosts a bird show and a lory walk (visitors enter an enclosure to feed and observe parakeets). *589 E. 1300 South; 801-322-2473.*

**Sugarhouse Park**

Sugarhouse Park, now a quiet expanse of grass and hills, reveals a colorful chapter of Salt Lake City history. It was formerly the site of the old Utah State Prison, a facility surrounded by 18-foot-high red sandstone walls, which was finally closed down in the 1940s. Labor activist Joe Hill, made famous in a folksong sung by Joan Baez, was executed here. So was a convicted murderer named John Deering, who was wired with an electro-cardiograph as a firing squad prepared to execute him. Seemingly unconcerned, his heart beat at the rate of 180 times per minute shortly before he was shot. The heart of a man doing violent exercise seldom beats faster than 120 times a minute. The prison physician said Deering would have died even if no bullet had been fired. A monument at Sugarhouse Park is a reminder of its grim past. *1300 East 2100 South.*

**Natural Areas**

A movement is afoot in Salt Lake Valley to preserve natural areas. The **Parleys Gulch Nature Center**, at the mouth of Parleys Canyon, and the **Dimple Dell Regional Park**, near Sandy in the southeast corner of the valley, have been preserved as such. The Jordan River, which almost cuts the valley in half as it flows from Utah Lake into the Great Salt Lake. Portions of that trail system are already in place. A trail system running the entire length of the valley along the Jordan River is nearly complete. The best part runs from 4800 South to 7800 North in Murry to Midvale, with parks along the way. We enjoy taking canoe trips from the Raging Waters waterslide complex at 1700 South, past Jordan Park and the International Peace Gardens, through the fairgrounds, to the Northwest Community Center. Despite its situation in the midst of a bustling city, this is a surprisingly scenic and quiet float trip. Portions of the Bonneville Shoreline Trail allows hikers a feeling of a walk in the mountains, and a view of the city. The trail follow, roughly, the shoreline of ancient Lake Bonneville. Joggers and bicyclists also enjoy **Memory Grove** and **City Creek Canyon**, located directly behind the state Capitol. The road up the canyon is often closed to automobile traffic, making it an excellent place to walk, run, or ride.

## LAGOON: A PIONEERING AMUSEMENT PARK

Peter Freed wanders through the well-manicured grounds of his Lagoon amusement park in awe of what he and his family have created. A new $7 million water slide park sits on the site of what was once a mere swimming pool. Nearby, people laugh and shriek as they are whirled upside down on the park's new metal roller coaster. High above the park, riders on the tramway peer down to the midway below, and the Lagoon band belts out a spunky tune in a place where entertainers as diverse as Duke Ellington and the Rolling Stones have performed.

Lagoon is the nation's second oldest operating amusement park. Only Pennsylvania's Dorny Park—which is three years older—predates the opening of the Utah park in 1886. It was founded by railroad magnate Simon Bamberger, who would later serve as Utah's fourth governor. Bamberger owned the railroad line connecting Salt Lake City and Ogden, and built the park in order to encourage people to ride his train. "Lakeside," as the park was originally called, was constructed four miles west of present-day Lagoon, on the shores of the Great Salt Lake, but met its demise when the lake receded. Eventually, the park was moved to a spot near a pair of ponds and some artesian wells, and renamed "Lagoon."

*The dancing pavilion at Lagoon.*

For many years the park was a tremendous success, but it was closed during World War II and by 1945 was derelict. "There were waist-high weeds all over the place," recalls Peter Freed, who with his brothers Robert and Dave took over the amusement park from the Bambergers in 1945. "It looked like a ghost town. You had to use a lot of imagination to envision it as an amusement park again."

A few remnants of the original Lagoon can still be seen. The oldest building, the Lake Park picnic terrace, dates back to the "Lakeside" resort. A turn of the century carousel, one of fewer than 200 of its kind in the United States, is still in operation. The park's first roller coaster, built in 1921, has retained its original design, although it has been rebuilt many times, and Freed believes it to be one of the oldest operating wooden coasters of its kind in the country.

When Lagoon was first conceived, it was, like most amusement parks of its time, relatively simple. "The big things in those days," recalls Freed, "were dancing and bathing. We put in the swimming pool, and it was the first one in the area. When we started buying rides, we started out slowly because we didn't have any money. There was nothing like we have now."

In 1953, a fire started near the roller coaster and destroyed most of the west midway. The Freeds rebuilt with a vengeance, and soon Lagoon was one of the largest amusement parks of its kind between the Mississippi River and the West Coast.

In the 1960s, legendary rock performers like the Doors, the Beach Boys, the Rolling Stones, and Janis Joplin performed at Lagoon's Patio Gardens. The Beach Boys even composed a song—"Salt Lake City"—which mentioned the park. But, with the advent of the drug culture, the Freeds decided to turn Patio Gardens into a

*Lagoon Park circa 1900. (Utah State Historical Society)*

spook alley and roller skating rink, because they were afraid that rock-concert patrons wouldn't mix well with wholesome families enjoying the rides. As an alternate entertainment, they built an opera house where they staged theater performances and musicals.

In 1974, the Freeds purchased the "Pioneer Village" collection of buildings and Utah artifacts then near the east bench of Salt Lake City and brought it all to Lagoon. Their interest in preserving and presenting Utah's pioneer history to the public is understandable. Their maternal grandfather was Brigham Young's older brother. Visitors to Pioneer Village get a sense of what it was like to be an early Utah settler. On view, in one of the best gun museums in the United States, are several of gun inventor John Browning's early prototypes, as well as his tools and workbench. Rare Civil War and Mormon Battalion flags hang near the safe of Mormon leader Porter Rockwell. Kids can be "locked" into an old rock jailhouse, ride a horse-drawn carriage through the streets of the little village, and imagine what school was like inside the old Wanship schoolhouse. Brigham Young's china, a tiny organ which survived the Mormon trek across the plains to Utah, the state's first soda fountain, a drug store, and a rock chapel moved piece by piece from Coalville, are on display. There's also the old Charleston post office, a train station moved from Kaysville, and the carriages of some of Utah's most prominent early citizens. The more modern thrills of a log flume ride—a modern-day equivalent of the water chute built at Lagoon at the turn of the century—and Old West shootouts on Main Street, add to the attraction of Pioneer Village.

Now, with the construction of the water slide park, Lagoon seems to have come full circle to its origins as a place to swim. The park draws over one million visitors annually, and on a busy summer day, it is not unusual to see 15,000 people enjoying the rides, playing games, listening to music, and viewing the gardens, exhibits, and fountains.

"My late brother Robert loved the amusement park industry," recalls Peter, "and made it his life. If he came back today, though, he wouldn't recognize it. The big change now is that the rides are so much more sophisticated. You really can't buy any kind of a ride at all for under $1 million. Some cost as much as $14 million."

Then, Utah's soft-spoken amusement park pioneer smiles, almost shyly. "The greatest thing about the business is that our product is fun."

*Located about halfway between Ogden and Salt Lake City just off I-80.*

## ■ ALONG THE EASTERN BENCH

The University of Utah sits on the eastern bench of Salt Lake City, a rise between the urbanized valley and the higher Wasatch Mountains. Some of the city's most interesting attractions are located on the bench.

### ◆ THE UNIVERSITY OF UTAH  *map page 102, D & E-5*

The University of Utah's roots date back to 1850 when the Territorial Legislature established the University of Deseret and placed it under the control of a chancellor and board of 12 regents. A month after the passage of the act, the regents solemnly announced: *PATRONS OF LEARNING: The citizens of the State of Deseret have established a University at Great Salt Lake City. . . . It . . . will teach all nations all useful arts and sciences. . . . instruction by means of lectures or otherwise will be brought to the level of the laboring classes. . . . It is neither arrogant nor extravagant to say this institution is forthwith prepared to teach more living languages classically than any other University on the face of the earth. . . . as to the matter of dead languages, we leave them mostly to the dead. Facilities for acquiring intelligence from every portion of the globe will be more perfectly secured to this institution than to any other of our acquaintance. Correspondence will be kept up with persons in the service of the University, living at London, Edinburgh, Paris, Rome, Copenhagen and Calcutta. Whatever is valuable in the laws and usages of nations . . . diversified languages . . . practical mechanism . . . fabrics of governments . . . physical laws . . . will be copiously poured into the lap of this institution.*

These lofty early aspirations were not, however, matched by available facilities or teachers. The home of the first "university" was the parlor of an adobe cabin owned by John Pack. Unfortunately, the $5,000 grant that the Legislature of 1851 appropriated for the school came from an empty treasury. The original venture into higher education lapsed into almost non-existence until 1867. Although the school lacked early success, it remains the oldest university west of the Missouri River.

The revival of the University of Deseret came in 1869 when Dr. John Park took over. He established a department and a training school. Although most of the institution's students were of high school ability, the schools of law, medicine, education, and mining were nonetheless quickly established. The name was changed to the University of Utah in 1892 and, in 1900, the institution was moved to its present site on the east bench of Salt Lake City, overlooking the valley. The university headquarters, located on a U-shaped road students call "The Circle," is called the Park Building, in honor of the man who helped revive the institution.

From those humble beginnings, the University of Utah has grown into a visually appealing architectural mix of traditional and contemporary buildings located in a lush, park-like setting. The campus consists of 1,500 acres and 280 buildings. It boasts a faculty of 3,400 and a student body of 27,000. In addition, the University of Utah Research Park, with 42 tenants in 28 buildings, is located on 320 acres adjacent to the campus. The university offers 74 undergraduate majors and 93 graduate degrees. In addition, several interdisciplinary degree programs enable students to design their own majors while working closely with faculty advisors.

While some of its recent scientific research has been controversial, the University of Utah continues to enjoy a reputation as one of the finest state-run institutions of higher learning in the country. Edward B. Fiske, the education editor for the *New York Times*, said the school's special academic programs "place the U. in the ranks of the most distinguished colleges."

The university continues to be a leader in the studies of technology, Middle Eastern culture, computer science, artificial limbs and organs, modern dance, genetics, and mining; and the culmination of a major research project in the 1980s brought it international notoriety. The first artificial heart transplant exemplified what University of Utah President Chase Peterson says brings many "highly promising as well as established scholars to the University for a sense of freedom that allows them to get things done."

The transplant of the Jarvik 7 artificial heart into retired dentist Barney Clark in December of 1982 by a team headed by surgeon William DeVries at the University of Utah Medical Center was the culmination of 15 years of research. Developed by Dr. Robert K. Jarvik, a design engineer who completed medical school at the U. in 1976, the heart consisted of two pumps that replaced Clark's right and left ventricles. The artificial heart was powered by an external air compressor linked to the patient by two hoses. Clark survived for 112 days.

The research project toward an artificial heart began with the establishment of the Division of Artificial Organs by Dr. Willem J. Kolff, a Dutch-born scientist, in 1967. He was appointed professor of surgery, research professor of engineering, and finally director of the Institute of Biomedical Engineering. The critical link for Kolff was the opportunity to join medical research with engineering disciplines.

Although the artificial heart has been used with mixed results and is now utilized primarily as a stop-gap measure for patients until a live transplant becomes available, artificial heart research is on-going at the University. It's possible that one day, tens of thousands of lives will be sustained with permanent totally artificial hearts, and many thousands of patients will lead more productive and gratifying lives with artificial hearing. "Our efforts to make these technologies widely available to the public and to build a large and profitable business are based on technological excellence and the early establishment of a strong position in the marketplace," noted Jarvik.

The U received $195.1 million for funding of research from external sources in 1998-99. It is a national leader in inventions per million dollars in research. In addition, the university's Huntsman Cancer Institute is a leading facility for study of that disease, and is currently greatly expanding its department to open even more labs for multidisciplinary research on cancer.

The partnerships formed by industry and the university have resulted in new companies that have added almost $600 million in annual sales and 6,000 new jobs to Utah's economy. This is double what it was five years ago. The state of Utah has partnered with the Technology Innovation Program of the University and the University of Utah Research Park to make this happen. Research Park houses 37 companies and portions of 30 academic departments.

Utah's Centers of Excellence work with these two entities. The University of Utah houses 11 of Utah's Centers of Excellence. Their goal is to convert university research and technology into marketable products, skilled jobs, and new high-tech businesses. Since 1986, seven new spin-off companies have been developed, 865 companies assisted, 96 patents have been issued, and 13 are pending.

In the computer graphics section, researchers are designing urban setting simulations to help planners visualize what cities of the future may look like. The school has also helped pioneer a "Service Learning Degree" in which students work on community aid projects. Students must complete a number of service hours as well as take specialized courses to earn this degree.

The University of Utah is not only a place where important research is conducted and where students attend class—it is an educational gathering place for the community, as well. The State Arboretum, the Utah Museum of Natural History, and the Utah Museum of Fine Arts are located on campus. The 45,000-seat Jon M. Huntsman Special Events Center and the 51,000-seat Robert L. Rice Stadium host cultural, artistic, and athletic events throughout the year. Rice Stadium is the site for the opening and closing ceremonies for the 2002 Olympics.

## ◆ THE CAMPUS AND OTHER EASTERN BENCH ATTRACTIONS

### Utah Museum of Natural History

Located in the old university library building, the museum houses more than 200 exhibits. These portray ancient Indian life in the West, explain the geologic forces which shape the earth, and feature Utah wildlife. Mounted skeletons of Jurassic period dinosaurs in combat and lifelike dioramas of animals in natural settings delight the youngsters who venture into the museum. Special events and exhibitions are held at the museum throughout the year. Perhaps the most important of these are educational outreach programs designed to introduce different aspects of the natural world to adults, families, and children. Our sons and daughter have enjoyed Junior Science Academy programs at the museum. The winter lecture series sponsored by the museum brings experts from all over Utah and the United States to address such themes as Wasatch Front geology, the importance of the Colorado Plateau, and ancient Indian culture. *President's Circle; 801-581-4303.*

### Utah Museum of Fine Arts

Though small in size, the museum is a fine facility for the visual arts. The comprehensive collection ranges from ancient Egyptian objects and examples of Italian Renaissance painting to European and American art from the 17th century to the present. The collections include sculptures from Southeast Asia, screens and prints from Japan, ceramics from China, Navajo textiles, and objects from African, Oceanic, and Pre-Columbian cultures. The Utah Museum of Fine Arts is open every day, and admission is free to the public. A new museum, three times as large as the existing facility, is being constructed, and is due to open in the spring of 2002. *Located on South Campus Drive; 801-581-7049.*

### State Arboretum of Utah

When you walk through the well-landscaped grounds of the University of Utah campus, it is difficult not to notice the collection of 8,000 trees. Three hundred varieties of trees were planted as a part of the state arboretum, including collections of hybrid oaks in Sotto Grove, beeches in Chapel Glen, conifers along North Campus Drive, and a California sequoia. Pick up a self-guiding tour map at the Arboretum Office in Building 436 on campus.

### Red Butte Garden

Two additional arboretum collections can be enjoyed at the mouth of Red Butte Canyon east of the university near Fort Douglas. A huge visitor center at the entrance to this area, known as Red Butte Garden, offers interpretive displays. There, the conservatory houses plants from tropical rain forests and deserts of the world, ranging from common plants to rare and endangered species. Enjoy a quiet stroll through the adjacent gardens—a place where the city seems to meet the forest. A meandering stream and waterfalls, quiet ponds, plant collections with explanatory signs, and rolling lawns add to the experience. *801-581-4747.*

## Fort Douglas

The fort dominates a site just east of the University of Utah, a position chosen by Colonel Patrick Connor for its commanding views over the defiant Mormon capital—defiant in Washington's view, at any rate. Five different examples of military architecture can be viewed at the fort. A museum on the grounds contains exhibits tracing military activities from the Escalante Expedition in 1776 to the present. The original cemetery on the fort's grounds dates back to 1862.

Part of Fort Douglas has been deactivated as a military base and has been annexed by the University of Utah, but the Army retains possession of the western portion. The Olympic Village, which will house the athletes at Fort Douglas, will become student dormitories after the Games. The Army parade ground and officers' quarters will serve as the commons area for the athletes during the Olympics. Afterwards, the historic buildongs will be used to house visiting professors.

## Hogle Zoo

The largest and best animal park of its type in the statet contains over 800 animals representing more than 300 species. Each visitor seems to have his or her favorite exhibit. Most children eventually con their parents into taking them for a ride on a replica of an 1869 steam train. Our favorite exhibit is a solarium full of exotic plants where tropical birds fly freely. As with many Utah institutions, Hogle Zoo has an aggressive outreach program which extends to more than 20,000 students and adults annually throughout the state. There are few school children in the Salt Lake Valley who haven't enjoyed a lecture from a zoo docent. Our kids will never forget the time the zoo teamed up with the Utah Symphony for a youth concert dedicated to animals that featured a musical piece built around "walk talk," and a classical rendition of "Pop Goes the Weasel." *2600 East Sunnyside Avenue, near the fort at the mouth of Emigration Canyon.; 801-582-1631*

## This Is The Place State Heritage Park

Spend a few hours here for a look back at pioneer times in the Salt Lake Valley, from its 1847 settlement to the coming of the railroad in 1869. Exhibits show how the homes developed from temporary dugouts to the comforts of substantial adobe. A town called **Old Deseret Village** has been established here and is managed by a private non-profit foundation. Original buildings have been moved to the site from all over the state. Guides dressed in pioneer garb take you on a tour of Brigham Young's Forest Farm House. Our kids are especially fond of the story of how the Mormon leaders' wives and children used silk worms at the farm to produce silk cloth. During the summer months, a variety of living history demonstrations are set up. Blacksmiths, adobe brickmakers, and various craftsmen encourage visitors to ask questions and even to join in the work. Special events are held during holidays.

SALT LAKE CITY

# UTAH MUSEUM OF FINE ARTS

JANUS MASK
Ejagham People,
Cross River Valley,
Nigeria

BLACK FIGURE NECK AMPHORA
Greek, in the manner of the
Antimines painter (c.510–500 B.C.)

CARVED HEAD
Maori people, New Zealand

CERAMIC CAMEL
Chinese, Tang dynasty (A.D. 618–906)

*Martha Rebuking Mary Magdalene* by Andrea Vaccaro, Italian (1604–1670)

*The Utah Museum of Fine Arts, housed at the University of Utah in Salt Lake City, has an impressive and eclectic collection. The museum exhibits span centuries, from ancient Egypt to the Italian Renaissance to the present-day United States, and feature a variety of objects, including European paintings, Chinese ceramics, Navajo textiles, and silk scrolls from Japan.*

*Mademoiselle Marie-Madeleine Guimard* by
Jean-Honore Fragonard, French (1732–1806)

*All photographs courtesy of the Utah Museum of Fine Arts.*

*Pioneer wagons at This Is The Place State Heritage Park*
*sits near the entrance of Emigration Canyon on the city's east side.*

At the entrance to the village is a visitors center, where visitors can hear the story of the Mormons' coming into the Salt Lake Valley. Sections of the last 35 miles of the Mormon Pioneer National Historic Trail from Henefer to the Salt Lake Valley can be viewed by driving up Emigration Canyon from the park. *Admission charged. Located directly north of Hogle Zoo at 2601 East Sunnyside Avenue; 801-582-1847.*

**Wheeler Farm**

Time stopped here at the turn of the century. Kids especially enjoy joining the farmer on his rounds of chores, one at 11 A.M. and one at 5 P.M., when they can help him gather eggs and milk cows. Old-timers may chuckle at the fact that kids have to pay (a small fee) to do these chores! Holidays are celebrated in the old-fashioned way on the farm. At Halloween the woods surrounding the old house become "haunted" as creatures suddenly appear on the trail. Entrance fees include a tour of the farmhouse and a wagon ride. Visitors during the Christmas season will see the grounds lit up with twinkling lights and holiday displays. *6351 South 900 East; 801-264-2212.*

# ■ THE SALT LAKE STAGE

From the beginning of the pioneer era in Salt Lake City, cultural events played a major role in society. Carl Arrington, writing in a 1977 issue of *New Era* magazine, observed that the Mormons had plenty of drama to provide them with inspiration.

"If we are actors in a drama, as the Bard would have us believe, then certainly Latter-day Saints have produced a script and players as dramatic as there have ever been," wrote Arrington. "The Mormon story is a complete drama with characters, conflicts, action, morality, tragedy, and comedy. Persecutions and hardships, combined with a yearning for that which is ennobling and uplifting, created a strong appreciation for culture and drama among the saints as they sought a place where they could establish a complete social experience centered around the gospel of Jesus Christ."

The first cultural organization in Utah was the Deseret Musical and Dramatic Society, organized in 1849 at the request of Brigham Young. It presented musicals, concerts, and pageants in the Old Bowery Building on Temple Square. The group's initial dramatic performances occurred in 1851 and included the melodramatic comedy, *Robert McCaire*, and the farce, *Dead Shot*.

"Theater continued to flourish," wrote Arrington, "and in the late 1850s a company called the Mechanics Dramatic Association was formed. The name was appropriately titled since all its members were busy giving their days to intensive physical labor and were committed to the fine arts in the evening. . . . In the early theater days, it was common practice to accept goods for the price of a ticket. One night the theater took in 20 bushels of wheat, five of corn, four of potatoes, two of oats, four of salt, plus two hams, one live pig, one wolf skin, one set of children's embroidered undergarments, one keg of applesauce, a dog, and a German silver coffin plate."

In 1862, when the Salt Lake Theatre opened, dramatic productions had become increasingly important to the cultural life of the community. Brigham Young had decided to build a real theater, the only one between the Comstock and the Mississippi at the time. A resident stock company started presenting productions. The company was so successful that, after starting with two performances a week, it was soon playing almost every weeknight. Its attractions were heightened by the traveling stars who stopped between Chicago and San Francisco to present their famous roles with the support of the local company.

That tradition was nourished when Maud May Babcock came to the University of Deseret as a part-time elocution and physical education teacher. When she retired 44 years later, she had founded two departments, a college, a professional theater company, and a university community theater. Her first major production, *Eleusinia*, was presented in 1895 in the Salt Lake Theatre. From 1918 to 1921, the first American professional company at a university, The Varsity Players, presented an ambitious series of plays in the Social Hall. Kingsbury Hall, a large performing hall on the University of Utah campus still used today, opened in 1930, two years after the final program was presented on the stage of the Salt Lake Theatre. When Dr. C. Lowell Lees came to the University of Utah in 1943 to chair the Theater Department, he also brought with him two dreams: to build a replica of the old Salt Lake Theatre and to form a theater company with a nucleus of professional actors. As chairman of the Drama Section of the Utah Centennial Pageant Committee, Dr. Lees brought internationally known actors, choreographers, dancers, singers, and conductors to Utah. He joined with the American National Theatre Association, a New York–based organization founded to decentralize theater, and within one season brought Judith Evans, Orson Welles, Jeanette Nolan, and Roddy McDowell to perform at Kingsbury Hall.

Finally, in 1962, the Ron W. and Elizabeth E. Simmons Pioneer Memorial Theatre was dedicated on the University of Utah campus, a full century since the dedication of its progenitor, the Salt Lake Theatre.

### Pioneer Theatre Company

Now, with an annual budget of close to $4 million and a full-time staff of 42, the Pioneer Theatre Company ranks in the top 25 percent of non-profit theaters nationally. Those familiar with the national "regional theater" scene compare the company's work favorably with the best that is being produced by the nation's top theaters. The company operates on a League of Resident Theatres contract with Actors' Equity Association, the same contract as major non-profit theaters in the country like Arena Stage, the Guthrie, Long Wharf, ACT, and Seattle Rep. The company stages seven productions a year. Actors working in the productions often come from Broadway, off-Broadway, television, and films. **Lees**

**Main Stage,** named after C. Lowell Lees is a 910 seat, 48-foot proscenium stage, equipped with state-of-the-art computerized lighting and sound systems. The downstairs **Babcock Theatre**, a 200-seat facility, features performances by the University of Utah Theater Department. *300 South 1400 East; 801-581-6961.*

### Salt Lake Acting Company

The smaller Salt Lake Acting Company, with an annual operating budget of $1,000,000, offers lesser known, more contemporary plays, which many might not expect to see in a town the size of Salt Lake City. Performing in a 200-seat theater in the Marmalade Hill Center, the company supports and develops new works by Utah playwrights and other regional writers, particularly those of national caliber. Patrons might expect to see examples of contemporary theater not available elsewhere in the region, including the works of such major writers as David Mamet, Emily Mann, Sam Shepard, John Patrick Shanley, Christopher Durang, and Tony Kushner. In 1982, SLAC's original production of Utah playwright Al Brown's *Back to Back* received the San Francisco Bay Area Theatre Critics' Circle Award for Best Touring Production. The theater doesn't shy away from plays with controversial themes and hard language, which sometimes challenge traditional conservative Utah values. *Marmalade Hill Center, 168 West 500 North. Call ahead and reserve seats well in advance; 801-363-0526.*

### Other Theater Companies

There are several smaller groups in the Salt Lake area. **City Rep**, the **Desert Star Playhouse**, and the **Hale Center** Theatre produce plays on a regular basis. In addition, the **Theatre League of Utah** brings Broadway touring productions such as Les Miserables into the Capitol Theater throughout the year. Community Theater at the **Salt Lake Community College's Grand Theatre** is popular.

### Utah Opera Company

One of the most popular features in the Utah arts scene, the opera company, was founded in 1978 by Glade Peterson, a Utah native who performed for the Metropolitan Opera in New York City. The company stages three fully costumed grand operas a year at the Capitol Theater. It often enlists

some of the great stars in American opera for its performances. The Utah Opera Company was one of the first of its size to use English super-titles to allow newcomers to opera to understand the words being sung in foreign operas. Some 80,000 Utah school children a year are introduced to grand opera as the company makes an effort to educate students about the pleasures of opera. Get your tickets well in advance since many operas in Salt Lake City sell out. *ArtTix.org; 801-355-2787 or 888-451-2787.*

### Capitol Theatre   *map page 102, D/E-2*

It was built in 1912 to host touring vaudeville shows, the Capitol Theatre but fell into disrepair in the early 1970s when it was used as a huge movie house. When Salt Lake County voters approved the construction of the Symphony Hall in the seventies, they also elected to restore the Capitol Theatre to its former elegance so it could be used as a performing arts center. The Capitol Theatre now serves as the home for the Utah Opera Company, Ballet West and the Ririe-Woodbury Dance Company. Touring national theater companies regularly perform there as well. *The Capitol Theatre is located at 50 West 200 South. ArtTix.org; 801-355-2787 or 888-451-2787.*

### Rose Wagner Performing Arts Center

Built in 1996 to add performance space for Children's Dance Theatre, Repertory Dance Theatre, Dance Theatre Coalition, Gina Bachauer International Piano Competition. *ArtTix.org; 801-355-2787 or 888-451-2787.*

# ■ SALT LAKE MUSIC

There is evidence of musical instruments and singing in pioneer times, but the classical musical tradition formed later. The first performance of Handel's *Messiah* took place in 1875 at the Salt Lake Theatre with a choir of 200 and a "full orchestra" of 45 members, making it the largest group of musicians ever brought together in Utah at that time. Salt Lake Oratorio Society perfroms Bach's *Christmas Oratorio* each Christmas season in Abravenel Hall.

The Salt Lake Symphony Orchestra Association was organized in the late 1800s. Most historians credit George Careless with conducting Utah's first symphony concert on May 17, 1892. Unfortunately, the orchestra disbanded at the end of that year, and it took 10 years for another symphony orchestra to be organized in Salt Lake City. In 1902, 22-year-old Arthur Shepherd put together an orchestra of 32 members. That group disbanded when Shepherd left the state. He would later be a two-time winner of the Society of American Composers' awards for musical compositions. The symphony was revived again in 1912 as the Salt Lake Philharmonic Orchestra by Anton Pederson. Two weeks after the first concert was given in 1914, Pederson died and his son, Arthur Pederson Freber, filled the vacancy. In 1924, the Philharmonic Orchestra was replaced by the Salt Lake Symphony Orchestra, which disbanded after two seasons. The forerunner to the current Utah Symphony was the Utah Works Progress Administration Orchestra, which was formed in 1935.

The **Utah Symphony**'s first season consisted of five concerts performed by 52 part-time musicians in 1940. The orchestra now numbers 83 members, tours internationally, releases acclaimed recordings, and plays year-round, performing in Salt Lake City and throughout the state. In in its first seven years under the direction of Hans Heniot and Werner Janssen, however, the Utah Symphony struggled artistically and financially. The most important event in its rise to prominence was the hiring of Maurice Abravanel as musical director in 1947.

"When President Fred Smith and the Utah Symphony board went after a new conductor in 1947," wrote Conrad B. Harrison in his book *Five Thousand Concerts, A Commemorative History of the Utah Symphony*, "they found, by some stroke of good fortune, not only what the orchestra needed at the moment, but just what it was going to need in the continuous battle for its very life as a major symphony organization. Maurice Abravanel had been fighting for music ever since he was a youngster, and he was prepared and equipped for the job, on and off the podium.

Ordinarily, an orchestra conductor of such skill and opportunities as this experienced cosmopolite might have chucked the local symphony's financial storms and moved on to milder climes. But he had loyalty, tenacity, and honesty as well as music in his temperament, and he remained to finish the job he had taken on."

Soon after Janssen resigned, the board compiled an impressive list of 40 applicants for the job of musical director. One story concerned the consideration of a brilliant 28-year-old conductor who was in the midst of a three-year whirl at the helm of the New York WPA Symphony. Smith and another symphony board member interviewed the young musician in New York City, but wrote off the prospective candidate as "too young and inexperienced." The prospect's name was Leonard Bernstein.

Still, Abravanel proved to be just the tonic the Utah Symphony needed. "Abravanel made it clear," wrote Harrison, "that he intended to build the Utah Symphony with Utah musicians and gave the assurance that he would stay on and complete the task he had undertaken. It was not until 32 years later, after giving Utah an internationally acclaimed major symphony, that he retired."

In a typical season, over a half million people enjoy Utah Symphony performances, including over 73,000 children. Audiences have ranged in size from 350 in Duchesne, Utah—about one-third the town's population—to close to 50,000 people who filled the University of Utah's Rice Stadium to hear a July Fourth concert in 1985. In addition to the 19 pairs of concerts performed at Symphony Hall each season, the Utah Symphony holds Pops and Classical summer series at both Symphony Hall and the Deer Valley and Snowbird ski resorts. There is a chamber orchestra series, special holiday concerts, and 65 performances a year in Utah schools. The symphony visits each school district at least once every two years and performs to nearly half of the state's public school enrollment. The orchestra also provides music for Ballet West and Utah Opera Company productions.

Perhaps the crowning moment for Abravanel came when Salt Lake County voters approved the funding for a new Symphony Hall and for the transformation of the old Capitol Theatre into a performing arts center. Though Abravanel retired for health reasons in 1979, the same year Symphony Hall opened, he was the inspiration for what *Time* magazine called "the most impressive of all (concert halls) in the country" in a 1983 article. Finally, after years of playing in the Salt Lake Mormon Tabernacle, the symphony moved into its stunning new home. The $12 million hall measures 160 feet in length, 90 feet in width, and 55 feet in height, with 2,811 seats. Six geometric chandeliers with 18,000 beads of hand-cut crystal imported from Austria and Czechoslovakia grace the interior. The exterior consists of a massive three-story wedge of glass and granite-like brick, enhanced by a 100-foot long diagonal fountain. The interior is a dramatic combination of brass, gold leaf, natural oak, and forest-green carpet. Dr. Cyril Harris, who was acoustical designer for the Metropolitan Opera House, Kennedy Center, and the remodeled Avery Fisher Hall in New York's Lincoln Center, was the acoustical consultant. Symphony Hall was eventually renamed **Abravanel Hall** in honor of the memory of the late conductor. *123 W. South Temple; ArtTix.org; 801-355-2787 or 888-451-2787.*

## ■ SALT LAKE DANCE

### ◆ BALLET WEST

If Abravanel was the guiding force behind classical music in Salt Lake City, then Willam Christensen was a pioneer in bringing ballet to the western United States. Christensen joined with Salt Lake City arts benefactor Glenn Walker Wallace in 1963 to establish the Utah Civic Ballet. The first fully professional ballet company in the Intermountain West originated in the classrooms of the University of Utah and performed at Kingsbury Hall on campus. The company was renamed Ballet West in 1968 to represent the western United States as the region's designated ballet company. Christensen, who served as the company's first artistic director, is recognized as one of the pioneers of American dance and is also noted for establishing the first ballet department at an American university—the University of Utah in 1951. He was the first American to stage full-length versions of *The Nutcracker*, *Coppelia*, and *Cinderella*.

When Christensen retired in 1976, he was replaced by Bruce Marks, an internationally acclaimed dancer and choreographer who had served as co-Artistic Director since 1976. Under Marks' direction, Ballet West received national acclaim for its production of *The Sleeping Beauty* and the re-created Bournoville classic *Abdallah*. "Only a truly classical company, which is what Ballet West has become, could carry this feat off," wrote *New York Times* critic Anna Kisselgoff after watching *Abdallah*. "Ballet West's young dancers bring the ballet back to life on new and valid terms." Marks was replaced by England's John Hart as Artistic Director in 1985, and Vonas Kage has been the director since 1997. With 40 members, Ballet West has transcended its regional status to become one of America's leading companies. *Ballet West is in residence at the Capitol Theatre, 50 West 200 South.; 801-323-6900 or ArtTix.org; 801-355-2787 or 888-451-2787.*

♦ MODERN DANCE

Classical ballet isn't the only form of dance Utah audiences enjoy. Salt Lake City is also a center for modern dance and boasts of two professional companies— the Repertory Dance Theatre and the Ririe-Woodbury Dance Company—in addition to the Children's Dance Workshop founded by Virginia Tanner.

### Repertory Dance Theatre

Known locally as RDT, this 10-member professional modern dance company was founded by Kay Clark and Linda Smith in 1966 with a grant from the Rockefeller Foundation. Members of the foundation with a love for modern dance sought a place where a modern dance company could preserve the work of the nation's top choreographers. With Virginia Tanner established as a modern dance instructor at the University of Utah, Salt Lake City was selected, and RDT was born. The company performs a variety of dance forms but does not use its own choreographers. It is one of the few modern dance companies of its size in the world currently operating without a budget deficit. In addition to two annual concert series at the Capitol Theatre in downtown Salt Lake City, RDT performs at the University of Utah and throughout the state. Like most of Utah's major art groups, it brings its specialty to school children and to rural areas. RDT also tours extensively in the United States. *ArtTix.org; 801-355-2787 or 888-451-2787.*

### Ririe-Woodbury Dance Company

Established in 1964 by University of Utah dance professors Shirley Ririe and Joan Woodbury, the Ririe-Woodbury Dance Company combines three major performances at the Capitol Theatre with national educational and performing tours. The two dancers take particular pride in the pioneering activities that have helped integrate dance into children's curricula throughout the United States.

We can attest to the magic of Shirley Ririe's teaching abilities. As students at the University of Utah in the early 1970s, we enjoyed a class called "The Artist in Each of Us," which was partially taught by Ms. Ririe. She soon had inhibited college students—most with little coordination or feel for modern dance—leaping around a dance studio waving long pieces of sheer cloth in the air and thoroughly enjoying the experience. The company, which employs six full-time professional dancers, is noted for its emphasis on humor, theatricality, and inventive use of media. In addition to performing the works of its co-founders, Ririe-Woodbury has performed works choreographed by dance innovators as diverse as Tandy Beal, Doug Varone, David Roussève, Murray Louis, and Alwin Nikolais. New additions to their repertory include pieces by Creach/Koester, Laura Dean, Douglas Nielsen, and Graham-Lustig. The company has performed throughout the world and in all 50 states, including three seasons in New York City and the Kennedy Center in Washington, D.C. *Capitol Theatre, 50 West 200 South; ArtTix.org; 801-355-2787 or 888-451-2787.*

# ROBERT REDFORD'S SUNDANCE INSTITUTE

"The first year," recalls Robert Redford, Sundance Institute's founder and all-around guru, "I couldn't get a loan from the banks. The waiters didn't show up so the owners had to wait on tables. The stablemaster was more interested in the female customers than in the horses, and horses from our stables wandered in confusion all over the canyon. The Sundance Summer Theatre was launched with a misfired rocket that lay fizzling on the stage.

Vehicles stalled, sewers backed up, we were robbed, and the tree in the Tree Room died. A potential early investor who spoke eloquently about his belief in our concept was hauled away by men in white shirts. But we endured."

Sundance Institute—named for Redford's character in the film *Butch Cassidy and the Sundance Kid*—did more than endure. Redford's extravagant vision of a combined resort, film workshop, artist colony, and environmental field laboratory in the mountains of Utah has prospered over the years. Recently, as Sundance has had to prune back some of its film-related activities, Utah's nascent environmental movement is looking to it more and more for guidance and inspiration. And the Sundance Film Festival (formerly the U.S. Film Festival), held each winter in Park City, has burgeoned into a full-scale entertainment industry phenomenon, attracting product-hungry media buyers from all over the world.

In fact, Sundance's present predicament has everything to do with its success. Redford's dream was always of an intimate, intense group of filmmakers, writers, and producers, working outside the relentlessly commercial purview of Hollywood. Provo, which was the Oscar-winning star's home base anyway, was a perfect venue.

Born in 1980, the Institute at first had a makeshift, improvisational feel to it, which both spurred artistic innovation and separated it from the slick, conformist feel of Hollywood. Sundance was to be a mecca for the rebels, for the independents, for those chafing under the restrictive yoke of commercialism. There, films would be treated as art, and the bottom-line box office mentality would be banished.

The idea was to bring novice movie-makers to Utah and cross-pollenate them with movie professionals. "The filmmakers' lab brings some of the most talented and successful filmmakers to Sundance to act as resource advisors," says John Genette, the institute's general manager. "It gets you away from the marketplace and the pressures of the marketplace. It could be done in some other remote place. But it takes the leadership of a person with vision."

And that person happened to live in Utah. So Utah it was; specifically, a down-at-the-heels ski resort east of Salt Lake City in the Wasatch Range. As Redford cajoled funds from contributors or poured in his own money from million-dollar acting fees, the place was transformed. Each year, the institute sifts through some 1,000 film proposals, project ideas, and inchoate dreams to select a baker's dozen as official institute projects. Sundance supports its babies in a variety of ways, from helping punch up a script to making the right connections with a producer.

The intermontane paradise at Sundance attracts movie industry heavy-hitters desperate to leave the smog-filled L.A. summer behind, and the Redford name pulls a few rabbits out of the hat, too. Actors Alan Alda and Sam Waterson, directors Oliver *(JFK, Natural Born Killers)* Stone and Sidney *(Out of Africa)* Pollack, screenwriters Ring Lardner and the late Waldo Salt have all been Sundance participants at one time or another.

But more and more, the Institute has been overshadowed by the Festival—the hugely successful Sundance Film Festival held January of each year in Park City, Utah, a couple of canyons south of the Sundance resort.

Normally a bustling haven for schussers, the mountain hamlet bulges at the seams during the festival, with producers, directors and wanna-bes stacked three deep in the town's favored hotel, the Stein Eriksen ("The Stein") as well as every ski condo for miles around. The town's theater venues become seriously overloaded, and the locals grumble about the "flatlanders" clotting up the sidewalks.

It can be comical, seeing all those flatland film hustlers getting tutored on the crucial difference between ski-slope moguls and movie moguls (there is no difference— both are hard, dome-shaped obstacles that are in your way when you're in a hurry). But after the festival, when the bar talk switches back to snowboards from storyboards, everything settles back down again. . . until next year.

All of this because the Sundance Festival has become the acknowledged premier showcase for independent film. As independent film has grown in importance as sort of a farm league for the studio majors, Sundance has grown in stature. Producers have begun to realize that there's a great deal of money to be made by catching a good buzz off a Sundance showing, and then marketing their movie as the latest indie sensation.

Stephen Soderburgh's *sex, lies and videotape* kicked off the phenomenon in 1988, but *The Blair Witch Project* (1999), as well as such groundbreaking documentaries as *Hoop Dreams* and *Crumb*, also went the same route. In fact, Park City has become so successful, so mainstream, that the original alternative festival has itself spawned an alternative festival: the **Slamdance Festival**, which itself is becoming an industry player. *For more information on the Sundance Film Festival, visit there web site at sundance.org, or call 801-328-FILM (3456).*

—Gil Reavill

# THE WASATCH FRONT

■ HIGHLIGHTS                              *page*

Brigham Young University            140
Alpine Loop                                142
Nebo Loop                                  145
Ben Lomond Peak                       149
Logan Mormon Temple              151
American West Heritage Center  151
Hardware Ranch                         152
Bear Lake                                   152

UTAH IS LARGELY RURAL, FULL OF WIDE-OPEN SPACES, ranches, and splendid mountain scenery. The Wasatch Front, a roughly 175-mile stretch of land which lies along the western base of the Wasatch Mountains in the north-central portion of the state, contains eighty-percent of Utah's residents. The cultural and urbane amenities of the Wasatch Front cities satisfy the demands of an increasingly sophisticated population, but Utahns and visitors still feel an occasional urge to escape into the nearby mountains to ski, hike, picnic, fish, or hunt.

## ■ THE MOUNTAINS

Stretching from the Idaho border in the north to the southern summit of Mt. Nebo, its highest point at 11,877 feet, the Wasatch Range endows one of the most spectacular urban settings on earth. A first-time visitor to the Salt Lake International Airport marvels at the peaks that seem to dwarf the city's modern skyline. Photographers use the reflection of the mountains in the windows of modern skyscrapers to illustrate the beauty of the contrast between urban and natural worlds. The mountains are dear to Wasatch Front residents because they provide water for the body and peace for the soul.

The Wasatch Mountains have always been a source of life to the Salt Lake Valley, providing the game that drew both the Indian and the early trappers into the area. Mormon pioneers used the water flowing from their snowcapped peaks to drink and to irrigate their crops. The early settlers quarried granite from the mountains to build their fine temple and cut wood from the forests to construct their homes. Members of Johnston's Army camped at their base and prospected for precious metals in the Wasatch canyons. Today, the mountains bring skiers from all over the world to experience the thrill of skiing on what Utah's car license plates proclaim to be "The Greatest Snow on Earth." Campgrounds, picnic areas, hiking trails, babbling brooks, small lakes, large manmade reservoirs, and seven Congressionally designated wilderness areas provide places both to escape urban life and to renew one's spirit.

A friend who is an avid outdoorsman points out that, on a typical Utah weekend, more cars, campers, and trucks pour out of Salt Lake City and into the mountains than come into the city. Salt Lake City is one of the few urban regions in the United States where residents can reach the trailhead of a 16,000-acre designated wilderness by driving 10 minutes from their home, or leave work at noon and be skiing at a world-class resort by 1 p.m. The numerous hiking trails, picnic areas, streams and lakes filled with trout, cozy little restaurants and country inns provide an easy escape from the hurry of urban life. John Veranth, author of *Hiking the Wasatch*, lists 207 hiking trails in his book without even leaving Salt Lake County!

Hikers can explore seven wilderness areas found along the Front. These include the 30,088-acre **Lone Peak**, 44,350-acre **Mt. Naomi**, 28,000-acre **Mt. Nebo**, 16,000-acre **Mt. Olympus**, 10,750-acre **Mt. Timpanogos**, 13,100-acre **Twin Peaks**, and 23,850-acre **Wellsville Mountains**. These wild places draw an amazing mixture of people—don't be surprised to see grandmothers at the top of mountains and fathers carrying babies.

Each canyon of the Wasatch, and there are many, holds its own secret. Hiking and fishing are the major summer activities in the canyons east of Salt Lake City. The Snowbird Tram in **Little Cottonwood Canyon** whisks visitors to the top of 11,000-foot Hidden Peak. Some ride it back down, while others choose to walk. When the snow finally leaves the area around mid-July, the high alpine meadows are covered with wildflowers. When we've ridden the tram to the top, we've hiked

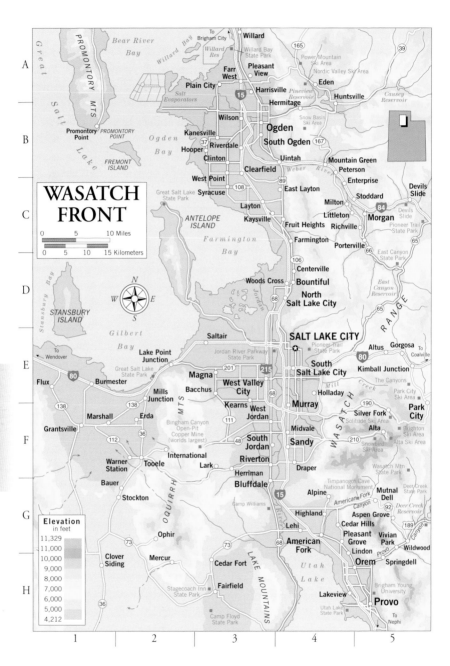

# WASATCH FRONT

0    5    10 Miles

0  5   10   15 Kilometers

ANTELOPE ISLAND

STANSBURY ISLAND

Elevation
in feet

11,329
11,000
10,000
9,000
8,000
7,000
6,000
5,000
4,212

over to nearby Mt. Baldy, enjoying the clear mountain air and spectacular views. And, speaking of views, the hike to the top of 9,026-foot **Mt. Olympus**, much of which lies in wilderness, is both difficult and rewarding —as are dozens of other hikes along the Wasatch Front.

The drive to the hamlet of Henefer through **Emigration Canyon** basically follows the route that the Mormons took into the Salt Lake Valley. Later, the Pony Express trail traversed this canyon. Markers along the way depict the progress the pioneers made as they completed their 1,500-mile journey.

Heading farther north, a scenic loop drive connects the towns of Farmington and Bountiful. Forest campgrounds and picnic areas are available along the steep, winding road.

■ PROVO AND UTAH COUNTY  *map page 138, G & H 3 & 4*

In many ways, Utah County and its county seat, **Provo**, serve as the quintessential models for a modern Mormon community. Where a considerable spectrum of influences exist in Salt Lake City and Ogden, the population of Utah County is primarily white, middle class, politically conservative, and of the Mormon faith. The influence and culture of the modern Mormon religion is more keenly felt here than in any other urban area of the world.

Ironically, two *Catholic* priests—Francisco Silvestre Velez de Escalante and Francisco Atanasio Dominguez arriving in September of 1776—are believed to be the first white men to visit Utah Valley. In his journal, Father Escalante noted that the group "ascended a low hill and beheld the lake and extended valley of Nuestra Senora de la Merced de los Timpanogotzis (as they called it) . . . surrounded by the peaks of the Sierra." Escalante noted that the river (later named the Provo) running through the valley watered plains sufficient to support, if irrigated, "two and even three large villages."

Provo is named after Etienne Provot, a young French-Canadian who explored the valley with a group of trappers in 1825. Though the Mormon pioneers explored Utah Valley three days after reaching the Salt Lake Valley, the first settlers didn't arrive until March of 1849, when John S. Higbee brought 30 families to establish a Mormon colony. As the story is told, the white men were greeted by members of the Ute Indian tribe. After promising not to drive the native Americans from their land, the Mormons constructed a fort, plowed 225 acres of land, and planted rye, wheat, and corn.

◆ BRIGHAM YOUNG UNIVERSITY

When Brigham Young University was founded (as Brigham Young Academy) in 1875 with the goal of turning its first 29 students into teachers, few could have imagined its modern scope of influence. Yet today, the Provo-based institution and its current enrollment of 27,000 students play a dominant role not only in Utah County, but around the country. It is no accident that the bumper stickers on the cars of a few of BYU's thousands of athletic fans declare the school to be "The University of Utah," a dig at the Provo school's arch rival to the north.

Brigham Young set the tone for the university he founded when, in 1876, he declared to students: "I want you to remember that you ought not to teach even the alphabet or the multiplication tables without the spirit of God." Dr. Jeffrey R. Holland, a modern BYU president, put things another way. "We want our students value-laden and moral," he said. "We want them to be a veritable rod of iron in what is too often a dark and misty ethical void. . . . There's a spiritual power here that goes out into the world. It is a result of our determination to place academic excellence in the context of committed religious faith and wholesome, broad development of the total person. It comes from our insistence on linking Virtue with Truth."

There are few gray areas in BYU's honor code, which students entering the university agree to obey. This includes following Mormon Church rules that encourage pride in maintaining a clean, strong, healthy body as a temple for the intellect and the spirit. The school's code of honor includes such commitments as being honest, observing university regulations, following the dress and grooming standards, refraining from sexual relations outside of marriage, avoiding drug abuse, and abstaining from alcohol, tobacco, tea, and coffee. Dress codes require students to be "modest, neat and clean in their grooming. Shorts, swimming suits, gym clothes and other extremely casual or grubby attire are not considered acceptable wear on campus. Beards are not permitted."

The beauty of the BYU campus setting is in keeping with the neatness of the students. The 646-acre campus, with 339 mostly modern buildings, is cradled between the lofty Wasatch Mountain peaks and the placid waters of Utah Lake. Facilities include an 837-acre farm, a motion picture studio, a 462-acre preserve in southern Utah, a 6,200-acre ranch in southern Idaho, radio and television stations, and a mountaintop observatory. Because Mormon leaders feel healthy bodies lead to healthy minds, some of the finest physical education and athletic facilities found on any campus in the world can be seen scattered through a campus dominated by grass and wide walkways.

Game day—be it basketball, football, track and field, or baseball—is a major event at BYU. The university's 65,000-seat football stadium fills for many community and university events, including the fantastic July 4th Freedom Festival. The school used its pass-oriented offense to win the national football championship in 1984 and is regularly ranked among the top 20 college teams in the United States. The 23,000-seat Marriott Center serves as the home for the BYU basketball team, a place for cultural events, and a setting for the regular Sunday meetings of students with Mormon church spiritual leaders. The modern track, one of the finest in the United States, is host to many major track and field events. The spring BYU Invitational, which dates back to 1915, brings high school athletes from all over the Intermountain West to compete.

Academically, BYU offers courses in 12 schools and colleges, along with a continuing education program. Through the graduate school and five professional schools, as well as in graduate studies and two areas of general undergraduate education, BYU offers bachelor degrees in 239 academic programs, master's degress in 799, juris doctorates in one, and doctorates in 32. In addition, researchers at BYU tackle such challenges as alleviating the world's food shortage through more efficient agriculture, developing synthetic antitumor agents in the fight against cancer, finding low-pollutant energy alternatives, and breaking language barriers with computer-assisted translation. The school's language program, which assists in training the thousands of young Mormon men and women who volunteer to serve on two-year missions all over the world for their church, offers 25 languages with classes available in 15 additional languages. Live-in language experience is available in 16 different language houses, and campus cable television broadcasts programs daily in many languages on its various stations.

BYU also serves as a cultural center for much of the Wasatch Front. Many of its 15 performing groups, including International and American Folk Dance ensembles, perform throughout the world. Theater-goers enjoy seeing live plays and musicals on campus.

Visitors to BYU can browse through four museums. The **Monte L. Bean Life Science Museum** exhibits a wide array of natural history scenes, mounted animals, insects, and plants, and also stores scientific collections. Artifacts of ancient Indian cultures from the United States, Central America, and South America can be seen at the **Museum of Peoples and Cultures** in Allen Hall. A major addition to the Harris Fine Arts Center, the **Museum of Fine Arts** houses some of the world's great traveling exhibits as well as a permanent collection of fine art.

The **Earth Sciences Museum** displays several full and partial dinosaur skeletons. Visitors can watch as paleontologists work on BYU's nearly 100 tons of fossils.

Though BYU dominates the list of places to see in the urbanized part of Utah County, there are other cultural and recreational attractions to enjoy.

◆ PROVO ATTRACTIONS

**McCurdy Historical Doll Museum**

Provo's doll museum features a collection of more than 3,000 dolls. Changing monthly exhibits spotlight dolls in such themes as folk dress of the world, dramatic episodes in history, provincial dress of Spain, or first ladies of the United States, both delighting and educating visitors. A doll shop and doll repair facility add a finishing touch to the museum. *246 N. 100 East; 801-377-9935.*

**Pioneer Memorial Museum**

The museum contains an extensive display of pioneer and Indian relics. The highlight of a trip here is seeing the Pioneer Cabin, a replica of an early Utah home furnished with rustic furniture. *500 W. 500 North; 801-852-6609.*

**Springville Museum of Art**

This art museum is among the finest in the state. If you happen to be in Utah during April, try to find time to see the museum's national art exhibit. *126 E. 400 South in Springville, seven miles south of Provo on US 89; 801-489-9434.*

**Utah Lake State Park** *map page 138, H-4*

The state's largest natural freshwater lake dominates the western portion of Utah County. Due to the murkiness of the water, the lake gets mixed reviews from boaters and anglers. There are three marinas on the lake: one west of Lindon, another south of American Fork, and a third at the state park. The state park marina offers swimming, camping, and ice skating at a beautiful rink. *4400 W. Center; 801-375-0733 or 800-322-3770 for camping reservations.*

◆ ALPINE LOOP  *map page 138, G-5*

North of Provo, the American Fork Canyon and Provo Canyon provide many recreational possibilities. They are connected by a narrow, winding road called the **Alpine Loop**. Take time to hike one of the trails found along the way, or to stop at a turnout and enjoy the view of the canyon. Our family likes to ski and fish at Tibble Fork Reservoir in the North Fork of American Fork Canyon. The Uinta National Forest operates a number of picnic areas and campgrounds in the area. Another nice side trip off the Alpine Loop will take you to **Cascade Springs**, a natural area where flowing water appears and then disappears out of the side of a mountain. Interpretive signs along a boardwalk trail explain the flora and fauna of

*Mt. Timpanogos rises from one of Utah's most popular wilderness areas, just north of Provo.*

the area. Kids like to look at the brown trout swimming in the clear water. The Provo River, flowing through Provo Canyon, is one of the top wild brown trout fisheries in the state. Since much of the stretch is governed by special fishing regulations, knowledge of the rules is a must. Another interesting attraction in Provo Canyon is **Bridal Veil Falls,** which drop 607 feet in two cascades. *Information and maps are available at the Uinta National Forest Headquarters in Provo or the Ranger District office in Pleasant Grove. See page 328.*

◆ TIMPANOGOS CAVE NATIONAL MONUMENT   *map page 138, G-4*

This monument is probably the most famous attraction of American Fork Canyon. The steep, 1.5-mile hike from the visitor center at the bottom of the canyon to the entrance of the cave entails an elevation gain of 1,065 feet, and is a summer tradition for many Utah families. The cave itself rewards those who make the hike on a summer day, both with its 43-degree temperature and the many limestone formations found inside. These include flowstone formations in subtle shades of green, yellow, red, and white. Martin Hansen discovered the first of three separate caves (tunnels now connect all the caverns) in 1887 while tracking a mountain lion. The other two weren't discovered until 1921 and 1922. The cave received both its lighting and national monument status shortly thereafter. Though a typical cave tour takes between 45 and 60 minutes to complete, plan three to four hours for both the hike and the cave tour. On busy weekends, it's an excellent idea to arrive at the visitor center early to purchase your tickets. Tours can sell out. Reservations are suggested for cave tours and can be purchased from one to 30 days in advance. If you're in the mood for a little more adventure, try taking the special flashlight tour offered very early in the morning during summer. *The Visitor Center is 2 miles into American Fork Canyon on UT 92; 801-756-5238.*

■ SOUTH OF PROVO

◆ PAYSON CANYON   *map page 183, C & D-4 & 5*

The mountains behind Provo are particularly beautiful. At the top of **Payson Canyon,** to the south of the city, are a series of little lakes stocked with trout. Fine Uinta National Forest campgrounds are at hand, some with facilities for people who bring horses. A paved nature trail, two small beaches, and some grassy day-use areas are found at the edge of Payson Lake. *Information and maps are available at the Uinta National Forest Headquarters in Provo or the Ranger District office in Spanish Fork. See page 328.*

WASATCH FRONT

If you have time, drive the entire length of the **Nebo Loop**, which rambles from Payson around the east side of magnificent Mt. Nebo, passing what looks like a miniature Bryce Canyon along the way, and ends near the town of Nephi on the southern boundary of the Wasatch Front.

◆ US HIGHWAY 89  *map page 183, C & D-5*

With the exception of the comparatively modern Snow Junior College in Ephraim and a few new subdivisions, the towns along the northern portion of US 89 seem barely changed from pioneer times. These quiet farming communities are perhaps best described as the Utah equivalent of Garrison Keillor's Lake Woebegon. Only a few franchises can be found. Old historic towns, such as Mt. Pleasant, Spring City, Ephraim, and Marysvale, are being discovered by artists seeking a quiet place to live and work. Between Fairview, Utah, and Page, Arizona, US 89 has been designated as Utah's Heritage Highway and is being promoted as a place to buy crafts made in Utah.

◆ MANTI  *map page 183, E-5*

A well-known figure in part of the state is a retired basketball coach/grocery store owner/philosopher named Wilbur Braithwaite. Braithwaite coached at Manti High School for over 30 years, and though he won but a single state championship, his emphasis on old-fashioned sportsmanship and his love for the pure, amateur ideals of high school athletics influenced countless students and peers throughout the nation. He exchanged ideas and letters with well-known college coaches like John Wooden, from UCLA, and Bobby Knight, formerly of Indiana. He mailed poetry and letters to friends, former students, and newspaper writers all over the world. Braithwaite's soft-spoken commitment to youth has been acknowledged. He was elected to the National High School Hall of Fame.

Wilbur also took the time to operate the Manti Grocery where he started working at age 10 as a delivery boy, packing bags of flour, sugar, and produce to nearly every household in town. By the 1980s, Wilbur's bag boys only delivered to the elderly and the home-bound, so the rest of the town's 2,080 residents turned Manti Grocery into something of a gathering place.

Although Braithwaite's old Manti Grocery store was recently torn down and replaced with a modern supermarket, the town's Main Street has retained much of its charm. It resembles something out of the fictional town of Mayberry of Andy Griffith Show fame. The quiet town does come alive in June each year when thousands of people come from all over the United States to watch the highly dramatic and spectacular Mormon Miracle Pageant on the grounds of the Manti Temple.

The center of **Manti** and, in fact, all of Sanpete County, is the stately **Mormon Temple,** which sits on the top of a hill at the north end of town. Brigham Young dedicated the site just three months before his death in 1877. It took workers 11 years to complete the magnificent structure. The highlight of the Sanpete County tourist season comes in June when church leaders, using the same story from the *Book of Mormon,* perform the Mormon Miracle Pageant.

For year-round recreation, locals and a few savvy out-of-state visitors venture east into the **Manti-La Sal National Forest.** Small canyons east of Ephraim, Manti, Fairview, and Mayfield lead to tiny fishing lakes, U.S. Forest Service campgrounds, and some fine nordic skiing and snowmobiling. *For information and maps, visit the Sanpete Ranger District Office in Ephraim. See Page 327.*

**Palisade State Park,** located in the lower part of Manti Canyon on the edge of the forest, provides perhaps the nicest public camping, with fishing, swimming on a pretty beach, and golf on the adjacent nine-hole golf course. *Information; 435-835-7275, camping reservations; 800-322-3770.*

Owners of four-wheel-drive vehicles—and the brave drivers of two-wheel drive vehicles with high clearance—enjoy negotiating the 150-mile **Skyline Drive,** on the top of the Manti Range, in summer and fall. The autumn leaf displays make this drive appealing. *For information and road conditions call the Ferron Ranger District Office. See page 327.*

■ OGDEN  *map page 138, B-3*

Though Mormon pioneers settled Ogden, Utah's third largest metropolitan area is named after a trapper. It possesses an exciting history shaped by the 1869 coming of the transcontinental railroad, and some awfully colorful characters.

It seems somehow appropriate that Ogden honors the memory of trapper Peter Skene Ogden, because the mountain men were the first non-Indian residents in the area. The current site of the city, built on the deltas of the Ogden and Weber rivers, served as a winter rendezvous site for six or seven years in the 1820s. A particularly memorable gathering took place in the summer of 1826, when General William H. Ashley arrived from St. Louis with a hundred well-laden pack animals. "It may well be supposed that the arrival of such a vast amount of luxuries from the East did not pass off without a general celebration," noted Jim Beckwourth, one of the mountain men. "Mirth, songs, dancing, shouting, trading, running, jumping, singing, racing, target shooting, yarns, frolic, with all sorts of extravagances that white men or Indians could invent, were freely indulged in. The unpacking of the medicine water contributed not a little to the heightening of our festivities."

Miles Goodyear became the first pioneer to settle in the Ogden Valley in 1841. The **Goodyear cabin**, oldest known dwelling constructed by a non-Indian in Utah, still stands at 2141 Grant Avenue. Goodyear moved out when the Mormons bought his property. Brigham Young sent a group of 100 families to settle the area in 1849. The community suffered through floods, drought, early frosts, insects, cholera, and Indian attacks. They supplemented their harvests with thistles and other wild plants. The sego lily, Utah's state flower, helped to save many pioneers from starvation.

The arrival of the transcontinental railroad in 1869 changed the character of the town and also created friction with Mormons who disapproved of the saloons and gambling halls that began to spring up.

Those animosities slowly dwindled as Ogden became an important railroad, manufacturing, milling, canning, livestock, and agricultural center. The increasing importance of nearby Hill Air Force Base as an employer helped the city continue to grow well into the 1980s. Established in 1939, the base occupies 6,600 acres just south of Ogden, and employs more than 8,700 people. Airplane buffs might want to stop at the **Hill Air Force Base Museum** and examine the thousands of aviation artifacts and numerous old airplanes. *Located five miles south of Ogden, east of I-15; 801-777-6818.*

◆ WEBER STATE UNIVERSITY

Another important event in the development of modern Ogden came on January 7, 1889, when 98 students gathered at the old Second LDS Ward meeting house on the corner of Grant and 26th streets for the first day of class at the Weber State Academy. In those lean times, school founders mortgaged their own homes to ensure that classes could be held. The school became Weber Academy in 1908 and broke into the college ranks in 1916 when two years of college work were added to the regular four-year high school curriculum. The name was changed again in 1918 to Weber Normal College and again in 1923 to Weber College, when the high school department was discontinued. The LDS Church transferred title of the college to Utah in 1933. Shortly after the college was moved from downtown to its present site in 1954, Weber State College became a four-year institution. The first senior class graduated in 1964 on the 75th anniversary of the school's founding. Now, 13,000 attend **Weber State University**; a modern institution offering undergraduate degrees in 98 fields of study. With its spacious Dee Events Center, Museum of Natural Science, Collett Art Gallery, Val A. Browning Center for the Performing Arts, and the Layton P. Ott Planetarium, all found on campus, Weber State serves as a center for culture in Ogden. *801-626-6975.*

### ◆ OGDEN MUSEUMS

John Browning, the foremost American inventor of firearms (building his first gun at the age of 13), helped shape the character of Ogden. Visitors to the city can see his collection of guns and learn about his life by visiting the **Union Station Museum.** Built inside the old railroad depot, the museum houses an auto collection and traces the history of the railroad. *25th and Wall Avenue; 801-629-8444.*

At the **Treehouse Children's Museum,** children can discover the wonders of literature, or attend a children's theater performance. *Located at the Ogden City Mall; 801-394-9663.*

### ◆ OGDEN PARKS AND NATURAL AREAS

Parks line the Ogden River as it winds its way through the middle of town The parkway includes a rose garden, a dinosaur parks, and an outdoor convention center. Bicyclists, hikers, and joggers enjoy a trail system while anglers catch wild brown and planted rainbow trout.

Also along the river, the **Eccles Dinosaur Park** is the habitat of over 100 life-sized reproductions of prehistoric creatures from the Cretaceous, Jurassic, and Triassic periods. They are placed in native Utah foothill vegetation. Kids often hear the creatures before they see them. A playground with dinosaurs to climb on is also a hit. *1544 E. Park Blvd.; 801-393-3466.*

A wildlife sanctuary, the **Ogden Nature Center** offers nature trails, tours, and many special events year round. *966 W. 12th St.; 801-621-7595.*

Fishing in the Weber and Ogden rivers can be excellent. Pine View Reservoir in **Ogden Canyon** is extremely popular with local boaters. The beaches are an ideal place to cool off when the temperature climbs in the valley.

One final note about Ogden. Don't be surprised if **Ben Lomond Peak**, which dominates the view to the east of the city, looks familiar. It served as the inspiration for the Paramount Pictures logo.

◆ NORTH OF OGDEN  *map page 205, B & C-7 & 8*

The venerable town of **Brigham City** was settled in 1851. This town of 20,000 people was originally named Box Elder Creek, but was later renamed to honor Mormon leader Brigham Young. Historic displays at the **Brigham City Museum and Gallery** show how residents lived in the 19th century. *24 N. 300 West; 435-723-6769.*

We like to visit the **Crystal Hot Springs** resort in neighboring Honeyville to soak in the naturally heated outdoor pools after a day of downhill or cross-country skiing in the nearby mountains. *8215 N. Highway. 38; 435-279-8104.*

During harvest time, Wasatch Front residents visit the fruit and vegetable stands located along old US Route 89 between Ogden and Brigham City, near the town of Willard. **Fruit Way**, as it is called, is a place where local farmers sell apples, apricots, peaches, pears, squash, corn, and pumpkins as they come into season.

■ CACHE COUNTY  *map page 205, B-8/9*

The Wellsville Mountains separate Cache Valley from Brigham City to the west. Cache Valley takes its name from the beaver trappers, who liked to cache their pelts here in the early 1820s.

◆ CHEESE

Some may travel to Logan, in the heart of Cache Valley, to attend a summer professional theater performance at the old Lyric Theater. Others might marvel at the beauty of Logan Peak, the 9,713-foot summit rising above the picturesque Mormon Temple. We enjoy coming to Logan and Cache Valley because of the cheese.

Cheese? The dairy industry is one of the major employers in this part of Utah, and some of the best cheese to be found is produced here. We like to tour the Cache Valley Cheese Plant, the Gosner Factory, and the Mountain Farms processing plant in Logan to treat ourselves to samples of different kinds of dairy products. We always take home boxes full of discounted cheeses for cooking or munching.

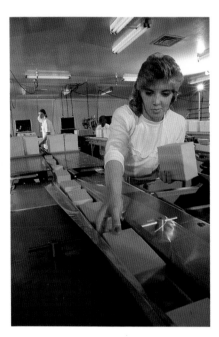

*The Cache Valley Cheese Plant at Amalga.*
*(Photo by Tim Kelly)*

♦ LOGAN   *map page 205, B-8/9*

It is not surprising that the agricultural industry still plays a key role in Logan's economy. **Utah State University**, a land grant institution established in 1888, is one of the leading agricultural research institutions in the United States! As a land grant school, Utah State supports basic and applied research. The school ranks 52 among public universities and colleges receiving contract and grant funds from the U.S. Government. With an enrollment of around 20,000 students, the school consists of 100 buildings located on 400 acres, with an additional 7,000 acres used for agricultural and other research. Colleges include agriculture, business, education, engineering, family life, natural resources, humanities, social sciences, arts, and science. The Extension Service administers classes and gives advice to farmers and homemakers at locations throughout Utah. Old Main Hill, where construction started on Utah State's historic administration building in 1889, was planned by the same landscape architects who laid out New York's Central Park.

More important to visitors, Utah State University contributes to the culture of the Beehive State by way of a variety of museums and performing arts centers. The **Daryl Chase Fine Arts Center** houses a theater and concert hall. The **Nora Eccles Harrison Museum of Art**, designed by the internationally acclaimed architect Edward Larabee Barnes, exhibits a fine collection of twentieth-century American art, examples of native American art, and fine ceramics. *University Public Relations Department; 435-797-0163.*

Designed by Truman O. Angell, the **Logan Mormon Temple** dominates the downtown skyline. Completed in 1885 after Brigham Young selected the site in

1877, the limestone temple with its beautifully manicured grounds ranks with the Salt Lake, Manti, and St. George temples for its striking appearance.

♦ AMERICAN WEST HERITAGE CENTER  *map page 205, B-8*

In the town of Wellsville, six miles southwest of Logan on US 91, is a different kind of museum, the **American West Heritage Center**. It is used as a laboratory in outdoor museum studies and living history for students who may go on to work as interpreters in state or national parks throughout the country. Graduate students operate the farm while completing master's degrees in history or American studies. Activity at the living history farm mirrors rural life circa 1917. Workers use farm equipment and techniques from that era. Kids especially enjoy helping workers

*A view of the Wellsville Mountains from Cache Valley may be*
*tonic enough for the city weary traveler.*

cut, bind, and stack wheat and barley. Threshing time usually takes place the second week of August, when farmers use a steam-engine tractor. Depending on the time of year, visitors can watch historic plowing demonstrations, sheep-shearing, a traditional wedding, fruit and vegetable canning, and cider pressing.

No Utah event celebrates the heritage of the American West and the trappers better than Wellsville's eight-day **Festival of the American West,** held anually at the American West Heritage Center. Some 25,000 people attend this event which traditionally opens the last Friday of July and continues through the first week of August. The festival gives visitors a chance to pan for gold, visit a military camp, see a Wild West show in a saloon, purchase Indian crafts, and get a feeling for what it was like to live in a mountain man camp. A pageant featuring dramatic action combined with music and dance helps bring to life the settling of the American West. *4025 South Highway 89/91; 435-797-1143.*

◆ BLACKSMITH FORK CANYON  *map page 205, B-9*

South of Logan, **Blacksmith Fork Canyon** strikes due east of Hyrum. It is one of our favorite canyons. Ducks and geese can be seen in the river and big game is common throughout the canyon. On one winter drive, a white weasel scampered across the road.

At the end of the road sprawls the **Hardware Ranch,** an elk preserve owned and operated by the Utah Division of Wildlife Resources. Workers at the site feed up to 700 elk every winter to prevent the animals from either starving or doing damage to farmers' lands in the valley below. Many families drive up to see the elk in winter when sleighs pulled by Clydesdale horses bring visitors right up next to the hulking beasts. *hardwareranch.com. 435-753-6206.*

◆ BEAR LAKE  *map page 205, A-10*

From Logan, you can also drive up **Logan Canyon** to marvel at the view of **Bear Lake** from the summit. Straddling the Utah-Idaho line at the extreme north end of the state, Bear Lake supports a state park and several private campgrounds and recreation areas. The lake contains four distinct kinds of fish thought to be the descendents of species found in ancient Lake Bonneville: the Bonneville cisco, Bear

Lake whitefish, Bonneville whitefish, and Bear Lake sculpin. Most fishermen, however, would rather catch the larger lake trout and Bear Lake cutthroat. In the summer, power boaters and sailboaters take over the lake. *Bear Lake State Park; 435-946-3343 or for campground reservations; 800-322-3770.*

If you're in the Bear Lake area in July or August, stop at one of the little drive-in restaurants in Garden City to enjoy a fresh raspberry malt or sundae. The area is famous for its crops of big berries. Many Salt Lakers make a special trip up to Bear Lake to pick or purchase raspberries for jams, jellies, and just munching.

*A spectacular ektacolor print of Bear Lake taken in July 1979 by artist Joel Sternfeld .
(©Joel Sternfeld, courtesy Pace/MacGill Gallery, New York.)*

# NORTHEASTERN UTAH
## MOUNTAINS & DINOSAURS

■ HIGHLIGHTS

| | page |
|---|---|
| Mirror Lake Highway | 158 |
| Flaming Gorge | 163 |
| John Jarvie Ranch | 165 |
| Dinosaur National Monument | 166 |
| Utah Field House of Natural History | 173 |
| Heber Valley Railroad | 175 |
| Wasatch Mountain State Park | 176 |
| Nine Mile Canyon | 178 |

THE WIND ROARED FIERCELY THROUGH THE PINE TREES above our cheap pup tent, bringing lightning, thunder, and rain. We huddled next to one another, for warmth and to keep from brushing against the side of the tent. Doing so would have brought a downpour of water on our heads. Eight miles from our automobile, we had no other choice but to hunker down for a long, frightful night. We had, of course, been seeking a wilderness experience, but this wasn't exactly what we had in mind.

We had come to climb 13,528-foot King's Peak, Utah's highest. Our attempted ascent earlier that day had failed a few feet from the summit when descending clouds turned the boulders slippery and clammy, and the frigid rain drenched us. Now, as a storm raged around us, a small rivulet of water slowly started trickling through the middle of the tent. By the time it was light, we were soaked. So was the firewood. Fortunately, a Peruvian sheepherder who had set up camp over the next hill spotted us and, in broken English, invited us to share a cup of hot chocolate and a cake he had baked the evening before. It was the kind of gesture strangers make to one another in such situations.

We packed our backpacks and began making our way down the muddy trail, certain that the adventures were over— until we noticed moose tracks in the mud.

# NORTHEASTERN UTAH

0        25        50 Miles
0     25     50     75 Kilometers

**Elevation**
in feet

13,528
11,000
10,000
9,000
8,000
7,000
6,000
5,000
4,000
3,000
2,780

Fresh moose tracks. It wasn't long before we spotted a majestic bull browsing in a meadow about 40 yards away. Confident we'd seen the last of the moose, we sauntered down the trail, only to be confronted by a cow and her calf. Mother moose wasn't pleased to have strangers around, and we quickly scrambled up a side hill, giving the huge animal and her baby the right-of-way.

When people ask what there is to do in northeastern Utah, we think back to trips like this one and know that anything is possible. We've paddled canoes down the remote White River in the springtime, watching geese and goslings scramble for cover. We've been drenched by white-water rapids when rafting down the Green River through Dinosaur National Monument's Split Mountain. We've spent a day bird-watching at the Ouray National Wildlife Refuge, and basked in the sun at remote Antelope Flat beach in the Flaming Gorge National Recreation Area.

The Uinta Mountains, the only major range in the lower 48 states which runs east and west, dominate northeastern Utah. Visitors can escape to rocky peaks, grassy alpine meadows, and thick, lodgepole forests in the 460,000-acre High Uintas Wilderness Area; it's Utah's largest designated wilderness, and the 17th biggest in the United States. Four of Utah's larger rivers—the Bear, Weber, Provo, and Duchesne—spring from 20 drainages and a thousand-odd lakes in the range. In the small towns and remote highways surrounding the Uintas can be found inns and cafes offering the comfortable charm of the rural West.

■ THE HIGH UINTAS *map page 155, B & C-1, 2, 3 & 4*

The Uintas look much the same today as they did in the days of the early pioneers. A passage from the book *Utah: A Guide to the State*, written in 1940 as part of Utah Writers Project under the Federal Works Projects Administration, tells part of their story:

"Wandering prospectors, cowboys and sheepherders penetrated the forests and climbed the peaks, leaving only burnt sticks and tin cans to mark their passing. A Swedish prospector was working with his partner in the Rock Creek country. The Swede felt that he had found what he always wanted—gold near running water, lakes, trees, flowers, and a fishing stream right in camp, but his partner yearned for the fleshpots of the mining camps. After many heated quarrels, the partnership was broken up in a fierce fight. The winner—the peace-loving Swede—sucked his bruised knuckles and yelled after his ex-partner: 'Yah, now run qvick to Park City vit its hussies and saloons. Anyhow! You are yust a snoose-chewing, coffee-

*Northern Utah's mountains are among the most rugged and wild in the West.*

grinding, visky-drinking, ski-yumping, fisk-eating yackass, anyhow!' Home-steading pioneers preferred better land in lower valleys, irrigable with water from these mountains. Some logging was done, but the roads were too rough and the distance to the large centers too far to make it profitable. All factors seemed to conspire to leave the High Uintas a primitive area. . . ."

The Uintas remain wild and undeveloped. Visitors searching for nightlife, ski lifts, and fine hotels can find them to the west of the Uinta Basin in Park City. Though a few rustic alpine lodges on the edge of the wilderness area (like Moon Lake, Defas Dude Ranch, or Spirit Lake) supply bedding and shelter, the Uintas are really for hikers, anglers, campers, and hunters. One doesn't need to backpack to enjoy the Uintas, however. The wilderness is surrounded by developed U.S. Forest Service campgrounds, which are easily accessible by car. A small fee is charged for use of the facilities here.

◆ **UINTA RECREATION** *map page 155 B & C-1–4*

### Mirror Lake Highway
*map page 155, B&C - 1 & 2*

The best known and most popular of roads to the Uintas is State Highway 150, known to locals as the Mirror Lake Highway. The road connects the town of Kamas, Utah, with Evanston, Wyoming. Closed by snow from late October until mid-June in most years, the highway climbs from 6,500 feet at Kamas to the 10,678-foot Bald Mountain Pass, and leads to dozens of developed campsites. Some of the campgrounds are located near lakes regularly stocked with rainbow trout. Trails off Mirror Lake Highway lead to popular backpacking areas. Most hikers are drawn by the wilderness designation on the east side of the road, but the west side (though not a congressionally designated wilderness) possesses many of the same qualities without the crowds. Wise backpackers check with rangers at the Kamas Ranger Station *(see page 328)* or the

Mirror Lake Guard Station to find the least visited lakes and routes.

Most Wasatch Front families seem to have a favorite lake or campground situated along the Mirror Lake Highway, and many make it a tradition to camp there at least once a summer. One of the largest camp-grounds surrounds **Mirror Lake**. The lodge on the lake burned down a few years ago, but the lake remains popular.

Campers willing to drive slightly farther can discover less crowded conditions at North Slope sites like Bridger Lake, China Meadows, and Hoop Lake. Located just south of Mountain View, Wyoming, these quiet places are tucked under some of the highest peaks in the range. Fishing for trout along the creek that flows through **China Meadows**, or just lying in the tall grass, can be a fine alternative to battling the crowds at better-known places. *Wasatch-Cache National Forest, see page 328.*

**East Slope**  *map page 155, B-3& 4*

Those wanting to go further afield will enjoy the camping areas at **Browne** and **Sheep Creek Lakes**, on the eastern edge of the Uintas. You'll need to follow dirt roads which head west from the Flaming Gorge National Recreation Area. Streams flowing from these small alpine lakes are teeming with cutthroat trout. Willing anglers should also hike from **Spirit Lake** into the nearby wilderness area, where they will likely be rewarded with excellent fishing. *Flaming Gorge Ranger District, Ashley National Forest Headquarters. See page 327.*

**South Slope**  *map page 155, C-2, 3 & 4*

We've spent many pleasant vacations camped near the **Moon Lake Lodge** on the South Slope of the Uintas in a developed U.S. Forest Service campground. As youngsters, we'd rise earlier than our parents and head for the stream flowing into Moon Lake to catch whitefish and trout for breakfast. We'd beg our parents to rent horses for an hour so we could ride into the forest or we'd paddle a canoe along the shoreline. Similar experiences were available at Defas Dude Ranch on the north fork of the Duchesne River. We would fish

*Mirror Lake at dawn in the High Uintas Wilderness Area.*

in Rock Creek or the Duchesne or Uinta rivers after our fathers had finished deer hunting. We enjoyed catching fish much more than "bushwhacking" through the aspens trying to scare a big buck into a hunter with a rifle. *Vernal Ranger District. See page 327.*

### Fishing

The Uintas are one of Utah's premier fishing regions. Anglers tell stories of walking to a nondescript, unnamed alpine lake and catching hungry trout on each cast. The simple technique of using a fly that imitates a mosquito, a plastic bubble for weight, and a traditional spinning rod works well here. Anglers soon get wise to the fact there are many lakes in each drainage. If one lake isn't producing, hiking 100 yards to the next can often change a fisherman's luck in a matter of seconds.

"We always suggest going into an area with more than one lake," says Glenn Davis, a retired fisheries biologist with the Division of Wildlife Resources. "That gives you some alternatives. The lakes closest to the highway get fished heavily. The Provo River drainage gets hit particularly hard. On the North Slope, there is high use on Henry's Fork (the trailhead to King's Peak) and Red Castle." Davis generally recommends fishing the east end of the Uintas where use is lighter.

The Division of Wildlife Resources manages 650 of these lakes, most of which contain either cutthroat or brook trout planted by airplane. A series of five booklets, called *Lakes of the High Uintas* ($2 each), giving detailed descriptions of lakes, types of fish stocked, trail access, and camping, are available from the DWR Salt Lake and Vernal offices. *See page 330.*

### Backpacking

Hikers seeking information on backpacking in the Uintas will find plenty of resources. Topographical and hiking maps of the areas can be obtained from the Wasatch National Forest headquarters in Salt Lake City, or the Ashley National Forest headquarters in Vernal. U.S. Forest Service district offices can be found along the roads into the mountains near Flaming Gorge, Vernal, Roosevelt, Duchesne, and Kamas in Utah, as well as Evanston and Mountain View in Wyoming. Bait shops and fishing guides sell other maps.

### Snowmobiling

Poor access, heavy snow, and extreme cold make winter access to the High Uintas Wilderness Area nearly impossible, but the Mirror Lake Highway is cleared to a snowmobile trailhead near Soapstone Basin. The trail is groomed regularly by the Division of Parks and Recreation. *See page 330.*

## ■ RESERVOIR RECREATION

Since Utah is one of the most arid states in the country, Wasatch Front residents rely on storage reservoirs to supply much of their water needs. One of the most complicated and expensive components of this water supply system is the Central Utah Project, a huge water-capture and delivery project conceived in 1956 to bring water from the eastern part of the Uinta Basin to the Wasatch Front. The large reservoirs of northeastern Utah, which provide drinking and irrigation water, also possess great recreational value for boaters, fishermen, and campers.

**Strawberry Reservoir**   *map page 155, D-1*
One of the premier trout fisheries of the western United States, this huge reservoir, located 23 miles southeast of Heber City near US Route 40, was originally built in 1906 as one of the nation's first reclamation reservoirs. It was expanded to 17,000 acres with the completion of the Soldier Creek Dam in 1973 and the joining with Soldier Creek Reservoir a few years later. Three immense U.S. Forest Service campgrounds give the thousands of fishermen who flock to Strawberry a place to spend the night. We've spent many a summer afternoon fishing for the large cutthroat trout that have made this place a popular angling spot for generations of Utahns. *Heber Ranger District. See page 328.*

**Deer Creek Reservoir**
*map page 205 G/H-9/10*
Just west of Heber City off US 189 is the Deer Creek Reservoir, also popular with anglers, sailboarders, and sailboaters. Its relatively low elevation draws waterskiers and swimmers. Campgrounds, showers, and picnic areas are at the lower end of the lake. *Deer Creek State Park, 435-654-0171 or 800-332-3770 for camping reservations.*

**Jordanelle Reservoir**   *map page 155, G-9/10*
Just up the Provo River north of Heber City is the newest Central Utah Project reservoir. It features fine facilities for campers and boaters, good trout fishing, and an interesting nature center. *Jordanelle*

*State Park, US 40, 10 miles north of Heber City; 435 649-9540 or 800-332-3770 for camping reservations.*

**Starvation Reservoir**   *map page 155, D-2*
Located near the town of Duchesne, Starvation Reservoir is a quiet alternative for Wasatch Front boaters. Although the fishing here is poor, the beautiful state park offers fine boating and camping facilities. *Off US 40, west of Duchesne; 435-738-2326 or 800-332-3770 for camping reservations.*

**Currant Creek Reservoir**   *map page 155, H-11*
This scenic, relatively new Central Utah Project lake, surrounded by pines and aspens, is located 19 miles off US Route 40 on a bumpy dirt road. Fishing can be spotty, but the Forest Service campground, offering a children's playground and some specially designed units for campers with horses, is one of Utah's best. *Heber Ranger District. See page 328.*

**Smaller Reservoirs**   *map page 155, E-2*
On the eastern side of the Uintas, south of Flaming Gorge, a handful of smaller reservoirs provide some interesting side trips from US Route 191. Bass and trout fishing, camping, and boating facilities can be found at Steinaker and Red Fleet Reservoir state parks. Calder, Crouse, and Matt Warner reservoirs on Diamond Mountain are also full of trout. The scenic 74-mile Red Cloud Loop leads to several small reservoirs, some beautiful forest, and Indian petroglyphs in Dry Fork Canyon.

# ■ FLAMING GORGE *map page 155, A & B-4*

The problem with visiting Flaming Gorge National Recreation Area is that there are almost too many interesting outdoor recreational possibilities. Flaming Gorge anglers tell stories about catching and releasing 30-pound lake trout. Below the Flaming Gorge Dam, fly fishermen cast nymphs, streamers, and dry flies to catch beautiful trout on the Green River, as rafters float down the gentle rapids on lazy summer afternoons. Boaters travel to remote campgrounds on the reservoir shore for a quiet evening under the stars and away from the sound of automobiles. As waterskiers zig and zag on the reservoir beneath 1,500-foot red-rock cliffs, swimmers bask in the sun on sandy beaches at Antelope Flat and Mustang Ridge. Hikers climb to the top of Bear Top Mountain for views across the canyons, enjoying close encounters with bighorn sheep. Children lead their parents on self-guided tours of the **Flaming Gorge Dam**, dropping 502 feet down in an elevator to the interior of the huge concrete structure, where they see the turbines, generators, and transformers, turning flowing water into electric power.

Best of all, visitors to Flaming Gorge can simply find a quiet, shaded campground, and spend their vacation relaxing. Our family will never forget a day spent at Antelope Flat beach. As the youngsters enjoyed swimming in the warm waters and building sand castles, two of us fished for smallmouth bass by casting spinners from the shoreline. We all marveled at the antelope and deer that wandered within a few feet of us. As we began to fry the fish we had caught, a surprise thunderstorm blew through the gorge. Lightning flashed on the red cliffs across the reservoir as we huddled in a sheltered picnic area. Then, as the storm blew over, a magnificent rainbow stretched from one side of the reservoir to the other. As the rain clouds dissipated, the sunset turned the entire surroundings into flaming orange embers. We watched the sun set and the sky turn dark before driving back to our campsite.

## ◆ FLAMING GORGE ATTRACTIONS

### Visitor Centers

First-time visitors to this national recreation area would do well to stop at the **Red Canyon Visitor Center**, located west of Dutch John on Utah State Highway 44. In addition to receiving information on things to do and places to camp, the interpretive display informs travelers about local plants, animal life, geology, and cultural history. The view of Flaming Gorge Reservoir, 1,360 feet below the plate glass window at

*Double rainbow stretches across the Green River and over Flaming Gorge.*

the Red Canyon facility, gives a feeling for the massive beauty of the gorge itself. Take some time to walk around the self-guided nature trail, an easy stroll designed to introduce visitors to the ecology of the area.

A second visitor center at Flaming Gorge Dam provides yet more local information. Visitors can view the movie *Flaming Gorge: A Story Written in Water*, which explains the natural and human history of Flaming Gorge from ancient times. *Flaming Gorge Ranger District, Ashley National Forest Headquarters at Ut 43/44 in Manila, UT; 435-784-3445.*

## Campgrounds

Developed campgrounds abound at Flaming Gorge. Some of the best include Firefighters Memorial, Lucerne Valley, Buckboard Crossing, and Firehole. Most camping sites are nestled in aspen and pine forests, while a few are found in sagebrush flats. Those who enjoy swimming might consider staying at Mustang Ridge or Antelope Flat, two campgrounds with beaches located nearby. *For camping reservations call Mistix; 800-283-CAMP.*

## Fishing

Though the main recreation season at Flaming Gorge runs from Memorial Day to Labor Day, you can fish on both the Green River and the reservoir itself year-round. Flaming Gorge Reservoir is famous for producing large lake and brown trout; lake trout of over 50 pounds are occasionally caught. Guide services and boat rentals are available at Cedar Springs Marina near the dam, Lucerne Valley near the Utah-Wyoming border, and Buckboard Marina in Wyoming. A number of Salt Lake City-based guides also take clients down the Green, which is easily Utah's best river fishery and one of the top trout waters of its kind in the United States. Nine ramps service the power boats and fishing crafts that ply the 66 square miles of the 91-mile-long reservoir. When you visit the Flaming Gorge Lodge near Dutch John, you can see the huge fish caught in the reservoir and often talk to anglers who have been out trying their luck. (Because of the complicated regulations designed to protect and produce trophy trout, anglers should study a Utah fishing proclamation closely.)

## Rafting the Green River

One of our favorite summer activities in the national recreation area is to rent a raft from the Flaming Gorge Lodge and Recreation Services, and take it down the Green. The river's small rapids provide thrills for experienced adventurers willing to guide their own rafts, as well as a good introduction for beginners with guides. Most enter the river at a ramp below the Flaming Gorge Dam and travel to the Little Hole pullout, just over seven miles downstream. A few ride the river all the way down to Brown's Park, a trip that takes the better part of a day, especially if you stop to fish. Concessionaires who rent the rafts will pick up clients. If you have two cars, it is less expensive to shuttle them back and forth, leaving one driver behind to travel the short distance over a dirt road between the dam and Little Hole to pick up rafters. If you have a shuttle vehicle available, the distances are short enough so you can make two or three trips from the dam to Little

Hole in a single day, giving everyone a chance to enjoy the ride. *Flaming Gorge Lodge and Recreation Services; 435-889-3773 or 435-885-3191.*

### Geology Driving Tours

There is much to learn about geology at Flaming Gorge. The loop road in **Sheep Creek Canyon**, on the west side of the reservoir, gives travelers an opportunity to view tremendous numbers of geological layers and formations exposed by erosion.

Another driving tour, the 30-mile "**Drive Through the Ages**" on US Route 191 between Flaming Gorge and Vernal, takes you across the edges of exposed layers, ranging in age from the one-million-year-old Uinta Mountain Group to the 80-million-year-old Mancos Formation. Inter-

pretive signs along the way point out the exposed formation. *For more information, pick up a free booklet from the Utah Field House of Natural History in Vernal, 235 E. Main St.; 435-789-7894, or from any Bureau of Land Management or U.S. Forest Service office. See pages 327-329.*

### Ute Mountain Lookout Tower

See how early foresters used lookout towers to detect forest fires at the Ute Mountain Tower. The only structure of its kind remaining in Utah has earned a place on the National Register of Historic Places. Visitors who climb the stairs to the top of the tower can see clear into Wyoming. Check with one of the visitor centers for hours and directions.

■ BROWN'S PARK   *map page 155, B-4 & 5*

Brown's Park is a remote valley lying across the borders of Utah and Colorado, just below the Wyoming boundary. It received its name from Baptiste Brown, an early fur trader. The area was frequently visited by the mountain men in earlier days. Today, the various parts of Brown's Park are managed by the U.S. Fish and Wildlife Service, the Utah Division of Wildlife Resources, the BLM, and the National Park Service *(see pages 326-330)*. Only one paved road leads into this area—from Maybell, Colorado. Dirt roads, however, lead from Dutch John to Clay Basin Creek, and from Vernal to the Brown's Park Waterfowl Management Area.

A point of historical interest in Brown's Park is the **John Jarvie Ranch**, on BLM property. In the late 1800s, the ranch contained a store, post office, river ferry, and cemetery, and was a regular stopping place for anyone traveling through this section of Utah, Colorado, and Wyoming. John Jarvie, a Scotsman, settled in the Brown's Park area in 1880. A colorful character, the well-educated Scotsman ran a ferry across the Green River, prospected in the nearby mountains, and entertained the locals by playing both the organ and the concertina. He knew, and occasionally hosted, outlaws like Butch Cassidy, the Sundance Kid, Matt Warner, Isom Dart, and Ann Bassett, who was known as the Queen of the Rustlers. Jarvie was murdered on July 6, 1909, by a pair of transient workers from Rock Springs, Wyoming, who were never captured. His body was placed in a boat and pushed out into the Green River. It was found a few days later, just above the Gates of Lodore in the eastern end of Brown's Park. Local legend has it that the dugout, which was Jarvie's first home, was often used as a secret meeting place for outlaws. John Bennett, a member of the Wild Bunch gang who was later hanged by vigilantes for his part in a local murder, built the stone house in 1888.

Today, the property consists of the stone house and dugout that served as Jarvie's homes, a blacksmith shop, and corrals built of hand-hewn railroad ties that drifted down the river from Green River, Wyoming, in the 1870s. Guided tours are available May through October, and visitors can take a self-guided tour year-round. To get to the ranch follow signs from US 191 that send you down bumpy Brown's Park Road. It's a long ride, but well worth the effort. *435-885-3307.*

### ■ DINOSAUR NATIONAL MONUMENT   *map page 155, C-5*

The lush, alpine forests of the Uintas and Flaming Gorge contrast with the stark, barren landscapes in the valleys of the Uinta Basin and Carbon County to the south. Looking over these desolate landscapes of tan, red, and white rock, it's hard to imagine this as a once-verdant land of ferns, cycads, club mosses, and clumps of tall conifers, where dinosaurs roamed. Yet fossils remain to attest to that history.

Giant vegetarians, like the *Apatosaurus* (once better known as *Brontosaurus*), *Stegosaurus, Diplodocus,* and *Camptosaurus,* as well as sharp-toothed and clawed carnivores like the *Allosaurus,* roamed this land 145 million years ago. When these dinosaurs died, some were washed by river floodwaters onto sandbars, where their bones mixed with the remains of turtles, crocodiles, clams, and other animals that lived in the river. Thick sediments piled up on top of them during later centuries. As the sea crept in and out, silica dissolved and percolated through the strata, turning the ancient riverbed into a hard sandstone, and mineralizing the bones buried within it. When the Rocky Mountains began to form to the east, the mountain building at what is now Dinosaur National Monument did not push the rock layers from below, but squeezed them from the sides. This action warped and tilted the rock. When rain, frost, and wind wore away the layers of sediment, a bit of the long-buried river bed—and its fossil treasure—began to appear at the top of a jagged ridge.

*(continues page 174)*

# UTAH'S JURASSIC PARK

Dinosaur National Monument provides us with a grand view of the Jurassic landscape of 145 million years ago, when the earth's continents were joined together in a single land mass now referred to as "Pangaea." As you look about you at the subtle greys and browns of the desert, try to imagine the brilliant green ferns, conifers, and mosses which once grew here, and the behemoth dinosaurs that wandered among them. One of these was *Apatosaurus* (a.k.a., Brontosaurus), a long-necked and long-tailed vegetarian—measuring over 70 feet in length and tipping the scales at 35 tons. Because *Apatosaurus's* brain was smaller than ours, though given the job of directing a body as big as 18 station wagons, some people assumed it was dull-witted and spent most of its time sloshing around in swamps. Yet, now we know from studying rock strata in such places as Dinosaur National Monument that *Apatosaurus* galloped around in herds, probably with its young in the middle, kicking up dust and trampling trees. The smell must have been awful, but they may have been fairly smart. After all, *Apatosaurus* belongs to one of the most successful groups of animals ever to live on the earth.

Other smaller dinosaurs shared Jurassic Park with these monsters, among them the comely *Stegosaurus* ("roofed reptile"), known for the bony knobs and bumps all over its body, the upright plates on its back and its tail spikes. These animals grew to 20 feet in length and weighed about one-and-a-half tons. Early researchers thought that the back plates served as a defensive weapon, but more recently scientists have suggested that they served as solar panels and radiators regulating *Stegosaurus's* body temperature.

Roaming around with these oversized vegetarians were meat-eating carnosaurs, who packed their weight behind large heads, powerful necks, stout hind limbs, and small forearms. These included *Allosaurus* ("strange reptile") and *Ceratosaurus* ("horned reptile"). Adult *Allosaurus* was close to 40 feet long with a skull that reached nearly three feet in length; it had sharp, recurved daggers for teeth—serrated on both sides—lining its jaws. Possibly, it sped around Jurrasic Park on its long, powerful hind limbs and grabbed its prey in the claws on its small, muscular forelimbs. *Allosaurus* probably fed on whip-tailed *Apatosaurus*.

As you climb into your two-ton station wagon to leave Dinosaur National Monument, you may feel vaguely relieved to return to the twentieth century, where the descendants of *Allosaurus* (birds) prey on insects and worms.

—Mark Goodwin, scientist at the U.C. Berkeley Museum of Paleontology

*(following pages) This famous mural of the Jurassic Period from Yale University gives an imaginative view of a world dominated by dinosaurs. (Peabody Museum)*

# DINOSAUR NATIONAL MONUMENT: TWO VIEWS

## *DINOSAUR'S HUMAN HISTORY*

*T*he colors of the rocks vary from a rich red-brown to vermilion, from gray to almost sugar-white, with many shades of pink and buff and salmon in between. The cliffs and sculptured forms are sometimes smooth, sometimes fantastically craggy, always massive, and they have a peculiar capacity to excite the imagination; the effect on the human spirit is neither numbing nor awesome, but warm and infinitely peaceful.

❖   ❖   ❖

*T*here passed nearly a thousand years after the last of the Fremont people departed during which, as far as history knows, these canyons were only wind and water and stone, space and sky and the slow sandpapering of erosion, the unheard scurry of lizard and scream of mountain lion, the unseen stiff-legged caution of deer, the unnoted roar of rapids in the dark slot of Lodore and the unrecorded blaze of canyon color darkening with rain and whitening with snow and glaring in the high sun of solstice.

❖   ❖   ❖

*A* place is nothing in itself. It has no meaning, it can hardly be said to exist, except in terms of human perception, use, and response. The wealth and resources and usefulness of any region are only inert potential until man's hands and brain have gone to work; and natural beauty is nothing until it comes to the eye of the beholder. The natural world, actually, is the test by which each man proves himself: I see, I feel, I love, I use, I alter, I appropriate, therefore I am. Or the natural world is a screen onto which we project our own images; without our images there, it is as blank as the cold screen of an empty movie house. We cannot even describe a place except in terms of its human uses.

And as the essential history of Dinosaur is its human history, the only possible destruction of Dinosaur will be a human destruction. Admittedly it would be idiotic to preach conservation of such a wilderness in perpetuity, just to keep it safe from all human use. It is only the human use that it has any meaning, or is worth preserving...

❖   ❖   ❖

And so it is plain that there is more to looking at a canyon or a mountain than merely filling the eye with scenery. The more we know about canyons and cliffs, buttes and ridges, valleys and terraces—their origin and their structure and the history of the strata that compose them—the more satisfying the scenery itself becomes. The further our curiosity probes back into the story of the rocks, openly revealed but in a language strange to most of us, the further our imagination is stretched by new revelations, and by a new concept of time.

—Wallace Stegner, "The Marks of Human Passage," *This Is Dinosaur*

### EDEN IN THE DESERT

You follow a stream course, now in it, now on a rock shelf above. After a time it will suddenly strike you: what happened to the desert? This surely doesn't belong—this sudden chill twilight, these firs and maples and birches and bowers of orchids and ferns. No rustle of cottonwoods or rasp of cicadas here—only the flute call of a hermit thrush and the tinkle of water under the sedges.

Some light shows through dark boughs up ahead. In a moment you emerge into a vast room, as high-walled as it is wide. Now the barrier is behind you and you're really on Split Mountain—not in the split itself, for that's where the noisy river is, but face to face with the naked castellated wall that hides it. If you are a climber, you'll be glad to find the rock firm and not slick. You will see that for all the depth of these massive formations, they run in layers, criss-crossed with ledges that will lead you to the top of the ridge high above the rushing Green. From this vantage point you can look into Dinosaur's Zion—more spiry than Zion but a true counterpart in color: chocolate and red, pink and purple and white and golden tan, its lower talus overgrown with sage and dotted with junipers, its heights dark with conifers.

And here on top you can stride along the wind-swept plateau past towering columns and steeples, past gulf after gulf of the kind by which you climbed from the valley. It has been a long climb, but the mountains always save their greatest rewards for climbers.

—David Bradley, "A Short Look at Eden," *This is Dinosaur*

*(following pages) The Green River exits Dinosaur National Monument and enters the Uinta Basin at Split Mountain Canyon.*

Thousands of tourists flock to Dinosaur National Monument each year to see this fossilized history of a time no man knew. Although hiking trails, river running, and some fine campgrounds can be enjoyed by visitors to the monument, most folks come to see the dinosaur fossils still in the rock at the dinosaur quarry. Remains of these ancient creatures dominate famous museums in New York, Washington, Chicago, Denver, and other cities throughout the world. Some of the earliest dinosaur skeletons ever assembled were excavated here in 1909 for the Carnegie Museum in Pittsburgh.

Earl Douglass, a Carnegie Museum paleontologist, was one of the first scientists to search for fossilized bones in the area. "I saw eight of the tail bones of a *Brontosaurus* in exact position," he wrote on August 7, 1909. "It was a beautiful sight."

Woodrow Wilson designated the place as Dinosaur National Monument in 1915. The national monument, which is now being considered for national park status, thus became America's most important natural display of fossilized dinosaur bones. It was increased in size by Franklin Roosevelt in 1938 to about 78 square miles. Additional land acquisitions since then have increased its size to about 325 square miles.

Douglass dreamed of the day when a museum could be built next to the quarry where he'd dug out so many unique dinosaur specimens. Visitors today enjoy the realization of that vision when they drive seven miles north of US Route 40 from Jensen to a dinosaur quarry enclosed in an architecturally novel building. Paleontologists used tools ranging in size from jackhammers to dentist picks to expose the fossils. They have ceased excavation at this site so that visitors can see how the bone were found in the rocks, and the paleontologist-interpreters here are more than willing to answer queries. In summer, rangers invite children to become "junior paleontologists" and get a behind-the-scenes look at the quarry. The kids can examine fossilized bones stored at the quarry, use tools to dig them out of a dirt pit, or take a walk with the paleontologist through the museum.

Most visitors spend too little time at Dinosaur National Monument. Take the time to contemplate and study the dinosaur bones entombed in the quarry rocks. Walk to the balcony overlooking the quarry and attempt to piece together the potpourri of fossilized bones into a single dinosaur, while imagining the giant creatures wandering through lush vegetation. Then spend an evening camped at Split Mountain watching the Green River roll slowly through the colorful canyon. Take a walk on the short, self-guided nature trail. You might be inspired to recall the words of John Wesley Powell, who stood near here on a bluff above the Green,

12 years after his 1869 expedition: "We are standing three thousand feet above its waters, which are troubled with billows, and white with foam. Its walls are set with crags and peaks, and buttressed towers, and overhanging domes. Turning to the right, the park is below us, with its island groves reflected by the deep, quiet water. Rich meadows stretch out on either hand, to the verge of a sloping plain that comes down from the distant mountains. These plains are almost naked rocks, in strange contrast to the meadows; blue and lilac colored rocks, buff and pink, vermilion and brown, all these colors clear and bright. . . . We are tempted to call this Rainbow Park." *Dinosaur National Monument, Quarry Visitor Center, UT 149, near Vernal; 435-789-2115.*

The **Utah Field House of Natural History** in nearby Vernal is an excellent place to learn more about dinosaurs. The outdoor Dinosaur Garden features many replicas placed in a natural setting, allowing visitors to view the creatures as something more than fossilized bones. In addition, skeletal reproductions, archaeological and geological exhibits, fluorescent minerals, and other natural history aspects of the Uinta Basin are found here. Pick up a free dinosaur hunting license from the visitor center. Our kids like to purchase souvenirs, such as fossils, children's books, or pieces of dinosaur bone, at the museum shop. *235 E. Main; 435-789-7894.*

## ■ TOWNS AROUND THE UINTAS

The little towns surrounding the High Uintas offer a special taste of Utah life for those willing to take the time to look beyond the gas stations and franchises. Stop in at the general store in one of these hamlets to chat with the proprietor about local history. We like to visit the little drugstore in **Kamas** to enjoy a freshly made malt with real ice cream, and when we visit **Roosevelt**, we always stop in at the mill in the center of town to purchase pancake flour. If you are in the area on the Fourth of July weekend you can experience one of the finest small-town rodeos in Utah, held every year in **Oakley**.

Heber City still has drive-in restaurants that serve great milk shakes and sundaes. And this is the home of the **Heber Valley Railroad** which takes travelers across the western part of Deer Creek Reservoir and down into Provo Canyon. There are special event trains featuring a sunset ride, murder mystery, pioneer day (July 24th), and others. *Call ahead for a schedule. 435-654-5601.*

This is a wild, hard land, away from the culture of the Wasatch Front's big cities and the fame of southern Utah's red-rock national parks. The lure of the Uintas and of Flaming Gorge, Dinosaur National Monument, and the small towns dotting eastern Utah's landscape draws those in search of solitude, wildlife, and a place still waiting to be discovered.

◆ UINTA PARKS AND RESORTS    *map page 138, F-5*

**The Homestead Resort**

Founded on hot springs in 1895, The Homestead has recently undergone a multi-million-dollar renovation, including the addition of an 18-hole golf course. You can climb the miniature volcano which produces the hot water for the swimming pool and peer down into the crater. Scuba divers and snorkelers can swim inside the crater. The Homestead Trail is joined with those at nearby Wasatch Mountain State Park. *homestead-ut.com, 700 N. Homestead Dr., Midway; 435-654-1102.*

**Wasatch Mountain State Park**

The park boasts a 27-hole golf course and a fine campground surrounded by scrub oak trees that turn a blazing orange in the fall. This is the home of the biathlon and cross-country ski events for the 2002 Winter Olympic Games. Coupled with trails on the golf course, this is the largest nordic ski area in Utah. *435-654-1791.*

■ PRICE AREA    *map page 155, E & F-2*

Moving west of Vernal to the town of Duchesne, and then southwest on US 191 to the settlement of Helper and the city of Price, travelers can discover another active dinosaur quarry and museum, and some colorful mining and railroad towns. Summer festivals, like Price's **Greek Days** during the second weekend in July, and **International Days** during the second week in August (in conjunction with the county fair) celebrate Carbon County's diversity.

◆ PRICE    *map page 155, E/F-2*

A city of nearly 10,000 residents, Price was named after Bishop William Price of the Latter-day Saints who led an exploring party through Spanish Fork Canyon in 1869. The city serves as a gateway to the canyonlands country to the southeast.

The **College of Eastern Utah Prehistoric Museum**, in the rear of the Price City Hall, contains a skeleton of *Allosaurus,* dinosaur footprints collected from nearby coal mines, fossils from the recently discovered Utah raptor, a hairy mammoth found at nearby Fairview Canyon, and Indian artifacts found in the area. Most of the fossils came from the Cleveland-Lloyd Dinosaur Quarry, south of Price. *(See "Stories in Stone" chapter, page 20.) 155 E. Main St.; 435-637-5060.*

*Fields of beeplant illuminate the desert floor in the San Rafael Wilderness south of Price.*

Price also serves as a gateway to the eastern edge of the Manti Mountains. State parks at Millsite, Huntington, and Scofield offer fine camping facilities, as do U.S. Forest Service sites near Joe's Valley, Ferron, and Electric Lake reservoirs. Utah's nicest and least-visited alpine scenery is set away from the Wasatch Front population centers.

◆ NINE-MILE CANYON   *map page 155, E-2 & 3*

Northeast of Price, this 50-mile-long canyon contains some of the finest examples of what archaeologists believe to be petroglyphs from the Fremont culture. Why is a 50-mile-long canyon called Nine-Mile Canyon? According to one story, when John Wesley Powell headed a government expedition through this part of the state in 1869, a mapmaker charting the area made a nine-mile triangulation drawing which he named Nine-Mile Creek. The name stuck with the canyon. Another tale states that the canyon got its name when the Miles family settled the area in the 1880s. Seven daughters and two parents added up to nine Miles. Free brochures to Nine-Mile Canyon—available from the Price Chamber of Commerce or the local BLM office *(see page 329)*—point out the locations of petroglyphs. These Indian tribes may have inhabited Nine-Mile Canyon as much as 1,700 years ago. The rock art itself depicts both humans and animals. No one knows exactly what the Indians were trying to say with their etchings, but part of the fun of visiting such a site is interpreting the writing yourself.

◆ HELPER   *map page 155, E-2*

Local railroad and mining industries have left Carbon County with a distinctive religious and ethnic flavor that can still be felt in downtown Helper. Though many of the old stores and hotels are boarded up, enough remain to provide glimpses of this coal-mining town's interesting past. With almost 3,000 present-day residents, Helper was named after the locomotives called "helpers," which were stored here in the late 1800s to help pull trains over the steep grade of nearby Soldier Summit and into the Wasatch Front. The **Western Railroading and Mining Museum**, located on Main Street, uses old photographs and memorabilia to trace Carbon County's roots. People from other parts of the state enjoy searching payroll lists to find old friends and relatives who once worked here. Other visitors may browse through the exhibits to get a feel both for the diversity of the region and for the hardships endured by miners.

# G R E A T     B A S I N

| ■ HIGHLIGHTS | *page* |
|---|---|
| Pony Express Route | 182 |
| Golden Spike National Historic Site | 186 |
| Bingham Copper Mine | 188 |
| Ghost Towns | 190 |
| Great Basin National Park | 192 |
| Great Salt Lake | 196 |
| Antelope Island State Park | 198 |
| Bonneville Salt Flats | 199 |

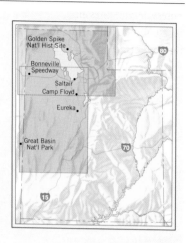

UTAH'S GREAT BASIN IS A LAND OF ISLANDS AND ILLUSIONS. Totally barren or covered with sagebrush and other desert-loving plants, often it is dismissed as wasteland. Yet in many places, water lies just beneath the surface. Alpine forests on the high mountain peaks and marshes around the Great Salt Lake sustain exuberant islands of life amidst the desolate mud and salt flats.

Mirages are among the first illusions encountered in the Great Basin. Motorists crossing the Great Salt Lake Desert see mountain ranges which seem to float on sky-colored water. Or are the mountains floating on air? But in approaching the mountains, the water slowly, mysteriously disappears. In other directions, where there are no mountains, the sky is indistiguishable from the horizon. All is bright and shimmering.

Closer to Salt Lake City, a strong ocean smell assails the nostrils. Seagulls fly overhead. Sailboats race across the bright blue water. Sun seekers wander along white sand beaches. It appears as if one has reached the coast. Yet, Utah's largest city is 500 miles from the Pacific, almost 1,500 from the Gulf of Mexico, and about 2,000 from the Atlantic.

Through the years, this great, nearly deserted wilderness has seduced thousands with the richness of her mineral deposits. Great Basin names like Disappointment Hills, Confusion Mountains, Skull Valley, and Little Sahara sound like the most

GREAT BASIN

uninviting spots on earth. This too, is illusory. Today Utah's western desert beckons with an extraordinary wealth of beautiful scenery and fascinating history.

While the masses of people living in Wasatch Front communities are inclined to avoid the Great Basin as much as possible, we have been increasingly drawn to the solitude. The view from the top of 11,031-foot Deseret Peak is breathtaking. Farther east rise the peaks of the Wasatch Range, and on most days, a light gray haze veils the buildings of Salt Lake City. The Great Salt Lake stretches to the north. To the west and southwest, countless basins and ranges, mostly uninhabited, drift off toward the horizon. One spring, we were lucky to follow cougar tracks down the mountain in the snow.

There are a handful of popular tourist destinations scattered around the Great Salt Lake, but to appreciate the rest of the Basin, it is necessary to explore with an adventurous attitude. Many a pioneer cursed the heat and the barren landscape of the salt flats and refreshed himself in the cool canyons of the mountains. With air-conditioned cars, modern tourists have the chance to appreciate the beauty of the desert in relative comfort.

About 12,000 years ago, humans lived in caves around the edges of Lake Bonneville, precursor of the Great Salt Lake. The lake at that time contained fresh water. Its salinity increased as the lake diminished in size. The Great Salt Lake reached its present level about 9,000 years ago. The Shoshone, Utes, and Goshutes may have collected salt on its shores. Mountain men explored the lake for a water route to the Pacific, but found none.

Immigrants bypassed the lake and salt deserts immediately to its west because they lacked water for their livestock. One hapless exception was the Donner-Reed party, which decided to cross after a California politician, Lansford Hastings, assured them it was a shortcut to the Golden State. Hastings himself had traversed the territory on horseback. What everyone failed to recognize was that the immigrants' heavily laden wagons would sink into the sludge, and their oxen would need more frequent water and pasture than did Hasting's horse. Delays in crossing caused the Donner-Reed party to reach the Sierra Nevada late in the season. They were stranded by the winter's first blizzard, bringing horrible suffering, starvation, and cannibalism. Forty of the original 87 members of the party died, making it the worst disaster of the California Trail. The story of their ordeal is told in the **Donner-Reed Museum** in Grantsville, northwest of Tooele and on the edge of the salt flats. The museum houses guns and relics abandoned by the party as it struggled to lighten its loads.

# SHERLOCK HOLMES IN UTAH

*I*n the central portion of the great North American Continent there lies an arid and repulsive desert, which for many a long year served as a barrier against the advance of civilization. From the Sierra Nevada to Nebraska, and from the Yellowstone River in the north to the Colorado upon the south, is a region of desolation and silence. Nor is Nature always in one mood throughout this grim district. It comprises snow-capped and lofty mountains, and dark and gloomy valleys. There are swift-flowing rivers which dash through jagged cañons; and there are enormous plains, which in winter are white with snow, and in summer are gray with the saline alkali dust. They all preserve, however, the common characteristics of barrenness, inhospitality, and misery.

There are no inhabitants of this land of despair. A band of Pawnee or Blackfeet may occasionally traverse it in order to reach other hunting-grounds, but the hardiest of the braves are glad to lose sight of those awesome plains, and to find themselves once more upon their prairies. The coyote skulks among the scrub, the buzzard flaps heavily through the air, and the clumsy grizzly bear lumbers through the dark ravines and picks up such sustenance as it can amongst the rocks. These are the sole dwellers in the wilderness.

In the whole world there can be no more dreary view than that from the northern slope of the Sierra Blanco. As far as the eye can reach stretches the great flat plain-land, all dusted over with patches of alkali, and intersected by clumps of the dwarfish chaparral bushes. On the extreme verge of the horizon lie a long chain of mountain peaks, with their rugged summits flecked with snow. In this great stretch of country there is no sign of life, nor of anything appertaining to life. There is no bird in the steel-blue heaven, no movement upon the dull, gray earth—above all, there is ab-solute silence. Listen as one may, there is no shadow of a sound in all that mighty wilderness, nothing but silence—complete and heart-subduing silence.

It has been said there is nothing appertaining to life upon the broad plain. That is hardly true. Looking down from the Sierra Blanco, one sees a pathway traced out across the desert, which winds away and is lost in the extreme distance. It is rutted with wheels and trodden down by the feet of many adventurers. Here and there are scattered white objects which glisten in the sun, and stand out against the dull de-posit of alkali. Approach, then examine them! They are bones: some large and coarse, others smaller and more delicate. The former have belonged to oxen, and the latter to men. For fifteen hundred miles one may trace this ghastly caravan route by these scattered remains of those who had fallen by the wayside.

—Arthur Conan Doyle, "A Study in Scarlet," from
*The Adventures of Sherlock Holmes,* 1902

■ THE PONY EXPRESS

The increasing wealth and population of gold-rich California, coupled with the threat of Civil War, convinced leaders in Washington of the necessity of improving communications between the East and West coasts. The Pony Express helped to ensure this. For 18 months between 1860 and 1861, young men (preferably orphans because of the risks involved) rode from one station to the next in stretches of approximately 11 miles each, linking the continent. At its peak, the Pony Express route incorporated 190 stations, 420 horses, and 80 riders. The fastest crossing took seven and a half days to carry Lincoln's Inaugural Message from St. Joseph, Missouri, to Sacramento, California. The Pony Express was thrust into sudden obscurity with the completion of the first transcontinental telegraph line.

Besides the daring mail carriers, the Pony Express route was also used by passenger stagecoaches and wagons hauling freight. Later, portions of the first transcontinental roadway, the old Lincoln Highway, would be built along the route.

Today a gravel road follows the trail through a hundred miles of Utah's Great Basin. Drivers can follow the Bureau of Land Management's interpretive signs

*The Pony Express. (Utah State Historical Society)*

**Elevation**
in feet

13,528
11,000
10,000
9,000
8,000
7,000
6,000
5,000
4,000
3,000
2,780

# WEST CENTRAL UTAH

0    10    20 Miles
0  10  20  30 Kilometers

GREAT BASIN

To Reno, NV

Bonneville Salt Flats State Park

Hill Air Force Range (no access)

Danger Cave State Park

Bonneville Speedway

Newfoundland Evaporation Basin (dry)

STANSBURY ISLAND

*Great Salt Lake*

ANTELOPE ISLAND

Bountiful

To Ogden

N Salt Lake City

65

80

Wendover

Knolls

Rowley Junction

SALT LAKE CITY

Great Salt Lake State Park

Magna

Park City

215

Flux

138

Mills Junction

Midvale

Wendover Range (no access)

GREAT SALT LAKE DESERT

Grantsville

68

Sandy

Tooele

Bauer

Stockton

Riverton

Draper

Iosepa

St John Station

Bluffdale

Bingham Canyon Open-Pit Copper Mine (worlds largest)

American Fork

189

CEDAR MTS

Ophir

73

Cedar Fort

Lehi

15

Orem

Clover

Mercur

Fairfield

Stage Coach Inn State Park

Provo

Dugway

Camp Floyd State Park

Utah Lake

Ibapah

Desert Test Center (no access)

Dugway Proving Grounds (no access)

Vernon

36

68

Spanish Fork

Gravel

Gravel

Wasatch Nat'l Forest

Genola

Payson

6

Thistle

Goshute Indian Reservation

Callao

Goshute

Fish Springs

Fish Springs Nat'l Wildlife Refuge

Simpson Springs

Eureka

Tintic

Elberta

Goshen

Old Pony Express and Stage Route

Silver City

89

Boyd Station Ruins

Haystack Peak 12,020

Topaz Mtn 7,113

Mona

Trout Creek

174

DESERT

Little Sahara Rec Area

6

Nephi

132

Baker Hot Springs

132

Moroni

NEVADA

SNAKE VALLEY

N W E S

Swasey Peak 9,669

Howell Peak 8,240

Antelope Springs

Lynndyl

Levan

HOUSE RANGE

SEVIER RANGE

Leamington

28

Ephraim

Sugarville

Sutherland

Abraham

Topaz

Delta

125

Oak City

Manti

Gravel

Old US 50/6

Hinckley

Deseret

Fort Deseret State Park

Fishlake National Forest

Scipio

Fayette

Robinsons Ranch

Notch Peak 9,725

Gunnison Massacre Monument

50

Gunnison

89

To Ely, NV

6

50

Clear Lake

BLACK ROCK DESERT

Holden

50

Centerville

Baker

487

Great Basin National Park

Sevier Lake (dry)

Flowell

100

Fillmore

Territorial Statehouse State Park

Aurora

Axtell

Salina

70

Garrison

257

Meadow

133

Richfield

Sigurd

To Green River

GREAT BASIN

21

Desert Range Experimental Farm

Gravel

Black Rock

Old Cove Fort

Kanosh

Fishlake

Cove Fort

Glenwood

24

Headquarters

Frisco Peak 9,725

Newhouse

Old Frisco Mining Town

Gravel

Elsinore

Monroe

Burrville

Koosharem

Freemont

Milford

15

Fremont Indian State Park

National

Sevier

Fishlake National Forest

PARKER RANGE

Greenwich

Loa

Marysvale

89

Piute State Park

130

Minersville

Greenville

MINERAL MTS

Manderfield

Beaver

Forest

Junction

62

Kingston

Lyman

24

Old Fort

Minersville State Park

To Cedar City

Otter Creek State Park

1    2    3    4    5

A B C D E F G H

along the route from Faust Junction (south of Tooele) through Simpson Springs Station and Boyd Station to Canyon Station, each in varying stages of reconstruction or disintegration. Before going, write to the BLM for information, or pick up the Utah Travel Council's maps that show Pony Express stations. *(See page 331.)*

◆ CAMP FLOYD/STAGECOACH INN STATE PARK   *map page 183, B/C-4*

A good place to to start off down the Pony Express route is at Fairfield's **Stagecoach Inn State Park** where you can obtain a printed guide describing the route and telling some of the wild tales associated with it. Here you can explore the Pony Express and stagecoach station where Mark Twain and Horace Greeley stopped on their journeys west. Fairfield was also the site of **Camp Floyd**, the army bivouac built by Colonel Albert Johnston when he was sent to put down a rumored Mormon rebellion that never materialized. *Camp Floyd/Stagecoach Inn State Park, 25 miles west of Lehi on UT 73; 801-768-8932.*

As you head farther west, you can sometimes see wild mustangs grazing in the valleys along the road. Ancestors of these animals were captured and broken to carry the riders through this unfriendly desert.

◆ SIMPSON SPRINGS STATION   *map page 183, C-3*

Captain James Hervey Simpson described the desert around his namesake outpost as a "somber, dreary wasteland, where neither man nor beast can live for want of the necessary food and over which a bird is scarcely seen to fly." In later decades, the spring water refreshed freighters hauling supplies to nearby mining towns such as Gold Hill. Today, there is running water at the BLM campground.

■ THE RAILROAD   *map page 205, B-6*

On May 10, 1869, at Promontory, Utah, the United States started on its way to becoming a world power. The American continent had been linked by rail! Golden Spike National Historic Site preserves this important piece of our history.

Before the railroad, land routes to the Pacific shore stretched over vast and often hostile terrain, a journey that took wagon trains months to make. The fastest voyage by clipper ship around the tip of South America still required at least a hundred days. With increased migration, Congress began to recognize the pressing need for a rail link between the East and West Coasts. Quarrels between the North and the South over which route the railroad should take kept it from being built until the outbreak of the Civil War. President Lincoln and Congress then decided to commence the job with a northern route in order to keep California with the Republic and to keep the war chest filled with California gold.

To spur interest in the construction project, Congress promised free use of building materials from the public lands, cash subsidies of $16,000 per mile of track on the plains and from $32,000 to $48,000 per mile through the mountains, and an outright bonus of every alternate, odd-numbered section of public land, which stretched checker-board fashion for 20 miles on each side of the tracks.

Employing mostly Irish workers to lay the tracks, the Union Pacific raced across the plains from Omaha. The Central Pacific snaked its way through the Sierra Nevada, employing workers mainly from China. Just as many modern contractors seek to bilk the federal government, the railroad companies, too, found ways to get rich. The most blatant example was the laying of 225 miles of parallel track in northern Utah before the government demanded that they bring the rails together at Promontory, joining a total of 1,776 miles of track. Completed in fewer than four years, the first transcontinental railroad is an engineering feat unequalled in American history.

*The railway lines from east and west finally met at Promontory on May 10, 1869. (Utah State Historical Society)*

Trains no longer pass through Promontory. Polititians and businessmen arranged to have it moved closer to established commercial centers, specifically Ogden, 45 miles to the south.

Visitors to **Golden Spike National Historic Site** can glean the significance of this momentous event through visitor center film shows and displays. The most riveting exhibition takes place outdoors on the anniversary of the event, May 10, and during the Railroaders Festival, usually the second Saturday in August. On those occasions, two full-sized replicas of the engines used in the original ceremony, the *199* and the *Jupiter*, recreate the historical meeting. Shiny and impressive, with thick, black smoke billowing from their stacks, they dwarf onlookers. Puffing and tooting, the engines ease together, head to head, to a squeaking, hissing stop. Engineers dressed in authentic uniforms jump from their cabs and take turns addressing the crowd, telling the tale of the joining of the rails and answering questions. *UT 83 west in Promontory; 435-471-2209.*

The original event was not without some humor. "California's Leland Stanford raised his hammer and swung a mighty blow," relates the WPA version from *Utah: A Guide to the State*. "He missed entirely, but the telegraph operator (a line was connected to the last spike to record the blow), a man of practical foresight, simulated the blow with his key and let tumult loose upon the cities of the country; fire bells, cannon, and factory whistles joined with shouting human voices to signalize the linkage of a continent. At Promontory the two locomotives gingerly nosed their cowcatchers together. To the world the telegrapher tapped out the historic message to the world:

*The last rail is laid*
*The last spike is driven.*
*The Pacific road is finished.*

Within two weeks of the joining of the rails, more than 300 frame buildings, shanties, and tents were erected at Promontory and nearby **Corinne**. The rough and lusty population grew to 7,500, including 5,000 Chinese railroad workers, and a temporary city government was set up to handle them. Colonel Patrick Connor, who had set out to weaken the Mormons' stronghold by bringing mining to the Utah Territory, headed the Liberal Political Party, based in Corinne.

Brigham City, 32 miles to the east of Promontory, tried to maintain its status as a quiet religious community by ignoring its unholy neighbors. Mormons took advantage of the railroad, however, to obtain jobs. They were not allowed to work on the trains themselves but kept busy grading the roadbeds.

In 1872, a diphtheria epidemic swept Corinne. Hundreds died. Many deserted the city. Indians surrounded the town and helped themselves to the ranches of the remaining inhabitants until soldiers from Fort Douglas drove them out.

In 1903, the Lucin Cutoff moved the rails across the Great Salt Lake to shorten the line, and Corinne was struck a crippling blow.

*Train replicas at Golden Spike National Historic Site.*

Present-day Brigham City celebrates the anniversary of the driving of the golden spike with many Chamber of Commerce promotions and community activities. Brigham Young's curse on Corinne for its lawlessness has been fulfilled. It is the tiny unprosperous place he prophesized it would become. The old railroad bed, abandoned in many places, is used by off-road-vehicles and mountain-bikes.

## ■ BOOMS AND BUSTS

With the coming of the railroad, mining became a more lucrative business. Brigham Young had discouraged his followers from prospecting, but gold and silver fever spread wherever the precious metals could be found. Boomtowns like Ophir, Mercur, Gold Hill, Eureka, Mammoth, and Frisco sprang up in the Great Basin seemingly overnight. Many still stand in various states of disrepair—fascinating and picturesque, they appeal to historians, antique collectors, photographers, painters, solitude seekers and dreamers. Rockhounds can use guides available in bookstores to help them locate specimens of fossils and minerals from sites all around the Great Basin.

The adventurous are invited to try their own hand at prospecting. There is treasure to be found if the searcher gets lucky. The treasure might be an ancient gold pan or century-old whiskey bottle. More often, it is a quiet day spent contemplating the past preserved in rusting machinery and dilapidated shacks. Visitors, however, should respect property rights and make sure buildings are safe and truly abandoned before entering.

As market conditions and milling methods changed, Great Basin towns repeatedly boomed and died. As new methods for extracting metals and minerals from the rocks are developed, some may be resurrected in the future. Until then, they struggle along and wait for better times, shadows of their former thriving selves.

◆ BINGHAM CANYON  *map page 183, B-4*

One of the first discoveries of precious metals was made in 1863 at Bingham Canyon, in the Oquirrh Mountains west of Salt Lake City. Although gold, silver, and lead first drew miners here, the modern quest is for copper. Today, the **Bingham Copper Mine** is the world's largest and most productive. Since 1906, when the open-pit method was first used, several towns have been bulldozed to make way for its ever-enlarging spirals. Visitors on the lip of the Bingham copper pit look out across uncounted spiraling cuts in the rock, which drop dramatically from a few remaining peaks to the rust-red, damp earth at the mine's lowest level.

At 2.5 miles wide and a half mile deep, the pit could easily hold all of downtown Salt Lake City; the tops of the city's tallest buildings would barely reach one-eighth the way up the walls of the mine.

The owner of the mine, Kennecott Utah Copper, was, at one time, the major employer of Salt Lake City residents (making the city a "boomtown"). Fluctuations in the copper market and the import of less costly ores from South America resulted in layoffs. Salt Lake City was forced to diversify its employment base, but mining continues to bring in 3.9 percent of Utah's industrial dollars.

*A tough customer prepares for another day at work. (Utah State Historical Society)*

Bingham Canyon and other mining towns throughout the state attracted people from all over the world: Scandanavia, the Balkan States, Western and Central Europe, Asia, and even, during World War II, the Navajo lands to the south. Each nationality settled into a separate neighborhood in the narrow canyon.

The immigrants kept a tight hold on their old-world languages and customs. Since mining at Bingham Canyon in those times meant dark tunnels, poor working conditions, and low pay, there were labor disputes and strikes. The old-world dislikes and prejudices crept into the new neighborhoods and there were fights. But as time passed, the disasters of fire, flood, and snowslide forced people of different nationalities to help each other and the old boundaries dissolved. Over time, the canyon evolved into a cohesive community.

John R. Wharton, principal of Copperton Elementary in the 1950s, had an unusual job heading a school with such an international makeup. "I thought I knew what a PTA meeting was like, but this one was different. I was told I didn't need to do anything except be there at a certain time and have a specific number of tables and chairs set up. I walked in as some women were setting up a big coffee pot. Shortly, parents arrived bringing specialties from their native countries. There was Italian food, Chinese food, Mexican food, everything you could imagine!"

Bingham Canyon has been designated a National Historic Landmark by the United States Department of the Interior. The visitor center is open daily from 8 A.M. to 8 P.M., April through October.

### ◆ BOOMTOWNS AND GHOST TOWNS

**Tooele**   *map page 183, B-4*
West of Bingham Canyon stands the town of Tooele (One of the tests of native Utahns is whether or not they can pronounce the name of Tooele: "Too-ill-uh.")

**The Tooele Railroad Museum** houses a collection of railroad and mining artifacts, including a scale railway and simulated mine. *Vine Street between Third East and Broadway; 435-843-2110.*

The town also has a Daughter of the Utah Pioneers museum. The log cabin next door to the museum, built in 1856, was one of the first houses in Tooele. *39 E. Vine; 435-882-0653 or 435-882-5470.*

**Ophir**   *map page 183, B-4*
South of Tooele is another of Utah's richest mining towns. Ophir was named after King Solomon's fabled mines. By 1900, the town had produced $13 million, including $1 million from the Kearsarge Mine alone. Even as it dimmed, Ophir's fabulous legacy was carried on beyond the boundaries of Utah by Marcus Daly, founder of Anacon-

da Copper, who earned his grubstake, and much of his know-how, while working at his Zella mine in Ophir. Although a few diehards still inhabit Ophir, it is a favorite of photographers because so much of the old appearance remains. Ophir Canyon is also an excellent place to view bald eagles during the winter months.

### Mercur *map page 183, B-4*

Few old buildings survive in Mercur, just south of Ophir. A fire on Statehood Day, January 4, 1876, burned the town completely. Rebuilt, it burned again in 1902 in a fire that began at a Chinese lunch counter. Flash floods rolling down the bare hills finished the job of ruining the city.

Mercur was named for the mercury ore mined there, which also contained large amounts of gold. In 1898, the Golden Gate Mill in Mercur became the world's first all-steel, non-ferrous mining plant and the first metallurgical plant in the Western Hemisphere to use transmitted electric power. Gold profits fell, however, and by 1917 Mercur became a ghost town. Seventy years later, mining began again—only to end again in the 1990s.

### Eureka *map page 183, C-4/5*

Farther south, Eureka has been called a living ghost town, not only because many of the buildings and mining paraphernalia have been kept intact for a century, but because a small population of old-timers still call it home. In 1868 it was the center of the Tintic mining district, one of Utah's biggest and richest. By the end of its first hundred years, the Tintic's production of silver, gold, and other metals and minerals

exceeded $500 million. Eureka's fortunes faded along with those of many other boomtowns, but 700 residents remain.

### Gold Hill *map page 183, C-1*

About 100 miles west of Eureka along the old Pony Express route, Gold Hill is one of the most picturesque and complete ghost towns in Utah. Gold Hill started as a gold boomtown in 1892. It died and was rebuilt during World War I when tungsten and other minerals were needed for the war effort. One former prospector who didn't strike it rich in Gold Hill but knocked out enough opponents to become the heavyweight champion of the world was Jack Dempsey. The town is 23 miles north of Callao on a dirt road.

### Topaz *map page 183, E-3*

A ghost town of a different nature was Topaz. In the wartime hysteria of 1942, about 9,000 Japanese, most of them American citizens, were brought to a camp hastily constructed here. The ghosts of the wrongly imprisoned souls can be felt around remaining streets and foundations. A monument to the injustice has been erected on the northwest corner of Topaz. To reach Topaz, drive six miles from Delta on US Route 50/6 to the small town of Hinckley, turn north, and continue 4.5 miles on a partly paved, partly graveled road to its end. Turning left (west), go 2.5 miles on a paved road to its end in Abraham, then turn right (north) and drive 1.5 miles on a gravel road to a stop sign. From there, turn left and drive three miles to Topaz on a gravel road.

**Near Delta**  *map page 183, E & F-3*
West of Delta, you can search for souvenirs in the trilobite fossil beds in the House Range.

South of Delta you can find the crumbling remains of **Fort Deseret**, an adobe-walled fort quickly built during the Black Hawk War of 1865.

About six miles southwest of Fort Deseret, is the **Gunnison Massacre Monument.** It marks the spot where Captain John W. Gunnison and seven of his men were killed by Indians while working on a federal railroad survey during the Walker War.

## ■ ISLAND RANGES, INLAND SEA

One of the greatest illusions of the Great Basin is that it is a deserted wasteland that must be crossed in haste as a traveler heads for California. The striking beauty of the mountains of the Great Basin are a well-kept secret. The magnificent desert, marsh, and alpine scenery of Utah's Great Basin is showcased in two designated and 19 proposed wilderness areas and seven wildlife refuges.

The mountain ranges of the Great Basin have been called islands of ecological diversity because slightly different species of plants and animals have developed on each. The intervening mud and salt flats and broad dry valleys kept the plant and animal species from migrating and interbreeding.

The upper reaches of the Stansbury and Deep Creek mountains are untouched wilderness areas. Deseret Peak in the Stansburys, Notch Peak in the House Range, and Haystack Peak in the Deep Creek Range provide fantastic views of the salt and mud flats of the Great Basin. The mountain ranges looming in the distance are home to thousand-year-old bristlecone pines. Miners, pioneers, and outlaws frequented their peaks and canyons. While hiking in the ranges, deer, pronghorn antelope, chukar partridge, bald and golden eagles, and peregrine falcons can be sighted. Obtain detailed topographical maps from the local U.S. Forest Service offices to help you explore these mountains. *(See pages 327 and 328.)*

### ◆ GREAT BASIN NATIONAL PARK  *map page 183, F-1*

US Route 50/6 which, from Delta, skirts the House Range to Baker, Nevada, has been called the loneliest highway in the United States. Just over the Nevada border, it passes Great Basin National Park, which preserves a spectacular stretch of mountain and high desert including 13,063-foot Wheeler Peak. Starting in a dry desert valley near Baker, where temperatures often soar over 100 degrees F in the summer, the park road switchbacks up through desert woodlands of mountain mahogany, pinyon pine, and juniper to alpine forests of Douglas fir, where it's always cool. *Park Headquarters; 775-234-7331.*

♦ WILDLIFE AND SAND DUNES

### Fish Springs National Wildlife Refuge
*map page 183, D-2*

No streams or rivers leave the Great Basin. The water running off from the mountain ranges ends up mainly in marshes. In the middle of seemingly barren desert, the United States government has established Fish Springs National Wildlife Refuge to act as a sanctuary for migrating birds, as well as local wildlife. The refuge is located on the old Pony Express and Stage Route. A self-guiding auto tour makes an 11 1/2 mile loop motorists may follow using a brochure that they can pick up at the entrance. The brochure describes various birds that inhabit the refuge seasonally or year-round.

### Waterfowl Management Areas
**Locomotive Springs State Waterfowl Management Area** is west of Golden Spike National Historic Site. **Bear River Migratory Bird Refuge, Harold S. Crane State Waterfowl Management Area**, and **Ogden Bay State Waterfowl Management Area** border the Great Salt Lake where the fresh water of the Bear and other rivers enters the salt water. **Clear Lake State Waterfowl Management** Area is the southernmost of them, over 20 miles from Delta in the Black Rock Desert. Bird watching in these areas takes patience but can be rewarding. A variety of birds frequent the refuges. In March, snow geese blanket the **Gunnison Bend Reservoir**, near Delta, during their northward migration.

### Great Salt Lake Islands
*map page 183, A-4 & 5*

The islands of the Great Salt Lake are always changing in relation to the lake's water levels. Stansbury Island closely resembles a peninsula now, but may, once again, be an island should the lake rise. All of the islands in the Great Salt Lake are actually extensions of the Oquirrh and Stansbury mountains. Bison, placed by early pioneers, inhabit Antelope Island. The diverse gene pool of this herd is utilized to keep bison herds elsewhere in the country healthy.

### Little Sahara Recreation Area
*map page 183, D-4*

Remnants of sandbars deposited by Lake Bonneville have accumulated in white dunes in the Little Sahara Recreation Area, managed by the BLM. Winds pushed the sands 180 miles to the northeast until they were deflected by Sand Mountain. Off-road vehicles and motorcycles can ply the sands but a separate area is set aside for foot traffic. The three campgrounds in the area have water. *For information or reservations, contact the BLM at 15 E. 500 North, Fillmore; 435-743-6811.*

disasters and insists that Utahns construct new buildings in the right place and in the right way. Disastrous earthquakes have shown many times that if you don't respect the power of the land—and prepare for it—the land will win.

While Atwood is pro-development, she has also spent much of her life in the outdoors studying Utah's scenic mountains, plateaus and deserts. Providing open space and access to those open spaces to preserve the quality of life they offer is as important to her as supplying jobs and homes. She prods policy makers and politicians to plan wisely to insure a prosperous future in the next century and beyond.

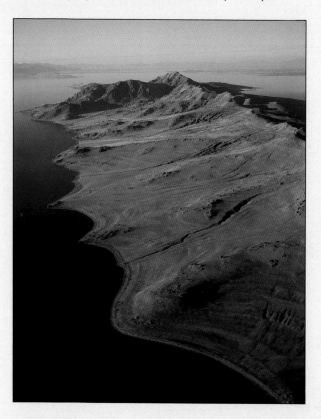

*Antelope Island, in the Great Salt Lake, is protected as a state park.*

# NORTHERN UTAH

0       10       20 Miles

0    10    20     30 Kilometers

To Twin Falls, ID

Yost   Standrod   Clear Creek   Cedar Creek

42

Lynn   RAFT   RIVER   MTS

Park Valley

Rosette

CURLEW   V

GROUSE   CREEK   MTS

Locomotive Springs National Wildlife Refuge

Grouse Creek

Etna

Gravel

30

DOLPHIN ISLAND

NEVADA

Lucin

GUNNIS ISLAN

Montello

DESERT

Hill Air Force Range (no access)

N
W   E
S

Oasis

To Reno,NV

80

*Newfoundland Evaporation Basin (dry)*

LAKE

Danger Cave State Park

Bonneville Salt Flats State Park

Bonneville Speedway

Wendover

Knolls   D

SALT

Wendover Range (no access)

CEDAR   MOUNTAINS

Skul In Rese

**Elevation**
in feet

13,528
11,000
10,000
9,000
8,000
7,000
6,000
5,000
4,000
3,000
2,780

GREAT

Ferguson

Desert Test Center (no access)

Dugway Proving Grounds (no access)

Dug

1     2     3     4     5

GREAT BASIN

# SOUTHERN UTAH

■ HIGHLIGHTS                          *page*

Cedar Breaks National Monument        213
Zion National Park                    215
Bryce Canyon                          224
Kodachrome Basin                      228
Grand Staircase–Escalante
    National Monument                 229
Capitol Reef National Park            236
Lake Powell                           243
Arches National Park                  250
Canyonlands National park             256
Trail of the Ancients                 266

SOUTHERN UTAH IS A PLACE FULL OF INCREDIBLE SURPRISES, contrasts, and pleasures. Summer tourists can watch Shakespeare performed in a replica of the Globe Theatre in Cedar City, ride a horse amongst the sandstone monoliths of Kodachrome Basin, or hike into a remote canyon miles away from the nearest town or person. Winter visitors can golf in St. George in the morning and ski at Brian Head in the afternoon.

"By whatever name it might be called," once wrote long-time Utah author Ward Roylance, "this great province is as distinctive in its own peculiar personality as, say, the Alps of Europe, the Amazon Basin of South America, the Sahara of Africa, the steppes or Himalayas of Asia."

The "Enchanted Country," as Roylance called it, is indeed a unique, magical, almost surreal place. Five national parks preserve a hunk of it; so do four national monuments, 19 state parks, three national forests, three ski areas, six currently designated wilderness areas (more are sure to follow in the future), two BLM primitive areas, and Glen Canyon National Recreation Area.

As more tourists discover the famous national parks, like Zion and Bryce, it is becoming more and more difficult to find the kind of solitude enjoyed by early

# WHAT ARE PARKS FOR?

The Park Service, established by Congress in 1916, was directed not only to administer the parks but also to "provide for the enjoyment of same in such manner and by such means as will leave them unimpaired for the enjoyment of future generations." This appropriately ambiguous language, employed long before the onslaught of the automobile, has been understood in various and often opposing ways ever since. The Park Service, like any other big organization, includes factions and factions. The Developers, the dominant faction, place their emphasis on the words *"provide for the enjoyment."* The Preservers, a minority but also strong, emphasize the words *"leave them unimpaired."* It is apparent, then, that we cannot decide the question of development versus preservation by a simple referral to holy writ or an attempt to guess the intention of the founding fathers; we must make up our own minds and decide for ourselves what the national parks are and what purpose they should serve.

—Edward Abbey, *Desert Solitaire,* 1968

There persists an old confusion between the National Parks and the National Forests—two very different things. The Forests provide the people, all the people, with magnificent facilities for recreation, and with vital watershed protection, and so do the Parks. But there the similarity ends. For the Forests are consistently put to economic use under policies prescribed by Congress and administered by the National Forest Service, a bureau of the Department of Agriculture. The Forests sell lumber and grazing, and can be developed for mining, irrigation, and power. The Parks sell nothing, although, like the Forests, they contract with concessioners to supply food and lodging and services to visitors. The Forests are open to grazing, under permit, and as a result have their troubles with some cattlemen. The same cattlemen yearn for grazing permits in the Parks, but there, in principle at least, they do not get them. Where cattle are seen in what appear to be Park lands, these are lands still held in private ownership within the Park's borders, and the Service is making every effort to eliminate them. Or the stock-owners are holders of pre-park permits which will not be renewed after their lifetime.

—Alfred A. Knopf, "The National Park Idea," *This is Dinosaur,* 1955

SOUTHWESTERN UTAH

visitors. Though the scenery remains essentially the same as in pioneer times, avoiding people on the trails and roadways can be difficult. But even the popular areas host secret times of the year and remote canyons, which modern-day explorers can find and cherish. People who visit south-central Utah often become possessive and secretive and try to hide their favorite spots from others, hoping somehow to keep them unspoiled.

Though getting lost on backcountry roads does have its pleasures, this region should not be toured by automobile alone. Take time to explore the many nuances of southern Utah by raft, mountain bike, horseback, jeep, or airplane. More simply, take a hike in a lonely canyon. In some ways, southern Utah might be called "the land of many choices." You can spend a lifetime exploring the area and never see it all. Visitors make a mistake when they try to see five national parks in six days, blowing through the landscape like tumbleweeds. Seeing less here actually provides a chance to see more.

This country challenges all five senses. Smell the sagebrush after a fall rainstorm. Feel the cool waters of the Green River as you enjoy a moonlight swim after a day of canoeing. Listen to the howl of a coyote on a dark night in Horse Pasture Canyon. Taste the dust stirred up after driving a four-wheel-drive vehicle over the challenging bumps of Canyonlands' Elephant Hill. Watch the sun set from the edge of Grandview Point on a late December afternoon, casting shadows over three mountain ranges and the canyons of the Colorado River.

Southern Utah can intimidate first-time visitors. Though civilization in the form of towns, gas stations, grocery stores, restaurants, and motels is seldom more than a few miles away, the dry desert and lonely roads can scare off the uninitiated.

## ■ SOUTH TOWARD CEDAR CITY  *map page 183, F, G & H-3 & 4*

### ◆ FILLMORE  *map page 183, F-4*

Interstate 15 leads south 160 miles from Salt Lake City to Fillmore, a town of over 2,000 residents. Because the site is near the geographical center of the state, Brigham Young designated Fillmore as Utah's original territorial capital in 1851, even though no town then existed. Visitors can tour the **Territorial Statehouse**, Utah's oldest government building, pioneer living quarters, and a jail. The first of four planned wings was completed in 1855, and several territorial legislatures met here. Lack of facilities, and antagonism between the U.S. government and the Mormons, eventually caused the legislature to move to Salt Lake City.

◆ UTAH STATE HIGHWAY 133   *map page 183, F4*

When traveling south along the interstate, we like to detour along the old Utah State Highway 133 into towns like **Meadow** and **Kanosh**. This is a part of Utah where getting off the beaten track pays dividends. There are few museums or tourist facilities; instead, visitors can stop at an old general store to enjoy a soft drink and some pleasant conversation with a local merchant, who often has the time to talk about the history of his city. Old pioneer homes, many restored to their original condition, dot either side of the four-lane main streets decreed by Brigham Young. The old pioneer cemeteries reveal interesting bits of history and family names. In the Kanosh cemetery, look for the headstone marking the burial place of old Chief Kanosh, the Paiute leader when the pioneers first settled this area.

**Corn Creek Canyon** leads into the Fishlake National Forest, east of Kanosh. A small, developed campground—ideal for family reunions—sits next to a clear mountain stream full of wild brown trout. Mule deer roam in the oak brush, and a few pieces of ruddy-colored stone jut out above the canyon, hinting at the red-rock grandeur farther south.

◆ BEAVER   *map page 183, H-3*

**Beaver** is a good town to explore. There are more than 200 historic houses of architectural interest scattered around town. Beaver began as an agricultural community. When gold and silver were found in the San Francisco Mountains to the west, non-Mormon miners rushed to Beaver. Tensions between the two groups, and threats of Indian attack, prompted the army to build Fort Cameron. One stone building from the fort still stands on the east edge of town, across the highway from the golf course. The ornate **Beaver County Courthouse** now houses a historical museum of pioneer and mining exhibits, as well as the courtroom and a dungeon-like jail in the basement. *Located on Center, one block east of Main.*

■ CEDAR CITY   *map page 208, C-4*

After passing through Beaver and Parowan, visitors reach Cedar City. With 11,000 residents, it's the second largest settlement in southern Utah. Boosters call it "The Festival City," because of numerous special activities built around Southern Utah University. The **Summer Games**, an athletic extravaganza where athletes representing many different sports compete in an Olympic-type atmosphere, ushers in the summer festivities at Cedar City. But the main event of summer is the **Shakespearean Festival**, which runs from early July through the mid-October.

◆ SHAKESPEAREAN FESTIVAL

At present, theater goers choose from three Shakespearean plays in the Adams Memorial Theatre, on the SUU campus, and three other classical or contemporary productions in the Randall L. Jones Theatre. The **Adams Memorial Theatre** is one of the world's most accurate reproductions of Shakespeare's Globe Theatre. "We searched worldwide to find a replica of Shakespeare's theater and found it in Utah," said Peter Wineman, a producer at the British Broadcasting Corporation. The 700-seat Randall Jones Theatre is the cornerstone of the planned Utah Shakespearean Festival Center for the Performing Arts. Planners proclaim that the center will provide "exquisite landscaping, ambling walks, idyllic streams of water, fountains, statuary and a central plaza complete with one of the most ambitious bronze pieces to be found in our state. This plaza will be surrounded by three theaters, each serving as a venue for its own unique theatrical offerings. A replicated old English village will feature shops, tea room, clock tower, and the Utah Shakespearean Theatre Administration Center. This entire complex will be walled in to shut out all 20th-century intrusions and will become a mecca for thousands of students, theatre patrons and tourists."

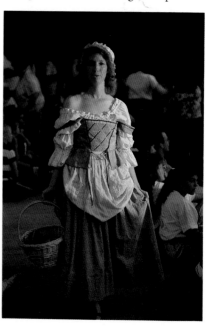

Literary and production seminars, special workshops, backstage tours, foyer entertainments, and an orientation to the evening's performance are also presented during the Shakespearean Festival. The nightly **Greenshow** adds to the festivities with jugglers, puppeteers, and vendors dressed in Elizabethan costumes. The audience is invited to join skits and impromptu plays. In addition, the popular **Renaissance Feaste** tempts tourists to dine in the lively manner of Elizabethan England. Patrons attending an outdoor

*The Shakespearean Festival in Cedar City attracts more tourists than any other annual event in southern Utah.*

play at the Globe replica can watch the sky change from blue to red to black. During the rare summer thunderstorms, they may be forced to move inside the adjacent auditorium until the storm passes over.

Southern Utah's love of Shakespeare actually dates back to pioneer times. According to R. Scott Phillips, marketing director for the Utah Shakespearean Festival, Mormons who settled nearby Parowan staged a Shakespearean play three weeks after moving in from the north.

Fred Adams, who left New York City to come West, tried producing a popular Broadway musical for southern Utah residents and discovered little interest. Challenged, he organized a production of *Romeo and Juliet*. Much to his delight, the play sold out its initial three-night run, and two more nights as well.

When Interstate 15 bypassed Cedar City's Main Street in 1962, city fathers became nervous that the town might die. The local Lions Club put up $1,000 for the first Shakespearean Festival in 1962. *The Taming of the Shrew, Hamlet,* and *The Merchant of Venice* were performed on an outdoor platform supporting a partial replica of an Elizabethan pavilion. The first festival drew 3,276 patrons, giving organizers enough of a profit to continue. The original company numbered 20 persons. In 2000, the festival was given a Tony award for best regional theater.

Nowadays, some 300 workers and actors—including 20 full-time employees—labor to produce the festival. Over 150,000 theater patrons enjoy a season lasting from late June through mid-October and featuring more than 120 evening performances. This mammoth undertaking produces $22 million for the local economy. *Information; 435-586-7790, box office; 435-586-7878.*

◆ Iron Mission State Park

For a glimpse of Cedar City's pioneer past, spend some time browsing through **Iron Mission State Park** on Main Street. The town earned the name of "The Iron Mission" because iron was produced here, making the city exceedingly important to the survival of Mormon self-sufficiency in the territory's early days. The park illustrates pioneer life with a collection of horsedrawn vehicles started by Gronway Parry in 1911, including a Wells Fargo Stagecoach, an original Studebaker White Top wagon, buggies, surreys, mail carts, horsedrawn farm machinery, an old milk wagon, and even a one-horse sleigh. The most popular item is probably the stagecoach that Butch Cassidy reputedly riddled with bullets during his gang's escapades in the Four Corners section of Utah. *695 N. Main; 435-586-9290.*

The Robert Redford-Paul Newman movie *Butch Cassidy and the Sundance Kid* gave even more notoriety to these two already famous Western outlaws. According to folklorist Dave Stanley, who chronicles the history and folklore associated with southern Utah's national parks and monuments, southern Utah abounds with tales and evidence of the outlaw Robert LeRoy Parker, alias Butch Cassidy.

"He and the Sundance Kid and the rest of the Wild Bunch have been tracked through Bryce Canyon, Capitol Reef, and Canyonlands, especially in the Robbers' Roost country between Hanksville and Moab," writes Stanley. "Many of the Butch Cassidy stories treat him as a Robin Hood figure who robbed the rich and helped the poor. One tale concerns a local widow whose ranch was threatened by foreclosure. Butch and the boys robbed the local bank and delivered the cash to the woman, who paid off a surprised banker when he showed up at the ranch to evict her. On the way back to town, Butch held him up again and made off with the money."

Cedar City's festivals and proximity to major national parks, monuments, and forests have brought many amenities not found in cities of similar size. Restaurants, modern motels, and a community that welcomes out-of-towners make Cedar City a comfortable place to visit.

■ CEDAR BREAKS NATIONAL MONUMENT  *map page 208, D-4/5*

Cedar Breaks National Monument sometimes does not open until mid-June, when the snow clears. With a drop of 2,500 feet and a diameter of more than three miles, Cedar Breaks is shaped like a gigantic coliseum. Stone spires, columns, arches, and canyons in hues of tan, red, and orange change color and texture as the sun moves across the sky. Particularly enchanting is the short walk along the Alpine Pond Trail in early summer, when high meadows are ablaze with wildflowers.

Cedar Breaks was named, erroneously, by Mormon pioneers who settled Cedar City in 1851. The "cedars" growing near the base of the cliffs were actually juniper trees. The pioneers referred to the steep badland topography as "breaks"; their past works still dot the park.

Cedar Breaks is not simply a summer park, as we discovered during a January weekend vacation to the area. Winter might just be the best season for visiting this national monument. The operators of the nordic center at the nearby Brian Head Hotel groom a loop trail on the property. The town of Brian Head marks miles of

cross-country ski trails. All are free, although there is a small charge for the trail maps. Brian Head nordic also offers tours and a variety of special programs, including ski tours under a full moon. Visitors fortunate enough to glide quietly on cross-country skis around the rim of the amphitheater will find the view on a clear winter day breathtaking. Ancient bristlecone pines frame vistas of snow-covered red and tan rock below, and the icy silence magnifies the majesty of the entire place.

In the summer months, hikers can take a rugged 10-mile backpacking trip into Rattlesnake Creek and the nearby U.S. Forest Service Ashdown Gorge Wilderness Area, located on the western boundary of the national monument. The trail descends an incredible 3,400 feet into the gorge. Smart backpackers arrange to be picked up at the bottom of the hike rather than hiking back out.

Those who don't enjoy camping in the summer months may wish to rent a condominium or hotel room at off-season rates at the Brian Head ski area. Excellent mountain biking opportunities can be enjoyed as one of the ski resorts' lifts is available to carry mountain bikers to the top of the resort, making for an interesting trip down. Information, trail maps, guide services, and rentals are available at the shop inside the hotel. Brian Head offers a variety of other summer activities, including photography workshops, star-gazing parties, music festivals, and hikes.

Summer visitors to Cedar Breaks often take side trips to **Panguitch** and **Navajo Lakes**. Both have rustic lodges and U.S. Forest Service campgrounds. Mountain bikers are discovering the challenging and scenic dirt roads and trails in this area.

■ ZION NATIONAL PARK   *map page 208, E-4*

The Great White Throne, Angels Landing, Temple of Sinawava, the Guardian Angels, the Pulpit, Mount Moroni, the Tabernacle: the names of Zion's canyons, peaks, and rock formations reveal much about the nature of this land and the reverence for it held by the pioneers who settled this rugged country. Zion is Utah's oldest national park and one of its most beloved tourist destinations.

Nephi Johnson is believed to be the first non-Indian to enter Zion Canyon, which he did in 1858. Isaac Behunin built the first cabin near the site of the present-day Zion Lodge in 1863. Zion first came under federal protection in 1909, when it was designated Mukuntuweap National Monument. Ten years later it became a national park.

*Snow lingers on rugged slopes at Cedar Breaks National Monument. The pioneers referred to the steep badland topography as "breaks".*

Zion may be Utah's most "civilized" national park. Visitors can enjoy a stay in its recently refurbished lodge, or walk along paved hiking trails to the more popular attractions. Large developed campgrounds, a children's nature center, visitor facilities at both Zion Canyon and Kolob Canyon, ranger-guided hikes, naturalist programs, and evening campfire talks provide even more options for visitors. Just outside the park's southern boundary in the tiny town of **Springdale** are restaurants, motels, stores, and the O.C. Tanner Amphitheater, where theater-goers enjoy live performance with Zion Canyon as a wonderful backdrop.

Yet, for all its civilized (and, in the summer, crowded) manner, Zion is essentially a wild place full of unexpected adventures for those willing to escape the confines of their cars and do some exploring. We'll never forget what appeared to be an easy spring stroll of just over a mile on the popular paved trail leading to the **Emerald Pools**. When a sudden thunderstorm hit the canyon, waterfalls began to

*The Great White Throne is a popular emblem of Zion, Utah's oldest national park.*

pour over the trail. We had to cling to the sides of the cliffs as we crawled under the flowing water. On a winter hike on the **East Rim Trail**, we explored a narrow passageway of twisted sandstone which almost formed a tunnel. We walked past ice frozen in bizarre shapes. Few who grip the chains on the **Angel's Landing Trail** to keep from falling into oblivion from the lip of a sheer sandstone cliff will forget the thrill.

Still, simply *driving* through the park is breathtaking (or park at the visitor center and take the shuttle). In Zion Canyon, the rock walls tower 2,000 to 3,000 feet above the road. Negotiating the switchbacks up to the **Mt. Carmel Tunnel** and motoring past windows cut in the tunnel walls, you hardly dare to glance down at the chasm below. Emerging into daylight again, you find yourself on the edge of a great petrified sand dune carved into a checkerboard pattern, where large trees grow sideways out of bare rock. Appropriately, the feature is known as **Checkerboard Mesa.**

Zion is a four-season park. Fall rewards visitors with sights of blazing orange oaks and yellow cottonwoods shimmering at the bottom of gigantic crimson cliffs. Winter brings snowcapped sandstone peaks, ice formations, and cold solitude. The sound of the Virgin River swollen with runoff roaring through the canyon, and the smell of plants coming to life after a winter hibernation, greet springtime visitors. Summer brings blazing heat, which sends visitors scrambling to a cooling waterfall or the shade of a narrow canyon.

Parents visiting the park in the summer may want to consider signing their children up for the Junior Ranger Program at the **Zion Nature Center**, whererangers teach kids lessons in ecology, ethics, and biology.

More and more adventurers explore Zion by backpacking into canyons. In the remote **Kolob region** of the park, some 45 miles east and north by road from Zion Canyon, backpackers can hike to Kolob Arch; with a span of 310 feet, it is the world's longest. Backcountry explorers may not always see wildlife like cougar, ringtail cat, bobcat, coyote, mule deer, and fox, but they can see signs of these critters in the dry sandy washes or on the banks of the tiny creeks which flow through this land of standing rocks.

*For more information call Zion National Park at 435-772-3256.*

*(following pages) Wiinter adds a touch of white to Zion's familiar reds and greens.*

photographers by the dozens to snap pictures. Fans of Paul Newman will recognize the town, with its schoolhouse, store, and cabins, as the setting of the bicycle scene in *Butch Cassidy and the Sundance Kid*. A nearby graveyard (you may need to ask locals for directions to find it) preserves interesting hand-carved headstones. But with the building of housing developments around it, Grafton is less of a ghost these days.

### Kanab    *map page 208, F-6*

This a pretty town, located 41 miles southeast of Zion on the Utah-Arizona border, isclose to both Lake Powell and Arizona's Grand Canyon. The town has been a center of the Western movie industry for many years. The **Frontier Movie Town** has been

built to show tourists a bit of the old West. Admission is free. Also, be sure to visit the **Kanab Heritage House**, an 1895 Queen Anne-style Victorian built by one Henry Bowman. He lived in it only two years before being called away on a mission. A photo of the next owner, Thomas Chamberlain, along with his six wives and 55 children, is in the sitting room. The house is open for tours most of year, though in winter the hours are 10 A.M. to 4 P.M. Saturday, 2 P.M. to 8 P.M. on weekdays.

### Coral Pink Sand Dunes State Park    *map page 208, E/F-5*

Stark, ruddy-colored hills of sand are the main attraction at this state park west of Kanab. The small campground provides an out-of-the-way experience that differs

*The color of the dunes at Coral Pink Sand Dunes State Park near the Arizona border is enhanced by the setting sun.*

greatly from the larger, crowded campgrounds at Zion. We once watched the sunrise while eating breakfast at a lonely picnic table on the edge of the dunes. The shapes of the few juniper trees growing nearby took on a surrealistic appearance in the early-morning light.

**Pipe Spring National Monument**
*map page 208, F-5*
One of the West's most vivid pictures of pioneer life is recreated in the living history program at Pipe Spring National Monu-

ment on Arizona State Highway 389, southwest of Kanab. Stepping through the gates of the visitor center is like being whisked away in a time machine. The place is just as it was in pioneer times. In the summer, docents dressed in period garb act the parts of pioneers and profess to knowing nothing about the 20th century. Descendants of the first settlers, the Heatons offer cattle drive and round up experiences to tourists along the Arizona strip (that part of Arizona north of the Grand Canyon).

■ BRYCE CANYON   *map page 208, C & D-6 & 7*

Bryce is not really a canyon at all. It's a series of 14 huge amphitheaters which extend a thousand feet down through the pink and white limestones of the Paunsaugunt Plateau. Bryce Canyon has been described as the most colorful national park in the world. Depending on the time of season, the hour of the day, and the weather, the fantastic formations of limestone visible from Inspiration and Rainbow points turn vivid shades of white, orange, yellow, red, and purple. When you first approach Bryce Canyon, take time to sit on a bench at the edge of one of the amphitheaters and contemplate the extraordinary scene before you.

Indian legend claimed that Bryce was built as a city for the people of Coyote. Because they worked too long beautifying their city, Coyote became angry. He turned the people all to stone and overturned the paints they were using. They are still standing there, rows and rows of them, with the paint dried on their faces.

Who can resist striking out on the trails for such enchanting destinations as Queen's Garden, Navajo Loop, Peekaboo Loop, Under-the-Rim, and Fairyland? Trails give hikers intimate views of formations like the **Chinese Wall**, **Mormon Temple**, **Fairy Castle**, the **Cathedral**, the **Alligator**, the **Sinking Ship**, **Wall of Windows**, and **Boat Mesa**. Unfortunately for hikers who may not be in the best of shape, the walks down into the Bryce amphitheater are deceivingly easy. Climbing back out with elevation gains of anywhere from 300 to more than 800 feet can be a real chore, especially during the hot summer months. The easiest hike is the 1.5-mile **Queen's Garden Trail**, which begins at Sunrise Point and takes about two hours to complete. Once, visiting Bryce with friends, we took the advice of a ranger and left one of cars at the bottom of the canyon near the tiny town of Tropic. Driving back up to the amphitheater, we made the four-mile hike, downhill all the way, and shuttled back to our campground.

Less crowded trails wander through the meadows of the **Paunsaugunt Plateau** on the west side of the park. In the spring, sego lilies, penstemons, asters, clematis, evening primrose, scarlet gilias, Indian paintbrush, and wild iris turn this part of Bryce into a garden full of wonderful color. Ancient bristlecone pines, alive during the time of Christ, still inhabit Bryce Canyon.

Though all of Utah's five national parks experience four distinct seasons, the extremes are greater at Bryce Canyon, mainly because of its high elevation, reaching 9,105 feet at Rainbow Point. This means temperatures in winter dip well below freezing. Winter is one of the best times to see Bryce.

A few years ago, our family ventured into an all-but-deserted Bryce Canyon in the dead of winter wondering what we would do. The spires of crimson red limestone in the Bryce amphitheater were dusted with snow. Three to five feet (one-two m) of the white stuff could be seen on the Queen's Garden and Navajo Loop trails as we admired the wintery scene from overlooks. The ranger at the visitor center suggested we try some (free) snowshoes.

At times it is possible to take a winter hike down into Bryce Canyon. The trails can be icy in spots and require a good set of boots, but the rewards are great. Hikers can watch snow crystals float down from the canyon walls. In some places the trail is so narrow that the towering rock formations all but hide the blue sky from hikers' eyes. In the winter hikers are alone; no trains of horses, sounds of automobiles, or long strings of other hikers can be heard. When we took our family down into the canyon, the winter silence gave us a sense of what this place must have been like when it was inhabited by the Anasazi Indians, or when Ebenezer Bryce, a New England shipbuilder and stockman, came here in 1875. *Bryce Canyon National Park; 435-834-5322.*

A mistake made by many who visit Bryce Canyon is that they end their exploration of this part of Utah with the national park and fail to keep driving east on Utah State Highway 12, where some of the state's best-kept secrets can be unlocked. This road brings travelers to some of the most remote and isolated towns and backcountry; the stately alpine forests give this part of Utah an entirely different look from that of Zion or Capitol Reef.

*A winter sunrise in Bryce Canyon (following pages)*

■ KODACHROME BASIN   *map page 234, F & G-2 & 3*

If our family were asked to pick its favorite place in Utah, we would probably select Kodachrome Basin State Reserve, a scenic little valley full of towering monolithic chimneys unlike anything else in the world. Yet, because Kodachrome Basin —which was named by the National Geographic Society—is located off the main highway on the northern edge of Escalante–Grand Staircase National Monument, it receives less visitation.

To our way of thinking, the 24-unit campground, located in the midst of the rock spires and pinyon/juniper forest, ranks among the best of its kind in the state, largely because each site is set so far from its neighbor. We've spent many an Easter weekend watching the children scramble up the sandstone walls, rolling Easter eggs in the soft, red soil, and soaking up the quiet solitude of this wonderful park.

Taking a hike to Shakespeare Arch, the small rock formation discovered by the superintendent of Kodachrome Basin while searching for a coyote den one after-

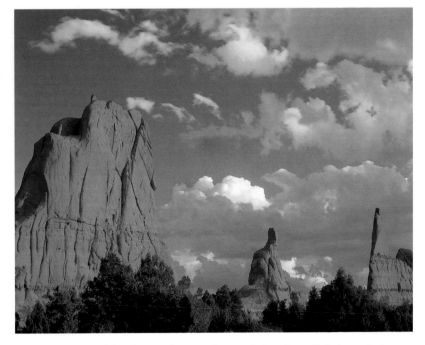

*Towering monolithic chimneys dominate the surrealistic setting at Kodachrome Basin.*

noon, helps introduce visitors to the ecology of the desert. Hikers walk past typical plants like juniper, sagebrush, buffaloberry, Indian rice grass, false buckwheat, saltbrush, snakeweed, yucca, Mormon tea, and rabbitbrush. The plants, animal tracks in the tan sand, gnarled trees, and potholes seen along the way give clues to the forces which shaped this strange, almost surrealistic setting.

**Kodachrome State Park** always had fresh water available to campers, but until recently, primitive facilities kept some visitors away. Using largely volunteer labor, park superintendent Tom Shakespeare constructed a modern restroom facility, complete with showers, at the reserve campground. A concessionaire provides guided horseback, wagon, and stagecoach rides, as well as cabins. *UT 12, Cannonville; 435-679-8562 or 800-332-3770 for camping reservations.*

♦ HEADING SOUTH THROUGH THE BASIN

**Grosvenor Arch** *map page 234, F/G-2/3*
The road which leads south from Cannonville to Kodachrome Basin is paved, but it becomes a considerably rougher dirt road beyond the park, so check with park rangers before attempting to drive it, and don't go when the road is wet. The road to Grosvenor Arch, an unusual, yellowish-tan span named in honor of the founder of the National Geographic Society.

**Cottonwood Canyon** *map page 234, G-2/3*
Farther south are the unusual rock forma-

tions of Cottonwood Canyon. These rocks have been named the Cockscomb because they resemble the top of a rooster's head.

**Paria Canyon-Vermilion Cliffs Wilderness Area** *map page 208, F-7 & 8*
The Paria River runs through the Kodachrome Basin, leading into the Paria Canyon-Vermilion Cliffs Wilderness Area on the Utah-Arizona border. Backpackers, who sometimes must wade through waist-deep water, tell many stories of the narrow, twisting canyons of the Paria River.

■ GRAND STAIRCASE–ESCALANTE NATIONAL MONUMENT
*map page 234, E–H - 2–5*

When President Bill Clinton designated the new Grand Staircase-Escalante National Monument in September,1996, he told millions what a few southern Utah red rock fanatics knew all along: that the new 1.7-million acre monument contains some of the world's wildest and most intriguing desert country.

"On this remarkable site, God's handiwork is everywhere," said Clinton. "In the natural beauty of the Escalante Canyons and in the Kaiparowits Plateau. In the rock formations that show layer upon layer millions of years of geology. In the fossil record of dinosaurs and other prehistoric life. In the remains of ancient American civilizations like the Anasazi Indians."

Unfortunately, the President never actually set foot on the monument he created with his signature. He made the announcement on the edge of Arizona's Grand Canyon—to the irritation of many of Utah's already disgruntled elected officials, who had boycotted the ceremony. They'd wanted a long-proposed coal mine on the Kaiparowits Plateau to be developed to provide jobs for rural Utahns and income for the state.

The new national monument may have detractors in Utah, but it does protect and highlight a region with great diversity of scenery: it's a wild land of arches, goblins, hoodoos, and assorted canyons. The Escalante River and its tributaries worked with rain and wind to form most of these natural areas. The river is believed by most historians to be the last major river "discovered" by government surveyors in the continental United States.

And the region is still hard to explore today. The Grand Staircase–Escalante National Monument's lack of access, difficult terrain, and challenging topography may keep some would-be explorers away. Both US Highway 89, on the southern border of the monument, and Utah Highway 12, on the northern edge, are paved, but in between, only a few rugged dirt roads (which will give visitors a brain-jarring ride) offer vehicle access into the rugged terrain. Inside the monument, there are few truly developed or marked trails into the interior. Some of the more popular hiking routes, such as those through **Coyote Gulch** and **Harris Wash,** have been worn in by hikers lured to the area by photos of lush gardens in the midst of desert terrain, narrow slot canyons, waterfalls and towering arches. But many other special places remain rather difficult to reach, largely untouched and explored only by those willing to take long day hikes or several-day backpacks— but it's well worth the effort.

There are multi-colored slot canyons so narrow in places that it is impossible to see the sky. The **Kaiparowits** offers unmatched vistas of wide open country in a seldom-visited desert that may be the loneliest wilderness this side of Alaska. Destinations on maps with foreboding names such as **Spooky Gulch, Devils Garden, Peekaboo Canyon,** and **Death Hollow** are inviting only to those willing to spend the physical effort to see the country on its terms.

*Lower Calf Creek Falls near the Escalante River.*

Before doing much exploring in this area, it's a good idea to stop at the **Escalante Interagency Visitor Center**. Literature, safety information, maps, and historical data will help visitors enjoy the new monument. *755 West Main, Escalante; 435-826-5499. (There is also a visitor center at Anasazi State Park, described below.)*

There are only two developed campgrounds within the national monument: the 13-unit Calf Creek campground and the 5-unit Deer Creek camping facility on the northern end of the monument. Nearby Escalante Petrified Forest State Park, Kodachrome Basin State Park, and Bryce Canyon National Park offer the best alternative camping facilities. Motels, restaurants and gas stations can be found in towns on the edge of the monument such as Kanab, Tropic, Escalante, and Boulder.

Not surprisingly, much of the area's colorful history involves pioneers searching for routes through the canyon and across the river. Hole-in-the-Rock Road, the Harris Wash–Silver Falls Canyon wagon route, the Boynton Road, the Boulder Mail (or Death Hollow) Trail and the Old Boulder Road were all valiant attempts. The first bridge over the Escalante wasn't completed until 1935, making the town of Boulder one of the last places in the United States accessible to automobiles.

Perhaps the best-known destination in the Escalante area is **Calf Creek Falls.** Small natural arches, 1,000-year-old Indian rock art, an Ancestral Puebloan dwelling and, after a moderate hike, the falls itself, make this a special destination. Summer visitors can fish in the pools along Calf Creek for brown trout. *Located 15 miles east of the town of Escalante.*

### ◆ HOLE-IN-THE ROCK  *map page 234, G-5*

The Hole-in-the-Rock expedition is perhaps the most colorful story about the pioneers who were searching for a short cut into southeastern Utah. Pioneers discovered the Hole in the Rock, a narrow slit in the 2,000-foot cliff overlooking the Colorado River. More than 200 people, 82 wagons with teams of two or more horses, about 200 additional horses, and more than 1,000 head of cattle made the 290-mile journey, traversing 1.7 miles per day.

Today, some of the **Hole-in-the-Rock Road** has been drowned by Lake Powell, but enough signs of the original trek remain inside the monument that boaters on Lake Powell or drivers willing to brave the rugged 61-mile county-maintained gravel road, can still view the places where pioneers struggled. The road passes **Dance Hall Rock**, a huge sandstone amphitheater where dances kept pioneer morale high, then leads to the crevice above the Colorado, where the party used blasting powder and picks to open a passage to the river.

Our most memorable trip along Hole-in-the-Rock Road came on an Easter weekend a few years ago. Mel Davis, who published Rudi Lambrechtse's excellent book *Hiking the Escalante* (which should be required reading for anyone planning to explore this part of Utah), served as our guide into **Spooky Gulch** and **Peekaboo Canyon**. Both consisted of nothing more than narrow cracks cut by water through the sandstone. Spooky Gulch was so cramped in one spot that only the children and slimmest adults could pass. At one point in the Peekaboo Canyon hike, it was possible to scramble to the top of the canyon and look down at hikers 20 feet below while straddling the crack.

Twelve and a half miles down the Hole-in-the-Rock Road you'll find this outstanding natural area with its fantastic collection of hoodoos reminiscent of Arches National Park and Goblin Valley.

◆ ANASAZI STATE PARK   *map page 234, E-4, or page 237, E-2*

The park conserves the remains of an ancient village constructed on top of a mesa. With a year-round water supply, fertile fields, a broad view of the surrounding countryside, and abundant wild game, wood, and stone, the village was able to support 200 people for 75 years. (The park retains the formerly used name for this culture—Anasazi, or "Enemy Ancestors"—but the preferred term is "Ancestral Puebloan," a name more acceptable to their descendants, the contemporary Native Americans of the Four Corners.) The park museum explains how the Ancestral Puebloans lived, while a reconstructed pueblo allows visitors to see for themselves. You can, for instance, try your hand at grinding corn the Indian way with a mano and metate. *460 North Highway 12 in Boulder; 435-335-7308.*

◆ BOULDER MOUNTAINS   *map page 237, C & D-1 & 2*

Passing through **Boulder**, UT 12 climbs north to the 9,200-foot summit of the Boulder Mountains in Dixie National Forest. It's a good place to go to escape the heat and to enjoy glimpses of Capitol Reef and the Waterpocket Fold to the east, the Aquarius Plateau to the west, and the Escalante canyons, Straight Cliffs, and Kaiparowits Plateau to the south. The temptation will be great to stay in one of three developed Dixie National Forest campgrounds along the road, from which you can hike into one of the many lakes on Boulder Mountain itself—lakes teeming with brook trout.

# SOUTHEASTERN UTAH

0    10    20 Miles

0    10    20    30 Kilometers

## ■ CAPITOL REEF NATIONAL PARK

Capitol Reef gets its name from two geological curiosities of the **Waterpocket Fold**, a 100-mile bulge in the earth's crust containing eroded pockets that catch water after each rainfall. Early settlers thought that the mountains, which dominate the landscape of the national park, resembled a coral reef. One of the white sandstone outcroppings, **Capitol Dome**, resembles that monument in our nation's capital. The area was designated a national monument in 1937 and transferred to national park status in 1971. *Visitor Center, UT 24, Torrey; 435-425-3791.*

Influences of Mormon pioneer settlers remain in and around the little town of **Fruita**: a barn, a farmhouse, rock fences, an 1896 one-room

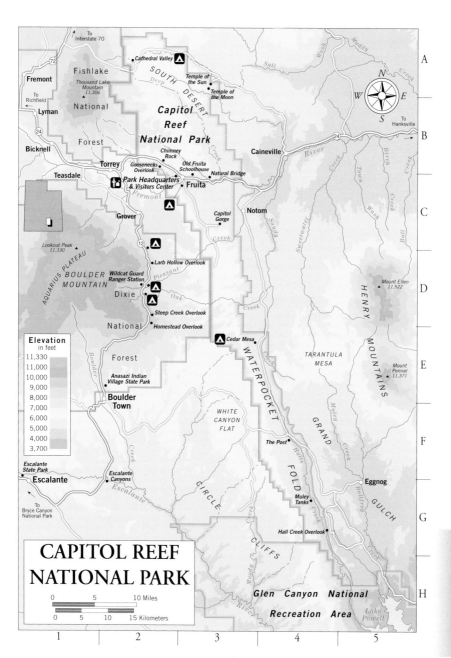

*Early Mormon settlers built the Fruita Schoolhouse circa 1896. It closed in 1941 due to a lack of students.*

schoolhouse, and acres of fruit orchards. These provide beautiful displays of blossoms in the spring, shade during the hot summer months, and fruit—apples, cherries, peaches, apricots, pears—in the late summer and fall. The public is invited to pick them and pay a small per-pound or bushel price. The campground is located in the midst of one of these orchards. Deer and skunks—which often get too friendly with campers—frequent the area. The old weathered barn, situated against the red-rock cliffs guarding the campground, is one of the most frequently photographed structures in southern Utah.

The **Fremont River** runs through the middle of the park along Utah State Highway 24, a lifeline for the fruit orchards and cottonwoods. Archaeologists believe the Fremont Indians inhabited this area as long ago as A.D. 800. They left petroglyphs and storage bins, called moki huts, along the walls of the canyons.

Capitol Reef has a fine paved road, but no trip can be complete without at least one short hike. Walking to **Hickman Bridge** or through **Capitol Gorge** and **Grand Wash** helps visitors appreciate the fascinating geology of the park with its water pockets or "tanks". Kids can scramble up the easy-to-climb sandstone and through the little stone alcoves, playing hide-and-seek, for hours. Longer, more difficult treks take walkers to **Cassidy Arch, Frying Pan Canyon** (where a shout turns into an echo heard several times over), **Spring Canyon,** and the **Golden Throne.** An excellent hiking guide detailing the most popular trails is available at the visitor center.

Only a small portion of Capitol Reef is unpaved, but it is good to check on conditions before setting out, as wet weather can make roads impassable. Solitude seekers can take longer hikes from the **Burr Trail,** a partially paved road cutting down the eastern boundary of the park, with one spur south to Lake Powell and another west to the town of Boulder. There are many washes to explore and arches to discover in this land. The **Muley Twist Canyons** are among the most popular backpacking destinations. As is the case in all of Utah's national parks, backpackers need a permit, which is free. This is dry country most of the year, so carry in your own water.

Four-wheelers can explore the rugged dirt road on the north end of the park leading to Cathedral Valley where huge monolithic sandstone remnants form jutting buttes that resemble cathedrals in the desert. To the south, the **Burr Trail** leads past farms and cattle ranches where lush green alfalfa and deep red soil color the landscape. After a harrowing drive up narrow switchbacks, the trail enters a sandstone canyon not unlike Zion's. Mountain bikers especially like traversing the Burr Trail in fall, spring, and even winter, taking advantage of the cooler weather.

While no accommodations or restaurants are found inside Capitol Reef National Park, tiny Wayne County hamlets like Torrey, Bicknell, and Loa furnish some unexpected treats. For example, stop at the **Sunglow Cafe** in Bicknell and try a piece of pickle or pinto-bean pie; the cafe is 10 miles west of the park oin UT 24. Or enjoy a fantastic contemporary Southwestern dinner at **La Cafe Diablo** in Torrey, at 599 West Main Street. There has been a recent building boom of franchise hotels, and several B&Bs have opened, especially in Teasdale. *(See page 312.)*

■ THE SAN RAFAEL SWELL   *map page 155, G & H-2*

The stretch of Interstate 70 between Salina and Green River cuts through Fishlake National Forest (watch for deer on the highway), the heart of the red-rock San Rafael Swell and Sinbad Valley, without passing through a town for over 100 miles. Some devotees argue that this is one of the most scenic portions of interstate highway in the entire national system.

*The Swell arches up from the landscape like a dinosaur's backbone.*

The Swell has been described as the jagged remains of a dinosaur backbone, an exposed sandstone coral reef, a saw blade, and a scene from the Arabian Nights. It's desolate but interesting country with a colorful history. Many believe it is worthy of national park status.

North of Interstate 70 at **Buckhorn Draw**, travelers can view the pictographs and petroglyphs left by ancient Indians who roamed this area thousands of years ago. Backpackers, horseback riders, and off-highway-vehicle enthusiasts can discover places like the Little Grand Canyon, Wedge Overlook, Temple Mountain, the Muddy River, Crack Canyon, Iron Wash, and Little Wildhorse Canyon. Outlaws and cattle rustlers once hid in the narrow, winding canyons of the San Rafael Swell.

Maps and information for exploring the San Rafael Swell are available from the Price Chamber of Commerce and BLM offices in Salt Lake City, Price, and Hanksville *(see page 329)*. There are also several good hiking guidebooks to the Swell.

### ■ GREEN RIVER   *map page 155, C—H -3 & 4*

The 57-mile drive on US Route 6/191 between Price and Green River gives glimpses of some of Utah's wildest, most desolate country. **Desolation Canyon**, a popular stretch of the Green River for rafting, is hidden from the road by the Tavaputs Plateau, Roan Cliffs, and Beckwith Plateau to the east. To the west, the northern portion of the San Rafael Swell looms on the horizon. On some stormy evenings, the sun plays tricks with the clouds. Thunderbolts slash across one part of the sky while a rainbow graces another. Save for the tiny coal-mining communities of East Carbon and Sunnyside to the east, there are no towns on this stretch of highway, leaving drivers free to relax while enjoying the grand vistas.

At first sight, **Green River** may seem desolate and bleak, but closer inspection reveals that this farm and tourist town has some interesting prospects. Built at an easy ford of the Green River, it's famous for its fine-tasting watermelons. Folks from all over Utah flock here in September to celebrate Melon Days, enjoy the early fall weather and, of course, buy melons from roadside stands.

For a taste of the rapids, canyons, and lore of the Colorado and Green rivers, the **John Wesley Powell River History Museum** offers telling glimpses of the famous explorer's journeys, as well as interpretive hands-on exhibits, art displays, a river runners' hall of fame, and a multimedia presentation. *885 E. Main; 435-564-3427.*

The **Green River State Park** south of town hosts campers in a lovely, shaded, grassy campground. It does fill at times during the summer, but there are nearby private campgrounds which almost always have space available. A nine-hole golf course winds its way along the river near the campground. The park serves as a launching point for some Green and Colorado rivers rafting trips, and offers a fine stretch of flatwater for canoes. The Memorial Day weekend Friendship Cruise, on which powerboaters take a scenic two- or three-day journey down the Green River to its confluence with the Colorado River, and then up the Colorado to Moab, begins here. *150 S. Green River Boulevard; 435-564-3633 or 800-322-3770 for camping reservations.*

## ■ GOBLIN VALLEY *map page 234 & 235, B/C-5/6*

Southeast of the town of Green River, Utah State Highway 24 heads back toward Capitol Reef along the edge of the San Rafael Swell.

One of our family's favorite destinations is **Goblin Valley**, on the edge of the Swell, roughly midway between Interstate 70 and Hanksville. Goblin Valley is 17 miles beyond a clearly marked turnoff.

Goblin Valley is filled with stone babies, goblins, ghosts, and toadstools that range in height from 10 to 200 feet. They stand like families of red goblins poured out, one by one, by a giant wizard and left frozen in time. The formations were made by uneven weathering of the sandstone; the softer material was removed by wind and water, leaving thousands of harder sections in unusual shapes. Water erosion and the smoothing action of windblown dust work together to shape the goblins.

There is something wonderful about wandering through the maze of goblins, toadstools, and hoodoos at night under a full moon. Children love to play hide-and-seek and turn this valley into a giant playground. It is easy to see the role rain plays in shaping Goblin Valley. We've witnessed an unexpected thunderstorm turn the hollows between the goblins into shallow streams resembling the chocolate river in *Willie Wonka and the Chocolate Factory.* Because there are few plants here, the mud flowed right off the formations. Minutes after the storm ended, the streams disappeared into the sand, and the goblins had taken new shapes.

Arthur Chaffin, who once owned and operated the Hite Ferry, stumbled upon Goblin Valley in the late 1920s while searching for an alternate route between Green River and Caineville. He called it Mushroom Valley. The area received

protection as a scenic area in 1954, when it was under the control of the Bureau of Land Management, and officially became a state park on August 24, 1964.

Plan on spending at least several hours there, or better yet, stay a night at the state park campground. Showers, drinking water, and a trailer dump station are all available. *435-564-3633 or 800-322-3770 for camping reservations.*

At **Hanksville**, travelers can either head west to Capitol Reef National Park, or south to Bullfrog and Hite marinas on Lake Powell in the Glen Canyon National Recreation Area.

■ LAKE POWELL  *map page 234 & 235, C—H-4—8*

Lake Powell, the second largest man-made reservoir in the world, is likewise Utah's second most popular tourist destination. Lake Powell receives some 3.2 million visitors a year—more than Yellowstone National Park. The Glen Canyon Dam, located near Page, Arizona, has created a 186-mile reservoir with a meandering, 1,960-mile shoreline. The recreation area itself consists of 1,869 square miles. Most of that is accessible only by boat, some of it can be reached by automobile, and other parts can be explored by hikers or rafters.

"There are few places on earth that cannot be adequately described," wrote Arizona author Bob Hirsch in his book *Houseboating on Lake Powell*. "Lake Powell is one of them. You'll know the first time you nudge the bow of your houseboat onto some sandy shore in a lonesome canyon far up the lake. It is quiet and peaceful and your eye delights in the patch of blue sky above, framed by soaring walls of buff and pink and light chocolate. The day is yours . . . from the time dawn tints a far-off butte from black to gray to the blush of rose, to the final hour storing up memories beside a driftwood fire, watching shadows dance on the ancient walls."

There is much to do at Lake Powell. At the very least, motorists should take highway 276 to **Bullfrog Marina** and ride the small John Atlantic Burr Ferry to Halls Crossing. Inaugurated in 1985, the ferry provides a different route to southeastern Utah for vehicles and trailers of all sizes. Bullfrog has campgrounds, luxury accomodations, and a good visitor center. **Bullfrog Basin, Hall's Crossing,** and **Hite** are the preeminent marinas at the upper end of the reservoir, offering powerboat and houseboat rentals, beaches, and campgrounds. Tourists who don't want to steer their own boat can stay in modern lodges overlooking the lake at either Bullfrog or Wahweap and take a guided tourboat ride. *Bullfrog Visitor Center; 435-684-2243.*

*Lake Powell's 1,960 miles of shoreline provide Utahns with a host of recreational opportunities.*

Houseboating is an especially popular way to see Lake Powell. Some of the larger boats sleep up to 12 people. With gas available at the Dangling Rope Marina near Rainbow Bridge, boaters don't have to return to the main docking areas for days at a time. There are arches to discover, Indian ruins to find, and narrow canyons that lead into fine hiking areas. Taking a moonlight summer swim in the warm waters, or renting a water-ski boat adds much to a trip to Lake Powell.

As avid fishermen, we like to avoid the crowds of summer by renting a powerboat in either April or May or from mid-September to late October. Fishing for large- and smallmouth bass, striped bass, crappie, northern pike, walleye, and channel catfish is best during those times of year. We like to pack all our tents, campstoves, and sleeping bags in the bow of the boat and head off to some secluded beach, where we can find some excellent fishing, swim, and enjoy a big driftwood fire in the evening.

Lake Powell boaters would do well to purchase one of Stan Jones's maps. Updated annually, these maps use a system of numbered buoys to help visitors find major landmarks, canyons, fishing areas, and other points of interest. Because this reservoir is so large, and because a boater can go miles before reaching the end of a flooded canyon, it is always possible to get lost or run out of gas.

◆ RAINBOW BRIDGE    *map page 234, H-5*

Probably the most famous sight along Lake Powell is Rainbow Bridge. With a height of 290 feet and a span of 270 feet, it is the world's largest natural bridge. This spot, sacred to the Navajo Indians, was made famous in Riders of the Purple Sage by Zane Grey. Tourists are asked not to walk under the bridge in respect for the Navajo culture. In Grey's day, only a few hearty souls made the long and difficult hike. Now thousands of boaters visit the monument annually.

◆ HENRY MOUNTAINS    *map page 234 & 235, D & E-5 & 6*

The Henry Mountains dominate the horizon to the northwest of the upper end of Lake Powell and furnish their own special kind of recreation. The dry, rugged character of the Henrys have kept them in a wild, natural state. Thousands of acres around the two highest peaks in the range, Mt. Ellen and Mt. Pennell, have been proposed for wilderness designation. John Wesley Powell named the range after Professor Joseph Henry of the Smithsonian Institute, one of his supporters. Prospectors have searched the Henrys for gold and other minerals since the turn of

*Rainbow Bridge is probably the largest natural arch in the world.*

the last century. Robbers' Roost, an important stopping point on the famed **Outlaw Trail** that stretched from Canada to Mexico, is found here. The remote canyons also made fine places for cattle rustlers to hide their bounty. The nearby **Dirty Devil River,** which now pours into Lake Powell, received its moniker because Powell and his men claimed "it stinks like a dirty devil." *Maps and hiking information are available at the the* BLM*'s Henry Mountain Field Station in Hanksville; 435-542-3461.*

The Utah Division of Wildlife Resources introduced 18 buffalo into the western foothills of the Henrys in 1941. Now hunters harvest surplus animals of what is one of the few wild, free-roaming buffalo herds in the country. In addition, the area is home to mountain lions, mule deer, snipe, chukar, blue grouse, and jackrabbits. Backpackers and four-wheel-drive enthusiasts seeking solitude enjoy dispersed recreation opportunities in this part of the state.

■ MOAB   *map page 235, B-9*

The town of **Moab**, with a population of just over 5,000, serves as the tourist hub of southeastern Utah. Though Monticello, Blanding, Mexican Hat, and Bluff to the south, all have a few tourist amenities, Moab offers much more than motels, concessionaires, restaurants, shops, and some unusual museums. Moab is, first and foremost, an incomparable base of operations for exploring the extraordinary canyonlands area of southeastern Utah, and in particular, Arches and Canyonlands national parks and the La Sal Mountains. It is also the preeminent base of operations for river trips, bicycle excursions, hikes, and four-wheel-drive expeditions through the red-rock country. On top of that, thousands of visitors from all over the United States come for the special yearly events, like the Moab Half-Marathon in March, the Easter Jeep Safari, the Friendship Cruise powerboat voyage on the Green and Colorado rivers, the Labor Day Jeep Jamboree, and the October Fat Tire Festival for mountain bikers. But most of all, Moab is the base for exploring some of the greatest canyon country in the world.

One word of advice to spring, summer, and fall travelers: arrive early in the day to get lodging, or better yet, make reservations. The campground at nearby Arches National Park is usually full from late March to late October. Though it occasionally snows in the winter and temperatures can dip down below freezing, off-season travelers to this part of Utah generally enjoy relatively mild weather. We think the ideal months to visit the Moab area are April and October.

Founded in the 1870s by Mormon farmers and ranchers after an 1855 mission attempt failed, Moab was named for the biblical kingdom at the edge of Zion, the promised land. The town itself is located in a green valley on the edge of the Colorado River and is surrounded by high sandstone cliffs. With Utah's "Zion" of Salt Lake City located almost 300 miles to the north, Mormon settlers must have felt that they, too, were living on the edge in this remote, often hot and dry place. Moab remained a quiet ranching community until the early 1950s, when a uranium boom tripled the town's population in three years and turned old prospectors like the near-legendary Charlie Steen into millionaires overnight. Steen earned and lost a fortune in just a few years. His home, named Mi Vida after the mine that made him rich, sits high above town and now houses a restaurant with a scenic view, the **Sunset Grill** *(see page 312).* The town also became a center of potash mining, but as is the case in many mining ventures, the boom went bust and Moab turned to tourism for its survival.

*The Colorado River town of Moab is the gateway to Arches National Park.*

Scenic country with a Western flavor helped turn Moab into a movie center. John Wayne films like *Rio Grande* and *The Comancheros,* the biblical movie *The Greatest Story Ever Told* with Max von Sydow, and more recently, *Indiana Jones and The Last Crusade* were filmed in the area.

First-time visitors to Moab should stop first at the **Visitor Information Center** for free brochures and videos on such fascinating subjects as Moab area movie locations, walking tours of the city, car tours, restaurants, mountain bike trails, jeep trails, rental equipment, winter activities, hiking trails, and other kinds of recreation. *Main and Center Streets; 435-259-8825 or 800-635-6622.*

◆ MOAB RECREATION

### Mountain Biking

Moab's reputation as the mountain-bike capital of the world grows each year. Some feel this town is to mountain biking what Aspen, Colorado, is to skiing. The first thing one will likely notice when driving toward this town is the number of mountain bikes being hauled on the top of automobiles and trucks. Though Rim Cyclery was among the first to recognize Moab's mountain biking potential, many other shops in town rent bikes and offer information. The **Moab Slickrock Bicycle Trail,** originally constructed for use by trail machines and motorcycles, has been taken over by mountain bikers who enjoy the challenges of riding their all-terrain bicycles over the pale orange Navajo sandstone "petrified" dunes. The formation is almost entirely devoid of vegetation and provides excellent traction for trail bikes. A 2.3-mile practice loop proved almost too much of a challenge for our family as we tried to negotiate the steep drops and rugged climbs with a guide from Rim Cyclery a few years

ago. Overlooks at Updraft Arch, Negro Bill Canyon, Shrimp Rock, Abyss Viewpoint, and the aptly named Echo Point provide glimpses of the Colorado River, the La Sal Mountains, and Arches National Park. *Rim Cyclery, 94 West First North; 435-259-5333.*

Those with more mountain biking experience may want to take a day to explore the 10.3-mile main loop ride. White arrows and caution zones painted on the rock keep bikers from straying into dangerous territory, but please make sure that your brakes are in good working condition. The four-wheel-drive roads and trails enjoyed by jeepers for years also provide excellent overnight or all-day mountain biking potential. Riding around the White Rim Trail in Canyonlands National Park, or exploring Monitor and Merrimac, Kane Creek Canyon Rim, Pritchett Canyon, Hurrah Pass, or the Gemini Bridges all provide challenging adventures. Still, the most exciting prospect for mountain bikers is the 128-mile Kokopelli's Mountain Biking Trail, which will run, when completed, between Moab and Grand Junction, Colorado. Free brochures that rate the difficulty of trail sections can be picked up at most bike shops. Drinking water is not available along the route. The trail was named after Kokopelli, a humped-back flute player depicted in Indian art, who wandered from village to village with a bag of songs on his back. Legend holds that he was able to drive back winter with his flute playing.

### River Rafting

Moab has long served as a base for river-running adventure. Day and night jet boat trips and one-day rafting trips make seeing the canyons relatively easy, but to really get to know the country, a longer expedition is in order. Most Colorado River trips into Cataract and Westwater canyons begin in Moab. When our family recently enjoyed a three-day Cataract Canyon trip, the thrill of shooting some of North America's most difficult rapids, coupled with the experience of swimming in the river, camping under the stars, exploring side canyons on foot, and enjoying the hospitality and knowledge of the guide, made for one heck of a vacation. We flew back to Moab in a small airplane, savoring spectacular views of the canyon country.

### Four-wheel-drive

Thousands of miles of old mining roads, many unmaintained relics from the past, offer some excellent and rugged, four-wheel-drive experiences. If you like a challenge for your machine, this is the place. The old jeeper's creed of "never move a rock if you can drive around it—or over it" certainly applies on dozens of routes. Rental vehicles and guided trips are available in Moab. Also keep an eye out in town for Fran Barnes's jeep safari books and maps, which are among the best for the backcountry.

### Hiking

The scenic route into Moab, via UT 128 from Cisco, crosses the Colorado River north of **Fisher Towers**. The towers, isolated remnants of a 225-million-year-old floodplain, gained some fame in 1964 and 1974 when helicopters placed cars atop the pinnacles to make some automobile commercials. A 2.2-mile hiking trail around the base of the towers takes about three hours to complete.

Hikers should also investigate the uncrowded trails that cross the country around Moab outside the boundaries of Arches and Canyonlands national parks. **Portal Overlook, Corona, and Bowtie arches, Mill Creek Canyon, Negro Bill Canyon, Hidden Valley,** and **Hunters Canyon** often reward explorers with contemplative solitude. Listen to the wind as it whistles through Corona Arch at sunset; it's an almost unearthly experience.

One of the more interesting stories involving the naming of these canyons surrounds Negro Bill Canyon. William Granstaff was a mulatto prospector who came to Moab Valley in 1877. Supposedly, he left in a hurry when other settlers charged him with selling whisky to Indians.

■ ARCHES NATIONAL PARK   *map page 235, B-9*

If there is a more spectacular hike in the world than the trek to Delicate Arch, we have yet to discover it. The arch, once dubbed "The Schoolmarm's Bloomers" by local cowboys, graces the covers of many Utah books and is the star attraction of Arches National Park.

Just driving into the entrance of the park, four miles north of Moab, is a thrilling introduction to what lies ahead. The park contains over 2000 natural arches, more than any other area in the world. Every year, more than half a million people come here for the spectacular scenery and the simple joys of hiking through soft sand and over slickrock.

Arches National Park is divided into six sections: **Courthouse Towers**, **The Windows**, **Delicate Arch**, **Fiery Furnace**, **Klondike Bluffs**, and **Devil's Garden**. Hiking guides and short, well-marked trails furnish glimpses of the natural arches, created by wind and rain in Entrada sandstone, which was laid down as coastal sand dunes some 150 million years ago.

Even lazy walkers can enjoy some of the trails of Arches, which for the most part are short, easy, and interesting. One of the best introductions to the park is taking the 2$^1$/$_2$-hour, two-mile ranger-led walk through the **Fiery Furnace**. Winding their way through a maze of narrow canyons, many hikers lose all sense of direction within moments and express relief that the ranger knows where he is going. Or does he? In places, visitors must squeeze through narrow spots on the trail, their bodies touching the walls on both sides.

Even toddlers enjoy short walks through **The Windows**. A quarter-mile hike leads to **Double Arch**, which appeared in *Indiana Jones and the Last Crusade*. Our children heard an echo here for the first time. Another favorite kids' hike is **Sand Dune Arch**, a .2-mile trek through a narrow canyon. Beneath the arch is a large sand dune. We've watched children spend an enchanted day playing in the fine, pink sand.

The longest series of maintained trails in Arches are found in the **Devil's Garden** area at the end of the paved road, just north of the campground. The five-mile loop trail, with only a gentle 200-foot gain in elevation, leads through narrow fins to **Double O Arch** and **Landscape Arch**. At 291 feet long and 188 feet high, Landscape is the longest span in the park and second longest in the world. No fewer than 60 arches, in fact, are found in this area. Take time to enjoy views of the fins, Salt Wash, and the La Sal Mountains along the way.

*Landscape Arch covered in a mantle of snow.*
*Arches National Park typically receives around 70 inches of snow every winter.*

Still, the most famous sight in the park is **Delicate Arch**, an improbable natural wonder of salmon-colored sandstone, about 65 feet high, and with an opening nearly 35 feet wide. The 1.5-mile trail to Delicate Arch begins at the historic **Wolfe Ranch**, built by Civil War veteran John Wesley Wolfe, who tried to make a living out of this desolate country in the late 1800s. The beauty of the hike is that the arch itself isn't visible until the last possible second. Viewing it for the first time can be compared to seeing the Statue of Liberty for the first time—a stunning sight that almost takes your breath away. Visitors tend to sit for hours contemplating the view in wonder and awe, especially at sunset, when the light and shadows play tricks with the arch and the natural amphitheater around it. Our most memorable trip to this place came on a cold, moonlit New Year's Eve. Frost on the willows near the swinging bridge sparkled like thousands of little fairies. The parking lot was empty, and snow covered parts of the trail. We reached sight of the arch just about midnight and brought in the new year in magnificent silence, standing in the moonlight, alone with the Delicate Arch. *Located five miles north of Moab on US 191; 435-259-8161.*

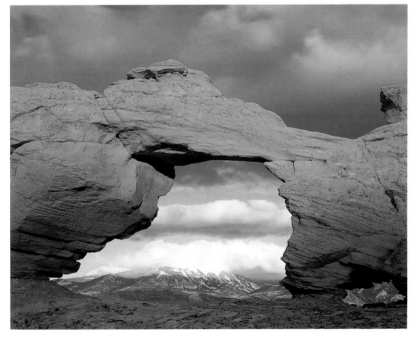

*The La Sal Mountains, seen through one of Utah's famous arches.*

# Utah's Natural Bridges

In November 1909, under the guidance of Dr. John Williams of Moab, we visited a natural bridge on the edge of Grand County that deserves to be classed with those of San Juan County among the great natural wonders of our continent. This is a graceful arch with a total elevation of sixty-two feet, and a span of one hundred twenty-two feet long and forty-nine feet high. It stands beside the cliff on the western edge of Pritchett Valley; and has been fashioned under somewhat different conditions from those prevailing during the construction of the other Utah natural bridges. Here there has been no narrow zig-zag canyon through which the waters surged in former times, but quite a large valley, some three miles long and from one-fourth to one-half a mile wide. On the sides of this irregular basin rise rugged cliffs that jut into the valley here and there in sharp points and rounded domes. The upper surfaces of these cliffs stretch back in bare undulating fields of sandstone much eroded by wind and water. Caves have been hollowed out of these cliffs and various and numerous natural reservoirs are found scattered on the surface of these bare rocks where soft places have been found in the stone, or whirling eddies in former ages have ground out cisterns. Some of these are mere shallow tanks, while others reach down twenty feet and more through the solid sandstone. Some are irregular and winding in their course, while others look as though they had been sunk by some Titanic drill when the gods were playing with the earth's crust. A few drain considerable areas of the cliff, and in time of storm many a rushing torrent loses itself in their depths. In a few instances such a reservoir has been formed directly behind a cave that was being hollowed out of the side of the cliff. As the walls of the cave gradually extended backward farther into the cliff, the reservoir was sunk deeper and enlarged little by little until its bottom broke through into the back of the cave. Then the waters formerly gathered into the reservoir and held surged through the cave and lost themselves in the valley below. Every downpour of rain and every driving wind carried the work a little farther until the former roof of the cave became an arch. When the reservoir held the waters until its depth about equalled that of the cave, then the gracefully curving arch of the cave became a real bridge as in the case of the fine arch already mentioned which we have christened Pikyabo (Pee-kya-bo), the Ute name for water tank.

—Byron Cummings,
*The Great Natural Bridges of Utah,* 1910

*(following pages) Delicate Arch rises above a sandstone bowl, with the La Sal Mountains looming in the distance.*

## ■ CANYONLANDS COUNTRY  *map page 235, C & D-7 & 8*

The late Edward Abbey, iconoclast, cynic, and author of some of the best essays and fiction written about the deserts of southern Utah, described the Canyonlands country of southeastern Utah best when he called the place "the least inhabited, least developed, least improved, least civilized, most arid, most hostile, most lonesome, most grim bleak barren desolate and savage quarter of the state of Utah—the best part by far."

In terms of acres, Canyonlands is the largest of Utah's five national parks. First designated as a park in 1964, it was expanded to its present size in 1971. It is the least developed and most difficult to tour. Check with the visitor centers for information on overnight backpacking, mountain biking, and four-wheel trip permits. *Park Headquarters is in Moab, 125 W. 200 South; 435-259-7164. There are visitor centers in the Needles and Island in the Sky districts, and at Hans Flat Ranger Station.*

The park is divided into four principal districts. Island in the Sky is a broad, level mesa wedged between the Green and Colorado rivers. It serves as a kind of observation platform for the other three wards of this rugged park: the Needles District, the Maze, and the River District. A separate chunk of parkland, the Horseshoe Canyon Unit, lies northwest of the main body of the park.

The **River District**, which takes in Cataract Canyon and the confluence of the Green and Colorado rivers, can be visited only by river runners and experienced hikers. The other districts can by approached by road—though in some cases, that means only by four-wheel-drive vehicle or on foot.

## ◆ ISLAND IN THE SKY  *map page 235, C-8*

The **Island in the Sky** is reached by Utah State Highway 313, which runs west from its junction with US Route 191, six miles north of the turnoff to Arches National Park. The highway is a dead-end. One spur leads to Dead Horse Point State Park, and another into Canyonlands.

You can survey much of the park from **Grandview Point**. On a quiet, cold winter morning, the distant peaks of the La Sal, Henry, and Blue mountains stand like snow-covered sentinels in the midst of twisting, convoluted canyons. To the south, the Needles jut like monoliths erected by some ancient culture. Rock formations with descriptive names like Lizard Rock, the Doll House, Chocolate Drops, the Maze, and the Golden Stairs rise up in the southern background near the canyon of the Colorado River. Take some time to be alone in this outpost, to contemplate the vast tract of wilderness below you.

Long hiking trails and rugged dirt roads lead down to the **White Rim Trail**, remote arches, and interesting side canyons. Only the hardiest backpackers and experienced four-wheel-drive enthusiasts should attempt these routes. Everyone else can enjoy shorter hikes into places like Mesa Arch, Upheaval Dome, and Whale Rock. Standing on the brink of the cliff at Mesa Arch is like walking on the edge of infinity.

Do you enjoy a mystery? Then come up with your own theory of how **Upheaval Dome** was formed. The latest thinking is that the three-mile long, 1,200-foot deep crater may have been caused by a meteorite, but geologists really don't

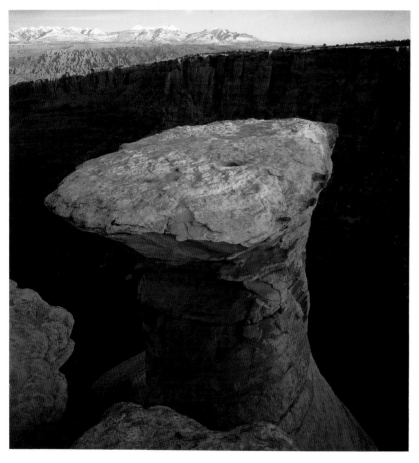

*A sandstone pinnacle in Dead Horse Point State Park rises above Long Canyon.*

know for certain. Before coming up with your own theory, you may want to hike the eight-mile trail that completely surrounds Upheaval Dome.

The eastern spur of UT 313 leads to **Dead Horse Point State Park** which offers a magnificent view from the lip of a 2,000-foot drop-off. Standing on the edge of this cliff gives a perspective of the depth, size, and majesty of the canyon country. Cowboys used to trap wild mustangs on the promontory by closing off the narrow neck of land. According to one legend, the gate was once left open so a band of corralled mustangs could return to the range. Instead, the mustangs remained on the point, dying of thirst within sight of the Colorado River, 2,000 feet below; hence the name of Dead Horse Point. *The state park has a visitor center and a campground. 435-259-2614 or 800-322-3770 for camping reservations.*

◆ CANYON RIMS AREA   *map page 235, C-8*

Traveling south from Moab, you can get a stunning glimpse of the Needles District by detouring to the **Canyon Rims Recreation Area** at the marked junction 32 miles south of Moab. The view from **Needles Overlook** is simply staggering. The reserve, run by the BLM, also offers camping, hiking, and four-wheel-drive recreation. Ask directions to **Jailhouse Rock**. Local legend has it that a sheriff's posse held a captured outlaw in the large pothole at the center of the rock. Another story says a rancher used to keep his wife there when he visited a local saloon. *BLM Montecello Field Office, 345 N. Main St., Montecello; 435-587-2141.*

Seven miles south of the Needles Overlook road, Utah State Highway 211 heads west from US Route 191 toward Newspaper Rock and the Needles District of Canyonlands National Park.

◆ NEWSPAPER ROCK   *map page 235, D/E-9*

A state park has been established here to preserve a wall of sandstone covered with Indian petroglyphs that date as far back as 1,500 years ago. Several theories have been proposed to explain the meaning of the rock graphics. Contemporary Indians recognize some symbols; the Hopi, for instance, still use some in their religious ceremonies. Some graphics have been found to have direct connections to astrological occurrences. Archaeologists have used some as maps to lead them to water. Others see the strange man-like figures as records of extraterrestrial visits. Or was all this writing simply the doodling of passers-by, like the graffiti found in our time? The fun of visiting places like Newspaper Rock is in forming your own conclusions.

*A view toward the Maze from the Green River Overlook in Island in the Sky.*

♦ NEEDLES DISTRICT   *map page 235, D/E-9*

The Needles District is an amazing landscape of wind-carved sandstone fins. Plan on spending a day or two here camping in their midst and hiking to the **Roadside Ruin, Cave Spring**, or **Pothole Point**. Lovers of cowboy lore should visit the reconstructed line camp next to Cave Spring.

Few jeepers will ever forget an expedition over **Elephant Hill**, one of the wildest, roughest, most challenging stretches of "road" in the entire West. Narrow slots barely wide enough for a vehicle to get through, silver stairs of sheer rock, and steep inclines force off-roaders to put their machines in the lowest possible gear. At one point in the 10-mile loop, four-wheel-drives are forced to back to the edge of a steep cliff in order to make the turn! (We know of one woman who left the vehicle in tears at this point, and walked until she perceived the trail to be safe again. It was a long walk.) A few backcountry campsites can be found in **Chesler Park** along this road.

You can also hike to Chesler Park, as we did one Thanksgiving weekend. As we wound our way through narrow sandstone slits, ate lunch huddled under an alcove during a snowstorm, and then watched the gray sky turn blue, we witnessed the canyon country in all its glory.

◆ MAZE DISTRICT   *map page 235, D-8*

The remote **Maze District,** located on the west side of the Colorado River, can be reached only by jouncing over some 60 miles of dirt road from Utah State Highway 24 near the Goblin Valley turnoff. Only hikers and four-wheel-drive vehicles should attempt the last few miles. Or you can do as we did: at Hans Flat Ranger Station, we rode borrowed dirt bikes for the ride down the steep, rocky, perilous Flint Trail to the verge of the Maze.

Few hikes anywhere compare with a turn through the Maze. We made the steep descent to the bottom while clinging to chains and feeling for footholds cut into the sandstone. Thankful to have a veteran guide along to show us the way out, we kept thinking of two friends who did not. They descended into the maze of canyons from this same point for a day hike, only to run out of water and become hopelessly lost. After trying for hours to find their way out, the two noticed their parents standing at the top of the canyon and were able to locate the trail out. The moral is, if you hike into this pristine area, bring a good topographical map and know how to read it. This is difficult, seldom-traveled country—that's why it's so special, of course.

◆ HORSESHOE CANYON UNIT   *map page 235, D/E-9*

The road to the Maze passes through a section of Canyonlands National Park detached from the main body of the park: the **Horseshoe Canyon Unit.** Some of North America's most outstanding ancient Indian rock art can be found there in the Great Gallery. The gallery's huge, ghost-like pictographs are believed to have been made by a culture predating the Ancestral Puebloans. Having seen the reproduction of these pictographs in Salt Lake City's Natural History Museum, we had long wanted to see the real thing in the sandy wash of Horseshoe Canyon.

Large graceful cottonwoods grow along the trail. In places the water surfaces to nourish cattails, horsetails, reeds, and willows. Seeping water in occasional alcoves

*After even a small rain, a trickle can explode into a roaring torrent, in time carving creek beds into canyons.*

nurse delicate flower gardens and lacy ferns. As we studied the land of the ancients, we tried to imagine how the residents of this canyon must have worked to make a living here. Would they have appealed to a higher force for help? Is that why the pictographs and petroglyphs are here?

The sand in the wash made walking hard. The dry wind blew sand into our eyes and plastered our hair. But we continued; we had seen other rock art before, but we knew this would be different. Perhaps it was partly exhaustion, partly the

## PURPLE SAGE

It was the moment when the last ruddy rays of the sunset brightened momentarily before yielding to twilight. And for Venters the outlook before him was in some sense similar to a feeling of his future, and with searching eyes he studied the beautiful purple, barren waste of sage. Here was the unknown and the perilous. The whole scene impressed Venters as a wild, austere, and mighty manifestation of nature. And as it somehow reminded him of his prospect in life, so it suddenly resembled the woman near him, only in her there were greater beauty and peril, a mystery more unsolvable, and something nameless that numbed his heart and dimmed his eye. . . .

Venters looked out upon the beautiful valley—beautiful now as never before— mystic in its transparent, luminous gloom, weird in the quivering, golden haze of lightning. The dark spruces were tipped with glimmering lights; the aspens bent low in the winds, as waves in a tempest at sea; the forest of oaks tossed wildly and shone with gleams of fire. Across the valley the huge cavern of the cliff-dwellers yawned in the glare, every little black window as clear as at noonday; but the night and the storm added to their tragedy. Flung arching to the black clouds, the great stone bridge seemed to bear the brunt of the storm. It caught the full fury of the rushing wind. It lifted its noble crown to meet the lightning. Venters thought of the eagles and their lofty nest in a niche near the arch. A driving pall of rain, black as the clouds, came sweeping on to obscure the bridge and the gleaming walls and the shining valley. The lightning played incessantly, streaking down through opaque darkness of rain. The roar of the wind, with its strange knell and the recrashing echoes, mingled with the roar of the flooding rain, and all seemingly were deadened and drowned in a world of sound.

—Zane Grey, *Riders of the Purple Sage,* 1912

spirit in the canyon, but after rounding the bend and seeing the Great Gallery, we all stopped in our tracks and gasped. Life-sized apparitions seemed to float out of the wall above our heads. The armless, legless figures wore mask-like, ghost-like faces reminding us of souls from another world. We talked in whispers of what their creators were trying to tell us. Knowing the language of the canyon country, we somehow read the message. It was a feeling that could not be translated into words. We knew the haunting figures were meant to be felt, not explained. The canyons, mesas, and rivers of the Colorado Plateau have spirits of their own. If one spends enough time silently learning their secrets, it is the feeling of the place that seeps into the soul.

## ■ MOUNTAIN ESCAPES

### ◆ LA SAL MOUNTAINS  *map page 235, D-8*

Though desert, vast and dry, seems to dominate the landscape around Moab, just to the east rise the cool, verdant peaks of La Sal Mountains, proffering summer respite in their forests of aspen and pine. Cleared of snow from May through October, the **La Sal Mountain Loop** transports drivers into the mountains from Utah State Highway 128 north of Moab, and US Route 191 to the south. The 60-mile loop takes about four hours to drive. As you gain elevation, the pinyon and juniper trees give way to oak, then to larger pines and aspen, and finally to spruce and fir.

Those planning to explore the La Sal Mountains on foot should stop by the Visitor information center in Moab for a copy of the U.S. Forest Service's excellent guide to the 18 hiking trails on the La Sal Mountains. Many of these trails were made by miners who explored the country a century ago. *Main and Center Streets; 435-259-8825 or 800-635-6622.*

**Pack Creek Ranch,** *(see page 312)* Utah's premier dude ranch, sits at the base of the distinctive, pyramid-shaped crest of 12,483-foot **Mount Tukuhnikivatz.** The mountain is named after a Ute word which means "the place where the sun shines longest."

Increasing numbers of cross-country skiers discover the fine, untracked powder of the La Sals each year. Novices enjoy gentle tours through the Pack Creek campground, while experts can drive to higher slopes. Rim Cyclery in Moab offers rentals and information on avalanche conditions. *94 West First North; 435-259-5333.*

◆ BLUE MOUNTAINS   *map page 235, E & F-8 & 9*

About 50 miles below Moab, west of Monticello, the Blue Mountains provide another welcome furlough from the desert heat. Also called the **Abajos**, the Blues rise to elevations as high as 11,360 feet. The high alpine country here is remote and little visited. After a horsepacking trip in the remote **Dark Canyon Wilderness Area** on the western edge of the Blues a few years ago, we enjoyed views to the north of the Needles District. A bobcat scurried across the road in front of us. At an evening campout, local cowboys cooked steaks over a blazing fire in Horse Pasture Canyon and listened to the howls of coyotes, which seemed but a stone's throw away.

*A high meadow in the Blue Mountains is painted with flowering vetch.*

*(opposite) The La Sal Mountains are the backdrop to a formation known as the Fiery Furnace.*

# ■ THE GRAND CIRCLE

The Grand Circle, the heart of Ancestral Puebloan country, embraces the Four Corners area of Utah, Colorado, New Mexico, and Arizona. Within the 500-mile circle, thousands of acres of public land have been set aside to preserve the ancient Ancestral Puebloans villages and ruins. Visitors can become acquainted with the Ancestral Puebloans and enjoy some spectacular scenery by following the **Trail of the Ancients** to the numerous Ancestral Puebloan points of interest. Brochures describing the trail can be obtained at any of the sites along the trail.

◆ EDGE OF THE CEDARS  *map page 235, E & F-8 & 9*

The ruins at **Edge of the Cedars State Historical Park** are being stabilized, and we enjoyed talking to the archaeologist working on this project. The remains of an immense kiva have been found there. Such structures are common around Mesa Verde in Colorado and Chaco Canyon in New Mexico, but the Great Kiva at Edge of the Cedars is the northernmost one of its kind in Utah. It was probably roofed and its flat surface used by many clans for dances and ceremonies. The roof of a smaller kiva nearby has been restored. Most kivas we have seen have not been open, so the kiva at Edge of the Cedars was our only chance to actually climb down into the chamber and sit awhile and contemplate. The monument museum traces the settlement of San Juan County by Ancestral Puebloans, Ute, Navajo, and Euro-American settlers, and also houses one of the largest Ancestral Puebloan pottery collections in the Southwest. You can buy Native American arts and crafts in the museum shop. *660 West 400 North, Blanding; 435-678-2238.*

◆ BUTLER WASH CLIFF DWELLING  *map page 235, F-9*

The rest stop at Butler Wash looked like a convenient place to wait out a late summer rainstorm. The one-mile roundtrip trail we took just after the storm led us on an adventure we'll never forget. Water from the storm flowed all over the smooth, salmon-colored slickrock. Streams and rivulets followed paths marked for them by previous cloudbursts. We tore off shoes and socks and scampered in the precious liquid. The source of life in this desert also brought us to life. We squealed with delight as newly formed waterfalls ran down our backs, drawn onward by the promise of more. Then suddenly, nestled far under the canyon's rim in a cozy alcove, we saw the Butler Wash cliff dwellings. Directly in front of the apartment-like complex, a waterfall cascaded like a curtain to the canyon floor. In the

*(opposite) The Ancestral Puebloans used natural landscape features, such as this cave, to quarry the stone for their structures.*

overhang to the right was a natural bridge where another waterfall plummeted over the edge. The ancient residents of this dwelling must have recognized the magic of this place. *Eleven miles west of US 191 on Utah State Highway 95.*

◆ NATURAL BRIDGES NATIONAL MONUMENT   *map page 235, F-7 & 8*

This national monument is famous for three impressive natural bridges. The trail down to White Canyon leads through a desert garden. It is easy to see why the Ancestral Puebloans wanted to live here. A stream runs through the bottom of the canyon, and tracks of coyote, ringtail cat, deer, and other small game line its banks. About 200 Ancestral Puebloan dwelling sites have been found there. Horse Collar Ruin is accessible from the trail between Sipapu and Kachina bridges.

The natural bridges were given Hopi names: **Kachina,** a representation of Hopi gods; **Owachomo,** a flat-rock mound; and **Sipapu,** the gateway to this world from the other world below. Hopi clan symbols can be seen near several of the dwellings. It is surmised that the White Canyon Ancestral Puebloans may have migrated south to join the ancestors of the present-day Hopi.

The national monument was established in 1908 by President Theodore Roosevelt after *National Geographic* magazine publicized the three great bridges. Unfortunately, fame also brought vandalism, as it does all too often today. Consider the story told by Zeke Johnson, who was the custodian of the monument in 1926:

> A group of boys was going out to the bridges from Blanding, and I told them not to scratch their names on rocks inside the monument. One man who went along with the boys (I will just call him John Doe) told his boy that man Zeke Johnson had no police authority over those rocks, and he and his son wrote their names on top of Sipapu Bridge and dug it deep.
>
> Well, of course I explained the law and told him to get back out and rub it off, and he told me to go 'places.' The invitation to go some place was repeated several times, and I found it necessary to write to the director of national parks in Washington, D.C. The defendant got a letter telling him that unless he immediately complied with Custodian Johnson's instructions he would have a ride at his own expense from Blanding to Washington, D.C., to be arraigned before the U.S. Government. He soon hunted me up and asked what he should do. I said just do as I told you, track back out there and take off those initials. He offered me twenty bucks if I would do it, but I told him nobody could do it but him,

and it was a five-day horseback trip in those days. Since then he has been a help to me. Several initial-cutters have been caught, and when they tried to lobby with me I just told them to step across the street and talk with Mr. John Doe. I can't give you chapter and verse, but the law is very plain, and I am obliged to enforce it.

*Located 40 miles west of Blanding on Utah State Highway 95; 435-692-1234.*

◆ GRAND GULCH PRIMITIVE AREA  *map page 235, F & G-7 & 8*

This area, south of the monument, preserves a winding, many-fingered canyon where numerous rock graphic panels can be found along the walls. Archaeologists have determined that the area was occupied as early as A.D. 200 by the Basketmaker Ancestral Puebloans, but was abandoned and reoccupied two centuries later.

If you're planning to explore Grand Gulch, it's wise to check in with the Kane Gulch Ranger Station or call the BLM Monticello Field Office *(see page 329). UT 261, four miles south of UT 95.*

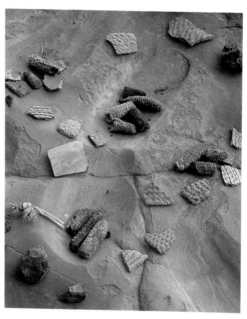

*Ancestral Puebloan artifacts near Junction Ruin in the Grand Gulch Primitive Area.*

◆ BLUFF  *map page 235, G-9*

Bluff, 27 miles south of Blanding, is another small Utah town on the Trail of the Ancients. Nearly every cliff or canyon slope within a 50-mile radius of town harbors some sign of its ancient inhabitants. As in all explorations of Indian ruins, visitors should beware of hazards. Many ruins are located in inaccessible cliffs. People have been injured trying to climb into ruins by treacherous routes. Rattlesnakes and scorpions can be found in this part of the country. Go slow and be observant. Backcountry trails and roads can become treacherous in a flash flood. Guided tours of the backcountry by foot or four-wheel-drive are available at Recapture Lodge Tours in Bluff, and to the south at Goulding's Trading Post near Monument Valley Navajo Park.

◆ HOVENWEEP NATIONAL MONUMENT  *map page 235, G-9*

Hovenweep is a Ute word meaning "deserted valley." All access to the monument, 42 miles east of Bluff, is on dirt roads that are generally passable by passenger cars, but tricky when it rains. Hovenweep is a curiosity in the Ancestral Puebloan world because of its distinctive square towers. The Ancestral Puebloans usually built round towers. Six separate ruined settlements are found here.

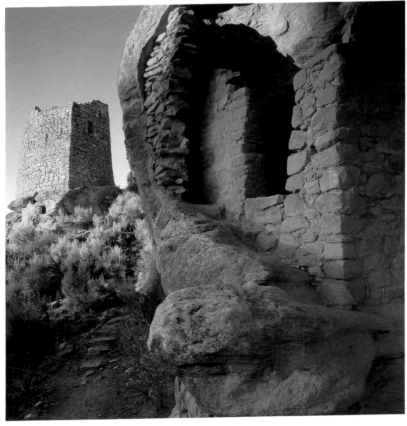

*Boulder House in Hovenweep National Monument was occupied by the Anasazi around A.D. 900.*

Hovenweep region was inhabited by Ancestral Puebloans who migrated from Mesa Verde, nearly 100 miles to the east, around A.D. 900. Perhaps they were migrants, maybe even outcasts. They lived in scattered villages and cultivated corn, beans, squash, and melons. From studying tree rings, it has been determined that by 1200, annual rainfall decreased substantially. The outlying farm villages were abandoned and new ones rebuilt near canyons with permanent springs. The style of the towers and the location of the dwellings in the cliffs suggest the inhabitants of Hovenweep may also have been preparing for attack by other Ancestral Puebloan clans or Shoshone raiders looking for food and water. Each tower contained only one small doorway protected by a parapet. Most towers also have peepholes pointing outwards—away from the canyon.

Archaeologists have offered another theory concerning the use of the towers. At least three sites at the monument, including the major ruin, **Square Tower**, may have been used as observatory sites. Certain windows in the towers are situated in such a way that sunlight enters only during the summer and winter solstices and the autumn and vernal equinoxes, striking particular points marked on the interior walls.

When the last springs dried up, the Hovenweep Ancestral Puebloans were forced to leave, archaeologists surmise, and join the Zuni Pueblo in western New Mexico. By 1300, the Hovenweep region was deserted.

*Hovenweep Visitor Center is located near the Hatch Trading Post, off UT 262; 970-562-4282.*

◆ MONUMENT VALLEY *map page 235, H-7 & 8*

The **Navajo Indian Reservation**, which covers large areas of Arizona and New Mexico, also reaches into Utah's rugged southeastern corner. Traditional Navajo hogans dot the landscape. Famous the world over, the majestic buttes of **Monument Valley** have served as the backdrops for many famous Western movies. **Goulding Trading Post** and the **Navajo Tribal Park** nearby provide meals and accommodations for visitors.

*(previous page) Looking through a window at Monument Valley.*

♦  FOUR CORNERS  *map page 235, H-11*

The Navajos also manage the entrance to a small monument at the Four Corners Monument, the only place in the United States where a visitor can stand in one spot and be in four states—Utah, New Mexico, Colorado, and Arizona.

## KEN SLEIGHT: PIONEERING RIVER-RUNNER

Ken Sleight struggled to keep the raft upright through the roaring foam of Skull Rapid in the Colorado River's Westwater Canyon. His passengers screamed in fright and delight. A wave of water engulfed the rubber boat, but somehow, some way, the guide and his passengers survived their run through the swirling rapids.

Relieved, the passengers slapped the river runner on the back and complimented him on the way he handled the boat. Sleight smiled but didn't let on that anything much almost happened.

"Shoot," he jokingly admitted years later, "I didn't have anything to do with getting us through there safely. I just got us out alive. I did a lousy job, but everybody thought it was really great stuff."

Ken Sleight belongs to an elite group of veteran Utah guides who pioneered river-running and backcountry touring in southern Utah during the early 1950s. Like many of these guides, he's spent his life living on the edge, greeting each day with the desire to learn something new and to introduce visitors to self-discovery and adventure, too.

"The biggest thrill in the world is to be able to lead a group of people up a canyon and let them discover something for themselves rather than to say, 'Okay, now we're going to see Rainbow Bridge right around the corner.' You see guide after guide after guide telling people to prepare themselves to see something. I think this is wrong. People who come on trips don't want to be classified as tourists or onlookers. I like them to feel like they're going to discover the river just like John Wesley Powell did.

"When I was a kid, my favorite pastime was going to the library and reading about all those people who were the first to discover something. When I went out and nobody else was in a place, I felt a thrill of discovery. People think a discovery is something that only happens once, but things are discovered anew in each and everyone's experience. I'm a watcher. And I love to watch people turn into the canyons for the first time. It blows their mind."

Sleight started running rivers commercially in 1951, and he's seen most of those in southern Utah. He took his boats through Glen Canyon before a dam created Lake Powell. He's run the Grand Canyon, Cataract and Westwater canyons on the Colorado, and most of the canyons on the Green River. As a horsepacker and hiker, the veteran guide helped explore famed Utah backcountry like Grand Gulch, Dark Canyon, Coyote Gulch, and the Maze. Though he enjoys giving his customers the feeling of adventure, like on the Westwater Canyon trip, he can't recall ever being in a life-threatening situation on one of his trips.

He is a man with definite opinions about what makes a good trip and what doesn't. He thinks, for example, that many modern-day river excursions are too short. "It takes time to bring a group together," he says. "The first day, when you meet the people, they're trying to analyze you, and you're doing the same to them. It usually takes three days for everyone to feel comfortable. The third day is the charm. Personally, trips six to 10 days long are my favorites."

Sleight loves taking excursions through canyons he's never explored before. "The more you've seen, the more you realize what you haven't seen. When I was a kid running the rivers, I thought I'd see them all, but there are so damn many, one guy in a lifetime couldn't see them all. That's the beauty of the canyons."

Sleight, whom many believe to be the prototype for the character of Seldom Seen Smith in Edward Abbey's novel *The Monkey Wrench Gang*, is, with one very big exception, the prototype of a typical conservative southern Utah businessman. He owns a small business, operating out of the Pack Creek Ranch 14 miles south of Moab at the base of the La Sals. He possesses a healthy distrust of government and its regulations. Like the prospectors, cattle ranchers, and farmers who struggle to make a living in this desolate country, Sleight is by nature independent.

He differs greatly, though, from many of his fellow southern Utah citizens in his concern for the preservation of wilderness in the canyonlands country where he lives and works. Many Utah residents want more developmStories in Stone: Utah's Geologyent. Sleight fights to preserve the country he loves. For example, he professes a profound hatred of Lake Powell, the huge man-made reservoir which inundated some of his favorite canyons and brought more motorized recreation to southern Utah. When it was built, he left the Moab area for a few years and ventured to Alaska. But the lure of his beloved red rock canyons drew him home again.

"The canyons are terrific," he says. "I guess that's why I'm so adamant that, if I'm going to stay here, I'm going to make damn sure they don't overdevelop them. If there was canyon country all over the world, I'd just move on. But it's so limited, really. It's just one section of the entire Earth. There's no place else to go. You have to make your stand. You have to keep it the way it ought to be and that's as wilderness."

So, Sleight does a bit of fighting politically. But, most of all, he helps people discover the joy of his beloved rivers and canyons on their own, knowing in his heart that the land will help them make up their mind about how much of it should be preserved.

*One of Utah's unnavigable slot canyons.*

# S K I I N G  U T A H
## THE GREATEST SNOW ON EARTH

THE SNOWSTORM RAGED THROUGH MUCH OF THE NIGHT, dumping prodigious amounts of fluffy powder on ski slopes throughout Utah. Cars full of skiers anxiously waited for the canyon roads to be cleared and for the avalanche rangers to declare the resorts safe.

As the road opened, the skies began to clear. A few fluffy white clouds rolled off to the eastern horizon just as the sun peaked over the mountain, bathing the ski slopes in light. Skiers quickly buckled their boots, snapped into their bindings, and hopped aboard the chairlifts. The untouched powder was knee deep. This was the kind of day Utah skiers love.

❄        ❄        ❄

When compared with their gigantic counterparts in California, Colorado, Europe, or the eastern United States, many of Utah's ski resorts seem quaint and small. But there is a certain magic that surrounds Utah ski resorts that has its source in what many have called the best quality skiing snow in the world. There's a reason Utah's snow conditions are often better than those in surrounding states.

"Most of the winter storms that affect Utah have their origin in the northern Pacific Ocean," said William Alder, chief meteorologist for the National Weather Service in Salt Lake City. "These storms move southeastward across the Sierra Nevada and Cascade Mountains, where they lose some of their moisture. When they hit the high Wasatch and Utah's south-central mountains, the orographic (air forced against mountains) lifting occurs and squeezes out much of the moisture. This is what produces the colder, drier powder snows for which Utah is noted.

"The secret of Utah's unique and wonderful powder is the structure of the individual snow crystals. Under cold, relatively dry conditions, light crystal-type snowflakes called dendrites are produced. These snowflakes are thin and symmetrical in shape, and they float down through the cold atmosphere, accumulating like fluffy down or powder on Utah's mountains. Many times cold northwest winds will follow a storm and prolong this powder snowfall over the higher mountains. When deep enough, the powder snow gives skiers the feeling they are floating on air as they ski down, and that's what makes the Greatest Snow on Earth."

There are 14 ski resorts in Utah. Visitors to the Wasatch Front have a choice of 11 ski resorts, all within an hour's drive of the airport. In addition, hundreds of roads in the national forests are ideal for cross-country skiing. Call or write to Ski Utah for their *Utah Winter Vacation Planner.* It contains information on specific resorts as well as on lodging, ski pass rates, seasons, hours, and other important details. *skiutah.com; 150 West 500 South, Salt Lake City, UT, 84101; 801-534-1779.*

## ■ HISTORY OF SKIING IN UTAH

Skiing started in Utah during the early 1900s when a few miners and trappers adopted skis for getting around the mountains during winter. Robert F. Marvin was one of the few miners to leave a first-hand account of early ski equipment and technique. "Let me tell you about Alta, before it became effete and a play-place for kids, before it was converted from a mining camp to a ski resort," wrote Marvin in an unpublished manuscript. "Let me tell you of the men who lived and labored there, of men who plied their trades as miners, as haulers of ore and freight, as hewers of wood. Let me describe the lives they lived and the works they wrought with strong backs and calloused hands and precious little help from things mechanical. I'll tell you about these things as they were in the early years of this century, as I first saw them in the closing days of 1916.

"To begin then, Alta was not in those days a ski resort. There were no hotels, no accommodations—and almost no skis. In 1916 the onset of winter found exactly two pairs of skis in the camp, not counting the stubby, broad and double-edged

*Early skiers used a single pole to "row" their way*
*through the deep snows of Utah's alpine meadows.*

# UTAH
# SKI AREAS

| | | |
|---|---|---|
| 0 | 5 | 10 Mi |
| 0 | 5 | 10 | 15 Km |

**Main map labels:**

Snowville · Richmond · Garden City · Beaver Mountain · Tremonton · Logan · Woodruff · Wellsville · Sherwood Hills Resort · Brigham City · Power Mountain · Road closed in winter · Ogden · Clinton · South Ogden · Morgan · Layton · Coalville · SALT LAKE CITY · Park City · Keams · West Jordan · Heber City · Grantsville · Tooele · Cedar Fort · The Homestead · Clover · Strawberry Reservoir · Provo · Vernon · Spanish Fork · Birdseye · Nephi · Fairview · Sugarville · Delta · Oak City · Ephraim · Scipio · Holden · Gunnison · Salina · Fillmore · Emery · Richfield · Cove Fort · To Green River · Capitol Reef National Park · Loa · Lyman · Milford · Junction · Torrey · Greenville · Beaver · Panguitch · Bryce Canyon Nat'l Park · Cedar City · Escalante · Henrieville · Zion National Park · Long Valley Junction · Grand Staircase-Escalante National Monument · To St George

WASATCH RANGE · WASATCH FRONT · Great Salt Lake · Utah Lake · Sevier River · WASATCH PLATEAU · AQUARIUS PLATEAU · Sevier River

To Wendover

N · W · E · S

**Salt Lake City inset:**

Nordic Valley · Harrisville · Huntsville · Ogden · Snowbasin · Mt Ogden · Clinton · South Ogden · Mountain Green · Uintah · Peterson · Syracuse · South Weber · Layton · Milton · Stoddard · Francis Peak 9,265 · Devil's Slide · Kaysville · Fruit Heights · Morgan · Henefer · Farmington · Porterville · Bountiful Peak 9,259 · Centerville · Great Salt Lake · Bountiful · Salt Lake International Airport · North Salt Lake City · SALT LAKE CITY · Kimball Jun · South Salt Lake City · Mt Aire · The Canyons · West Valley City · Mt Olympus · Park City · Deer Valley · Murray · Solitude · Alta · Brighton · West Jordan · Snowbird · Twin Peaks · Sandy · South Jordan · Lone Peak · Draper · Deer Res · Road closed in winter · Bluffdale · Point of the Mountain · Sundance · American Fork · Pleasant Grove · Lindon · Wildwood · Orem · Olmsted · Utah Lake

N · W · E · S

**Beaver / Cedar City inset:**

Manderfield · Elk Meadows · Beaver · Road closed in winter · Minersville · Greenville · Dixie Nat'l Forest · Summit 7,910 · Little Creek Peak 10,135 · Paragonah · Panguitch · Summit · Parowan · Brian Head · Enoch · Cedar City · Summit 11,315 · Brian Head · Hatch · Dixie · National · Forest · Summit 9,900 · Summit 7,530 · Long Valley Junction

# UTAH SKI RESORTS

| SKI RESORT | INFO: GENERAL LODGING | VERTICAL RISE FT. | NO. RUNS | NO. LIFTS | TOP ELEV. | SKIING ACRES | MI. FR. SLC ARPT |
|---|---|---|---|---|---|---|---|
| **Alta** Map left, D-3. | 801-742-3333 888-782-9258 | 2,020 | 39 | 8 | 10,650 | 2,200 | 26 |
| **Beaver Mountain** Map left, B-1 | 435-753-0921 | 1,600 | 16 | 3 | 8,840 | 464 | 111 |
| **Brian Head** Map left, C-7 | 801-677-2035 888-677-2810 | 1,707 | 53 | 7 | 11,307 | 500 | 260 |
| **Brighton Resort** Map left, D-3 | 801-532-4731 800-873-5512 | 1,745 | 64 | 7 | 10,500 | 850 | 29 |
| **The Canyons** Map left, D-3 | 435-649-5400 888-226-9667 | 3,190 | 58 | 7 | 9,990 | 2,000 | 33 |
| **Deer Valley** Map left, D-3 | 435-649-1000 800-558-3337 | 3,000 | 66 | 13 | 9,400 | 1,100 | 34 |
| **Elk Meadows** Map left, D-5 | 435-438-5433 888-881-7669 | 1,400 | 40 | 5 | 10,400 | 400 | 228 |
| **Nordic Valley** Map left, C-1 | 801-745-3511 | 1,000 | 12 | 2 | 6,400 | 85 | 49 |
| **Park City Resort** Map left, D-3 | 435-649-8111 800-222-PARK | 3,100 | 89 | 13 | 10,000 | 2,200 | 32 |
| **Powder Mountain** Map left, B-1 | 801-745-3772 | 2,005 | 33 | 7 | 8,900 | 1,600 | 54 |
| **Snowbasin** Map left, C-1 | 801-399-1135 801-627-8228 | 2,400 | 39 | 5 | 8,800 | 1,800 | 52 |
| **Snowbird** Map left, D-3/4. | 801-742-2222 800-453-3000 | 3,240 | 47 | 8 | 11,000 | 2,500 | 24 |
| **Solitude** Map left, D-3 | 801-536-5700 800-748-4754 | 2,047 | 63 | 7 | 10,030 | 1,200 | 27 |
| **Sundance** Map left, D-4 | 801-225-4107 800-892-1600 | 2,150 | 41 | 4 | 8,250 | 450 | 51 |

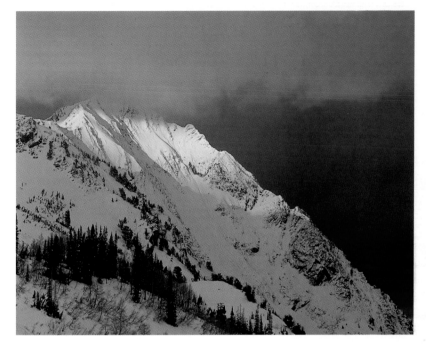

*Spring sunrise on Superior Peak as seen from Alta in the Wasatch Mountains.*

skis the Finlander miners brought in from the old country. I had to send far away for my first pair, all the way to St. Paul, where someone had begun to manufacture them. When the skis came, they were hickory, thick and heavy and exactly 11 feet long. The thinking was that the longer the skis were the better they would ride atop the snow and not sink in. I was about the only person in camp long-legged enough to make a kick turn with them, and it was an effort like a high-kickin' chorus girl's. Ski poles we had none; they were to us an unknown. Instead, we had a single long pole, usually cut from creek-side brush, preferably water birch because the bark was so smooth. This pole we used like an oar or gee-pole, always on the uphill side, right or left. Also, there was no ski harness, only a leather toe-strap (sometimes tied to the ankle with a short length of cord to prevent the skis going home by themselves in case of a tumble). With this primitive gear, we 'rowed' ourselves uphill and down to all the places your tows and lifts take you now, and beyond; to the top of Baldy on occasion."

The Utah ski industry grew from these humble beginnings. Alta, second only to Sun Valley, Idaho, as the oldest resort in the United States, constructed its first lift in 1938. It was followed by Snowbasin in Ogden Canyon and Brighton in Big

Cottonwood Canyon. Construction of the huge Park City complex—one of the few Utah resort areas which can compare in size and scope to Aspen, Vail, and Mammoth Mountain—started in 1963. The Canyon and the exclusive Deer Valley followed, as did other Wasatch Front resorts, like Robert Redford's Sundance east of Provo, Powder Mountain and Nordic Valley in Ogden Valley, Solitude in Big Cottonwood Canyon, and Beaver Mountain in Logan Canyon. Snowbird, a huge, modern complex located below Alta in Little Cottonwood Canyon, appeared on the scene in the early 1970s, bringing with it an often acrimonious debate over how much development should take place in the canyons east of Salt Lake City. With Utah now hosting the Winter Olympics in 2002, the controversy over how much development should be allowed in the precious Wasatch Front canyons continues to rage. For an account of these controversies, as well as the most detailed information on the colorful history of Utah skiing, pick up a copy of Alexis Kelner's *Skiing in Utah: A History.*

Each Utah resort occupies its own niche. The giant resorts, like Park City and Snowbird, rank with the top ski areas in the world in terms of facilities, number of runs, and nightlife. Smaller resorts, like Beaver Mountain, Brighton, and Alta, bring to mind simpler times in the ski business when only the quality of the snow and the ski runs seemed important.

## ■ LITTLE COTTONWOOD CANYON  *map page 278, D-3&4*

Little Cottonwood Canyon is just a short drive east from Salt Lake City. Alta and Snowbird, the two resorts located just a few miles from one another at the top of Little Cottonwood Canyon, could not be more different.

*An early snowfall in Big Cottonwood Canyon dusts aspens as they turn from green to gold.*

SKIING

## Alta
*map page 278, D-3*

*UT 210, information: 801-742-3333,*
*reservations: 888-782-9258*
*www.alta.com*

With its world-famous powder and comparatively low lift rates, Alta provides a reminder of what skiing in the United States used to be like. Its eight lifts service a mountain which compares favorably to any on earth as a place to ski. Its lodges are small, quaint, and few in number.

Even on holiday weekends, when a skier may have to wait in line for 40 minutes before boarding an Alta lift, the wait seems worth the effort. Resort managers haved bucked a national trend toward building high-speed lifts, invoking a philosophy that too many people on a hill at the same time can ruin a skier's experience.

Alta has a well-deserved reputation for some of the best powder in the world and is also an excellent place for beginners to learn the sport. Its slopes are well-groomed and the Sunnyside Lift services one of the longest and best beginners' slopes found in Utah. Moguls, tree skiing, and deep powder off the Wildcat Lift challenge even the most expert of skiers.

Lodging at the resort ranges from elegant to rustic. But the Utah Transit Authority bus service which brings skiers from downtown to Alta for a $2 roundtrip fare makes staying in town and then skiing at Alta a relatively easy proposition.

## Snowbird
*map page 278, D-3/4*

*UT 201, information: 801-742-2222*
*reservations: 800-453-3000*
*www.snowbird.com*

Snowbird is an unabashed giant, working hard to create an image of technological wonder. From the monolithic cement condominiums at the resort base to the gleaming red and blue trams which whisk skiers to the top of 11,000-foot Hidden Peak, Snowbird presents itself as a gleaming, well-planned, modern ski area. The shopping centers, restaurants, tennis courts, swimming pools, convention center, spa, and bars reflect the vision of founders Dick Bass and Ted Johnson. Skiers straight off the slopes can head to a spa where they can enjoy a massage, nail care, herbal wraps, and hair care, or visit the shops, restaurants, bank, post office, laundry, medical clinic, and pharmacy.

Snowbird is a slightly more difficult resort to ski than Alta. Some runs range up to $3^{1}/_{2}$ miles in length. Only 25 percent of the runs are rated for beginners with 30 percent for intermediate and a whopping 45 percent for experts. Fine skiers like the challenge of taking the tram and the Peruvian and Little Cloud lifts to ski the expert runs. Snowbird skiers can choose from two high speed quads, seven double chairlifts, and the tram. The vertical drop of 3,100 feet is the sharpest at any Utah resort.

*(opposite) Big Cottonwood Canyon in a winter storm.*

# ■ BIG COTTONWOOD CANYON  *map page 278, D-3&4*

## Brighton
*map page 278, D-3*

*information: 801-532-4731*
*reservations: 800-873-5512*
*www.skibrighton.com*

Named after William S. Brighton who constructed a small hotel in 1874 in Big Cottonwood Canyon, Brighton bills itself as the place Utah learns to ski. Dave Farmer, a lift supervisor at the resort, put things another way. "People learn to ski at Brighton and then go on to enjoy all types of expert powder skiing at the other resorts, only to return here when they get older and their knees start going bad."

Alexis Kelner, in his book on the history of Utah skiing, says simplicity and sincerity were the hallmarks of the original 1870s' Brighton venture. These days, some of that simple charm has been replaced by high tech with two high-speed quad lifts, three double and two triple chairs.

Brighton boasts good powder skiing and about 39 percent of its runs are rated for experts. Powder hounds love blasting through the deep stuff on the Scree run near the Millicent Lift or skiing between the pines under the Snake Creek triple chair after a heavy snowfall. The Crest and Great Western Express quads service a wide area, all but eliminating lift lines. The resort features some of the state's best night skiing, good snowboarding, and several trails that connect to its Big Cottonwood neighbor, Solitude.

## Solitude
*map page 278, D-3*

*information: 801-536-5700*
*reservations: 800-748-4754*
*www.solitude.com*

Solitude might be described as a poorman's Snowbird. The skiing terrain, like Snowbird's, possesses many mogul hills and places to enjoy great powder after a heavy storm. The resort offers a high-speed quad detachable chairlift, a lift capable of moving skiers up the mountains twice as fast as a normal chair but which slows up to allow skiers to load and unload. There are also four double chairs and two triple chairs servicing 63 different runs.

Solitude was opened in 1957 by a colorful miner named Bob Barrett, an independent sort who believed in doing things his own way. He ran into trouble with both Salt Lake City officials trying to protect the Big Cottonwood Canyon watershed, as well as U.S. Forest Service bureaucrats charged with issuing special-use permits for the part of the resort which rested on its property. Barrett was a do-it-yourself buff and his lifts, unique to Solitude, became legendary for both their construction and numerous breakdowns. The new phase of Solitude began in 1975 when Richard Houlihan took over the resort, adding three state-of-the-art chairlifts. Now under new ownership, solitude's base facilities resemble a Swiss village.

■ PARK CITY SKI AREAS   *map page 278, D-3&4*

Not long ago, Park City's Main Street was on the verge of turning into a ghost town. Old mining equipment, an abandoned railroad station, and wooden shacks hanging precariously on the hills seemed to litter the landscape. Mining activity in the old community, which had produced some of Utah's richest and most eccentric community leaders, had all but ceased. A few curious tourists made the 32-mile drive from Salt Lake City during the summer to shop for antiques or have a soda at the old fountain. Park City still served as the home of Utah's oldest weekly newspaper, *The Park Record.* Some colorful characters would tell visitors of the fires, different cultures, 30 Main Street saloons, and the wealthy mining magnates that were all part of the history of this place. Fewer than 2,000 residents lived in what was once a booming town.

What a contrast to the current day's bustling atmosphere brought on by the development of Park City, the Canyons, and Deer Valley—three of Utah's largest ski areas. Though Main Street is still listed on the National Register of Historic Places, the town has become a huge ski resort. Park City houses some of Utah's poshest eateries. In addition to skiing, visitors now can ride a hot-air balloon, go ice skating, take a moonlight sleigh ride, ski cross-country on groomed trails, take a snowmobile journey, and play tennis and racquetball. Live theater performances and the Sundance Film Festival add to the allure of the town. In the summer, visitors can entertain themselves with golf and miniature golf, bicycling, hiking, and an alpine slide that careens riders down a mountainside on a wheeled car. The Park City Arts Festival in August is one of the biggest events of its kind in the state. The landscape of this once quaint mining town is now dotted with hundreds of condominiums, built in many different styles and catering to numerous incomes and tastes. Park City is as close as Utah gets to imitating the atmosphere and nightlife of huge ski areas like Vail, Aspen, or Sun Valley.

In 1923, *The Park Record,* published an article predicting that Park City would turn into a mecca for winter sports. It may have taken three-quarters of a century, but that prediction has become a reality. The world will discover that reality in the 2002 Olympics. Deer Valley will host the slalom and freestyle ski events. Park City is the site of snowboarding and the giant slalom alpine races. And the nearby Utah Winter Sports Park will be the site of bobsled, luge, and ski jumping.

The way Park City caters to out-of-state skiers is reflected in the price. Skiing at Park City is more costly than anywhere else in the state, and the exclusive Deer Valley has among the highest lift ticket prices in the United States.

## Park City Resort
*map page 278, D-3*

*information: 435-649-8111*
*reservations: 800-222-PARK*
*www.parkcitymountain.com*

With 14 lifts, Park City Resort is easily Utah's largest. It can handle 23,000 skiers an hour on its 100 designated runs, 650 acres of wide-open bowl skiing, and more than 3,300 acres of skiable terrain. Nobody has to ski the same run or use the same lift twice in a day. In addition to a lift running from the old part of town, there are runs catering to children, and Jupiter Bowl at the top of the resort for powder hounds. In terms of the services offered and variety of terrain, nightlife, and facilities, Park City provides more of everything. The town serves as headquarters for the United States ski team and as the site of numerous professional and World Cup skiing races. When Utah hosts the Winter Olympics in 2002, Park City will be the site for many alpine skiing and snowboarding events.

## Deer Valley
*map page 278, D-3*

*information: 435-649-1000*
*reservations: 800-558-3337*
*www.deervalley.com*

Just east of Park City, Deer Valley spoils skiers. *Skiing* magazine calls it "the crème de la crème of ski destinations, devoid of most hassles that vacationing mortals are heir to, with uncrowded runs groomed to silky perfection…advanced terrain as good as anywhere… a cornucopia of slope-side extras, which in the aggregate spell the difference between routine and luxury."

Even the moguls appear groomed at Deer Valley. Expect help unloading the skis from your vehicle and look for attendants clad in elegant green ski suits to help load you on the lifts. Deer Valley is a place to beat the holiday crowds because the number of skiers allowed on the mountain at any given time is limited by a reservation system. Lighted signs advise Deer Valley skiers about lines in the restaurants. There are even places to recline in the snow on lounge chairs during skiing breaks. Don't expect paper plates and plasticware in even the least expensive cafeterias at the resort—everything is served on china. The Stein Erikson Lodge at the resort is considered one of Utah's most elegant dining spots.

Those who use Deer Valley's 17 lifts and one gondola notice a feeling of quiet elegance. Each run seems perfectly groomed. Details like keeping the lifts free of snow, the walkways shoveled, and tissue boxes at the bottom of the lifts are not ignored.

Skiing takes place on five areas—with 15 percent of the runs rated as easy, 50 percent as more difficult, and 35 percent as most difficult. Not many locals can afford the stiff lift-ticket prices at Deer Valley, but the few who splurge enjoy being treated like royalty.

## The Canyons
*map page 278, D-3*

*information:* 435-649-5400
*reservations:* 888-226-9667
*www.thecanyons.com.*

Situated north of Park City near Snyder-ville (and once known as Park West, and later as Wolf Mountain), the Canyons has been transformed from a sleepy, inexpensive ski area into Utah's newest mega-resort. In terms of acreage, its 3,700 acres make it the state's largest.

Resort managers continue to add runs and lifts, as well as a completely new base and a large new hotel. With eight quads, eight triple lifts, two doubles, and a gondo-la, the Canyons is aresort where skiers and boarders rarely wait in line.

Those who drive by the resort can only see a small part of the mountain. There are actually 125 runs—the most of any Utah ski area: 14 percent beginner, 44 percent intermediate, and 47 percent advanced runs. The Canyons is at the top of the list for many snowboarders.

■ SUNDANCE   *map page 278, D-4*

## Sundance
*map page 278, D-4*

*information:* 801-225-4107
*reservations* 800-892-1600
*www.sundanceresort.com.*

A skier can explore the many nuances of Utah County's only ski resort for years and never catch a glimpse of its famous owner, Robert Redford. Yet Redford's spirit seems to live in every part of Sundance.

In 1969, the actor purchased a tiny ski area in the Uinta Forest called Timp Haven. He renamed it after the character he played opposite Paul Newman in the movie *Butch Cassidy and the Sundance Kid,* and slowly turned it into a film and arts center, ski resort, and home. Redford also filmed a movie about mountain man Jeremiah Johnson close to his resort. Views of 11,788-foot Mt. Timpanogos dominate both the movie setting and the ski resort.

Sundance is not a flashy resort—one has to search to find the few condominiums located on the site. The base facilities are small, quiet, and tasteful.

Sundance is located on a fine ski hill east of Orem. Though relatively small even by Wasatch Front standards, the resort's three lifts lead to 41 trails on 450 acres. Beginners can find places to fit their abilities at Sundance, but the terrain also challenges good skiers, especially after a heavy snowfall. As a rule, the higher the elevation of the lift at Sundance, the more difficult the runs.

## ■ OGDEN VALLEY RESORTS *map page 278, C-1*

Some might question why a skier would want to travel the longer distances from Salt Lake City to ski Ogden Valley's three resorts—Snowbasin, Powder Mountain, and Nordic Valley. Variety is one reason, the quality of snow is the other. Some of the highest quality powder in Utah can be found at tiny Powder Mountain, a resort consisting of three mountains and three lifts.

"The greatest snow. . . .What are we really talking about," wrote Williams in his Utah Geographic Series *Utah Ski Country.* "The amount? The moisture content? Yes, but for a ski resort there is more. Is it easy to get to, and does it last? And, my big question—Are powder skiers happy? At Powder Mountain, the answer is 'yes' all around."

### Powder Mountain *map page 278, B-1*

*information: 801-745-3772*
*www.powdermountain.com*

The view from Powder Mountain, northeast of the tiny community of Eden, is alone worth the price of a lift ticket. One can see the sun setting over the Great Salt Lake, peer into Cache Valley to the north, or see the distant ski runs cut out of the mountainside of Park City to the south.

Those who have never skied Powder Mountain may be deceived into thinking that a resort with only four lifts is small. The resort's one triple and two double chairs are smartly constructed to cover the largest possible skiing area. In some cases, shuttles are used to transport skiers from one lift to the next.

Another oddity is that the resort facilities are located near the top of the ski area instead of at the base. One actually needs to ski down from the main resort complex to reach a lift. There are 81 runs here, including an excellent night skiing hill serviced by the aptly named "Sundown Lift."

### Nordic Valley *map page 278, C-1*

*information: 801-745-3511*
*(Located west of Powder Mountain)*

The smallest ski resort on the Wasatch Front, Nordic Valley consists of two double chairlifts capable of serving 1,800 skiers. There are only 12 runs, but all of them are lighted at night, making for some of the best night skiing along the Wasatch Front. With its excellent teaching programs, Nordic Valley is a good place to introduce the kids to the sport of skiing.

## Snowbasin
*map page 278, C-1*

*information: 801-399-1135*
*reservations: 801-627-8228*
*www.snowbasin.com*

Expect the 2002 Winter Olympics to put this once-sleepy resort into the big leagues of skiing. Snowbasin has only recently become one of Utah's super resorts. As host of the the premier alpine skiing events of the 2002 Olympics, the downhill and super G events, the mountain is undergoing massive changes to prepare for the Games, including the addition of two high speed gondolas (one takes skiers to the edge of the mountain, providing views of the Great Salt Lake below). A high-speed quad and small tramway provide access to the Olympic downhill run. Add one double

and four triple chairs, and Snowbasin ranks among the largest of Utah's ski areas. It will do nothing but get bigger. The Olympics have provided the impetus for expansion of other resort facilities including a golf course, and other amenities.

For an intermediate skier, Snowbasin is ideal. The runs are steep enough to be challenging but well-groomed enough not to contain many surprises. Its vertical drop of 2,400 feet—ranking third in Utah for steepness—gives skiers a chance to enjoy long, scenic runs.

The thing we like best about Snowbasin is the scenery. Mt. Ogden is magnificent. On the drive up to the base of the resort, keep an eye out for wintering moose foraging in the willows at the side of the road. Don't forget to take along your cross-country skis! Have a picnic and enjoy the view. Located on UT 16, Trappers Loop Hwy.

## ■ NORTHERN UTAH  *map page 278, B-1*

## Beaver Mountain  *map page 278, B-1*

*information: 435-753-4822 or*
*435-946-3612*

At the top of Logan Canyon, on US 89 near the Utah-Idaho border, you'll find Beaver Mountain, a small, family-operated resort which serves the outdoor-oriented students of nearby Utah State University.

In many ways, Beaver Mountain resembles a small-scale Brighton. Its three double

chairlifts service 22 major runs and provide access to beginner and intermediate hills and to a few expert runs, as well.

We enjoy skiing cross country over the groomed U.S. Forest Service trail near the side road that leads to the resort. We then spend the evening soaking in the outdoor pools and hot tubs at Crystal Hot Springs, located in nearby Honeyville. Some fine condominiums are found at neighboring Bear Lake, which are seldom, if ever, crowded during the winter months.

■ SOUTHERN UTAH RESORTS *map page 278, C & D-5, 6 & 7*

One might not expect to find places for nordic and alpine skiing in the midst of what many picture as red-rock desert. But the Brian Head and Elk Meadows ski areas feature high elevations, good powder, uncrowded conditions, and modern facilities.

## Brian Head
*map page 278, C-7*

*information: 435-677-2035*
*reservations: 888-677-2810*
*www.brianhead.com*

Located south of Parowan on UT 143, Brian Head possesses a bit of the alpine atmosphere of Utah's northern ski areas but looks more like southern Utah. Skiers taking the resort's Giant Steps Lift, one of six at the resort, find themselves standing under 11,307-foot Brian Head Peak— an impressive red sandstone mountain some say may have been named (but misspelled) after the famed bald-headed politician William Jennings Bryan. On a clear, cold winter day, skiers peer down on a scene of fire and ice, looking out toward Zion National Park and the red-rock deserts.

The town of Brian Head comes alive in winter. The resort is large enough to provide for thousands of skiers, while retaining a quaintness that makes it a quiet alternative to the huge California and Colorado resorts. Smaller lodges near Duck Creek and Panguitch Lake offer rustic, out-of-the-way settings to visitors looking for "big city" escapes. Less expensive lodging can be found in Cedar City and Parowan.

## Elk Meadows
*map page 278, D-5*

*information: 435-438-5433*
*reservations: 888-881-7669*
*www.elkmeadows.com*

Elk Meadows, one of Utah's newest resorts, is a fine place for families and has one of the best "learn-to-ski" packages in the state.

The resort lies east of Beaver on UT 153, nestled in an alpine canyon at an elevation of 9,200 feet. The runs reach as high as 10,400 feet, and this quiet ski area receives 350 inches of snowfall annually. Its two newest lifts serve primarily intermediate runs. Skiers can choose from three double chairs, one quad chair, one poma lift, and one T-bar at a resort that is rarely crowded. Lodging is available at the ski area itself or in nearby Beaver.

*Snowfall in southern Utah tends to be wetter and less persistent than in the north.*

the High Uintas and the Wasatch Range are a sight to behold on a crisp, clear winter day. Snowmobiles can be rented at Wasatch Mountain State Park, the state's finest and most complete snowmobiling facility.

Trailheads at **Midway**, **Park City**, and **American Fork Canyon** offer plowed parking areas, restrooms, designated play areas, warming stations, and 60 miles of groomed trails.

Snowmobilers searching for a chance to view red-rock canyons coated with snow usually head for the Cedar Mountain Complex, just east of Cedar City on a high plateau. Trails lead into Cedar Breaks National Monument, which is closed to automobile traffic in the winter. Much of the trail leads through the pines and aspens of the Dixie National Forest, but views of the red-rock country are common. Access to the complex is available from the Brian Head, Duck Creek, Strawberry, Navajo, and Midway trailheads, with some package tours offered out of Brian Head.

One of our favorite complexes is the Logan Canyon-Monte Cristo-Hardware Ranch area in northern Utah. The 150 miles of groomed trails here connect with hundreds more trail miles in neighboring Idaho. Be sure to stop by the Hardware Ranch to see the winter feeding grounds of the wild elk. Though snowmobiles are not allowed near the huge animals, visitors can take a horse-drawn sleigh ride near the elk herds. The visitor center provides heated restrooms, a warm fire, vending machines, and information about the elk. The wide-open spaces on Ant Flat between Hardware Ranch and Monte Cristo and in the Sinks area of Logan Canyon give snowmobilers plenty of area to enjoy untouched powder.

In central Utah, you might enjoy a snowmobile ride across a portion of Skyline Drive where elevations reach nearly 12,000 feet. About 75 miles of trails are groomed in this scenic complex, with trailheads found on both sides of the Manti Range. We like the ride from Huntington Canyon into Joe's Valley Reservoir.

On occasion, the Division of Parks and Recreation also grooms snowmobile trails near Strawberry Reservoir and in the Vernal area. This depends on the availability of groomers. If you are in the mood for a bit of adventure and have confidence in your snowmobiling abilities, these are two good areas to try.

# ■ 2002 WINTER GAMES

As Salt Lake City and Utah prepare to host the 2002 Winter Olympics, many of those who fought for and against hosting the Games find themselves in a retrospective mood.

Since 1961, John W. Gallivan, publisher emeritus of *The Salt Lake Tribune*, Utah's largest daily newspaper, has dreamed about the time when the state will host the Olympics. That is when a few visionaries first thought about the idea. "In those days, we were going nowhere with tourism, which was an obvious industry for the state," said Gallivan. "Mining was in the doldrums. Agriculture was falling off. We had all these God-given wonders, but no place for people to stay." Business, civic, and church leaders joined together to form the Downtown Planning Association, dreaming of new hotels, a convention center , and a downtown arena.

While unsuccessful Olympic bids in 1968, 1976, 1988, and 1998 discouraged local leader, their dreams of a bustling downtown became a reality, in some ways fueled by the bids, and others by tourism. The new Salt Palace convention center, expanded again in 2000 to meet growing needs, has now been rebuilt four times. Its arena was replaced with the Delta Center. New hotels, an expanded and redesigned freeway system, and light rail mass transit have all become a reality.

So has the Olympic dream. Utah was awarded the 2002 Games. That has fueled even more growth, as ski areas, that will host the Games such as Park City, Deer Valley, and Ogden's Snowbasin, are bustling to get ready for the skiing and snowboarding races. Snowbasin, once a sleepy ski area known only by a few locals, is using the Games as an excuse to transform itself into the West's next mega-resort. It is owned by Sun Valley and Sinclair Oil tycoon Earl Holding. He is also building a new grand hotel in Salt Lake City.

A new winter sports park has been completed near Park City for ski jumpers, bobsledders, lugers, and skeleton racers. The E Center, a sparkling new concert and hockey facility, was built in West Valley City to host hockey. A new speed skating oval has been constructed at Oquirrh Park in the west part of the Salt Lake Valley. The Delta Center, home of the Utah Jazz professional basketball team, will be the figure skating venue. And Rice-Eccles Stadium on the University of Utah campus has been totally renovated and expanded to host the opening and closing ceremonies. The coyote, bear, and snowshoe hare, three animals native to Utah, were picked as official Games mascots. And thousands of Utahns have volunteered their time to help stage the Games.

"The exciting thing about the Olympics is that if we can get people to come here once and see what we're like, they'll come back again with tourist dollars," said Gallivan.

Yet, in some ways, Utah's Olympic dream has turned into a nightmare. No matter how good the facilities, and how friendly the hosts, the adjectives "scandal tainted" will likely be placed in front of the 2002 Winter Olympics when they conclude in February 2002.

When a Salt lake City television reporter revealed a letter from the Salt Lake Organizing Committee files that showed the bid committee paid the tuition of the daughter of an International Olympic Committee member on November 24, 1998, few realized the impact that revelation would have.

That letter, leaked from a file, proved to be only a small part of what Salt Lake bid organizers— and other bid cities— had done to secure the games. The revelations showed the crass side of the Olympics bidding process. Stories of gifts, cash payments, lavish vacations, and free medical care, given in an effort to influence International Olympic Committee members to vote for Salt Lake City, soon followed. So did investigations by the U.S. Justice Department and the Federal Bureau of Investigation. Frank Joklik, the Salt Lake City Organizing Committee chair, stepped down. So did senior vice president Dave Johnson. It was also revealed that Australian officials used cash payments to secure the 2000 Winter Games.

This left Mitt Romney, a Mormon, Brigham Young University graduate, businessman, and former U.S. Senate candidate from Massachusetts, who took over as Salt Lake Organizing Committee president, in a difficult situation. With the luster off the games, many major sponsors began to back out, creating cash-flow problems. The budget for the 2002 Games was soon slashed from $1.453 billion to $1.34 billion.

None of the scandal surprised long-time Utah Olympic opponent Alexis Kelner, a Salt Lake City environmentalist. Long before the state was successful in winning the 2002 bid, Kelner penned these words in a 1989 book called *Utah's Olympic Circus*: "...the International Olympic Committee, the various national Olympic associations, and numerous international sports federations have developed a fail-safe pyramid scheme to rival that of the ancient Pharaohs."

In retrospect, Kelner identified many problems with the Olympic movement that surfaced with the scandal. And he predicts that the worst is yet to come, "when the public gets stuck with the bills."

distinct seasons. (St. George is mild enough in winter for golf!) Almost everywhere else in Utah, including Salt Lake City, winter can be cold.

Summer temperatures throughout most Utah valleys hover around 85-100 degrees F (26-38° C), while the nearby mountains might enjoy a cool 60 degrees F (16° C). At night, temperatures in the mountains may cool off to 40-50 degrees F (5-10° C).

Spring and fall are the most comfortable seasons in southern Utah with day-time temperatures in the 60-70 degree F (16-19° C) range. In northern Utah, during April and May, you might ski in the morning and golf in the afternoon.

## ■ ABOUT UTAH LODGING

Utah's urban areas offer modern, full-service hotels operated by major national chains. You'll get more specific information—and better rates—by calling locally once you arrive in town. Most are listed in the Utah Travel Council's free Travel Guide, published annually and available free of charge; call Utah Travel Council, 801-538-1030. With an increase in tourism in recent years, there has been a building boom of sorts. And some of the older hotels have been razed or converted to office spaces. This means that while the state's hotels and motels tend to be clean and modern, they can also be somewhat sterile.

Visitors looking for a spot with more character should try staying at one of Utah's charming bed-and-breakfasts, many of which are colorful old mansions re-stored to their former glory. Some of the lodges at major ski areas draw a wealthy clientele. For a taste of the Wild West, consult the Utah Travel Council for a list of rustic dude ranches or cabins near fishing areas.

For detailed information on accomodations, contact the Utah Hotel Associa-tion at 9 Exchange Place, Suite 812, Salt Lake City, UT 84111; 801-359-0104

---

### *Hotel & Motel Chains*

| | |
|---|---|
| Best Western  . . . . . . . .800-528-1234 | Marriott Hotels . . . . . . .800-228-9290 |
| Comfort Inn  . . . . . . . .800-228-5150 | Motel 6  . . . . . . . . . . . .800-4-MOTEL-6 |
| Days Inn;  . . . . . . . . . .800-329-7466 | Quality Inn  . . . . . . . . . .800-221-2222 |
| Embassy Suites . . . . . . . .800-EMBASSY | Ramada Inn . . . . . . . . . .800-228-2828 |
| Hilton . . . . . . . . . . . . . .800-HILTONS | Super 8  . . . . . . . . . . . .800-800-8000 |
| Holiday Inn  . . . . . . . . .800-HOLIDAY | TraveLodge  . . . . . . . . .800-578-7878 |

# ■ ABOUT UTAH RESTAURANTS

The great number and variety of restaurants found throughout the state, especially along the Wasatch Front, prove that eating out is a major Utahn pastime.

In Salt Lake City, for example, it's possible to find a sampling of many different ethnic specialties as well as traditional American meat-and-potato fare. The area around the Salt Palace convention center and the Delta Center is fast becoming *restaurant* center, with many fine establishments setting up in renovated historic buildings. There are many excellent restaurants in Trolley Square.

One can also find a surprising number of good restaurants in places like Ogden, Provo, Cedar City, Moab, St. George, and Brigham City. Eating in smaller Utah towns can be an adventure. Often, restaurants are operated by colorful characters who not only serve a fine meal but can tell you about local history and attractions. When in doubt, order the chicken-fried steak at a cafe or diner in rural Utah. You won't be disappointed. Meanwhile, in Navajo country in southeastern Utah, pick up a Navajo taco instead of a hamburger. Small town drive-ins (not franchises) often mix up a fine milkshake or malt—especially when local fruit is ripening. For example, drive-ins around Bear Lake serve great raspberry malts and sundaes in late summer. Try some fresh peach pie in the Willard area in the fall.

# ■ UTAH'S LIQUOR LAWS

Outsiders view Utah's liquor laws as a bit difficult to figure out. They have, however, been liberalized in recent years, so most visitors will find it relatively easy to purchase an alcoholic beverage. The state owns liquor stores in convenient locations throughout the state. The stores are open every day of the week except Sundays and holidays, with varying hours. Beer (which is 3.2-percent alcohol) is available in most grocery stores. There are also a number of microbreweries in Salt Lake, Park City and Moab. Most fine restaurants and fine hotels in Utah have liquor licenses. Patrons may purchase mixed drinks, wine, and beer—with a meal after noon—in restaurants with these licenses. If in doubt, ask your server about the availability of wine and liquor.

For a nominal fee, visitors can purchase a membership to a private club where liquor is sold by the drink. Many of these clubs can be found inside the larger hotels, some of which offer free club memberships as a courtesy to guests. Alcoholic beverages are sold in private clubs throughout the day. Lounges and taverns sell only 3.2 beer; they do not offer wine or mixed drinks, nor can patrons bring their own liquor or wine into these establishments.

## ■ FOOD & LODGING

Complete listings of lodging and restaurants for all of Utah's cities can be obtained from the Utah Travel Planner *(see page 331)* or from individual travel councils. Those listed on the following pages are our personal favorites. The map shows towns with hotel and/or restaurant listings in this book.

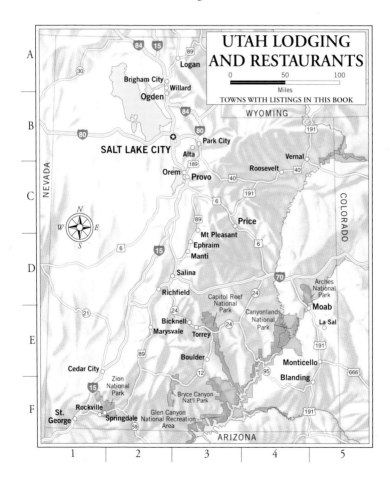

UTAH LODGING AND RESTAURANTS

0    50    100
Miles

TOWNS WITH LISTINGS IN THIS BOOK

## *Room Rates*
per room, per night, double occupancy:
$ = under $50; $$ = $50-75; $$$ = $75-125; $$$$ = over $125

## *Restaurant Prices*
per person, excluding tax, tip, and drinks:
$ = under $10; $$ = $10–15; $$$ = $15–30; $$$$ = over $30

### Alta
*map page 305, B-3*

🍴 **Alta Lodge.** Little Cottonwood Canyon; 800-707-ALTA  $$$-$$$$
A rustic but elegant throwback to traditional European ski lodges. Though wonderful during ski season, try staying here in July when rates are lower, the pace is quiet, and the canyon wildflowers are blooming.

*ALTA LODGE*

🍴 **Cliff Lodge at Snowbird Resort.** Little Cottonwood Canyon; 800-453-3000/ Salt Lake: 801-521-6040/Alta: 801-742-2222  $$$$
In addition to world-class skiing at Snowbird, there is a splendid spa at the top of the lodge, a climbing wall, fine restaurants, and Rocky Mountain splendor a short distance from downtown Salt Lake City. A varied calendar of performances and countless activities keep guests busy all year long.

### Blanding
*map page 305, E/F-4/5*

🍴 **Grayson Bed & Breakfast.** 118 E. 300 South; 435-678-2388 or 800-365-0868  $$
Private baths and lovely antiques in each of seven guest rooms, some with kitchenettes. Quiet. Full country breakfast; pancakes, etc.

*GRAYSON BED & BREAKFAST*

🍴 **Rogers House B&B.** 412 S. Main St.; 435-678-3932 or 800-355-3932  $- $ $
Five rooms in Western decor. Private baths and generous breakfasts.

## Boulder
*map page 305, E-3*

⊞ **Boulder Mountain Lodge.**
Corner of UT 12 and Burr Trail;
435-335-7460 $$-$$$$
Built in a newer Southwestern style, with
pine beams, sandstone bricks, stucco, and
weathered metal roof. Rooms have balconies
and picture windows overlooking wetlands.

*BOULDER MOUNTAIN LODGE*

✕ **Hell's Backbone Restaurant.** Corner of
UT 12 and Burr Trail; 435-335-7464
As if a wall of windows showing off the
spectacular scenery weren't enough, this
restaurant, in the Boulder Mountain Lodge
complex, serves up the best of regional fare
featuring organic ingredients.

## Brigham City
*map page 305 A-2/3*

⊞ **Howard Johnson Inn.** 1167 S. Main
St.; 435-723-8511 $$
Modern rooms; hot tub and swimming pool.
Close but not too close to I-15.

✕ **Maddox Ranch House.** 1900 South,
US 89, Perry; 435-723-8545 $$$
A northern Utah classic. The beefsteaks,
chicken steaks, and especially the turkey steaks
are prepared in a traditional American style.
We'll bet that few places in the country serve
better basic meat and potatoes.

✕ **Idle Isle.** 24 S. Main; 435-734-2468 $
In business since 1921. The decor of the soda
fountain, candy store, and restaurant has
changed little. A good place to order turkey
steak or pot roast.

## Bryce Canyon
## Nat'l Park *map page 305, F-2/3*

⊞ **Best Western Ruby's Inn.** 1 mi. north
of the park entrance; 435-834-5341 or
800-468-8660 $$$
Operated by the Syrett family for several
generations, this sprawling facility is one of
the largest full-service hotels in southern
Utah. It features ski touring and snowmobiling in the winter, helicopter rides and
rodeos in the summer; hot tubs, a swimming
pool, general store, gift shop, and restaurant.
Nothing fancy, but the hospitality and variety
of things to do make it the area's best.

⊞ **Bryce Canyon Lodge.** Inside the park;
303-297-2757 or 435-834-5361 $$$ -
$$$$
Built for the Union Pacific Railroad in the
1920s and since refurbished, this lodge
nonetheless retains its old charm. Open mid-
April through October.

FOOD & LODGING

## Bryce Canyon Nat'l Park *continued*

▭ **Bryce Canyon Pines.**
UT 12, 6 mi. west of the park turnoff; 435-834-5441 or 800-892-7923  **$$**
Modern rooms with beautiful views in a relatively secluded setting. The restaurant and swimming pool are open from spring through fall.

✕ **Bryce Canyon Lodge Restaurant.**
Inside the park; 435-834-5361  **$$**
Some of the best dining in the area. Specialties include trout and prime rib. Breakfast and lunch are also served and box lunches can be arranged by calling 12 hours ahead.

## Capitol Reef Nat'l Park *map page 305, E-3*

▭ **Best Western Capitol Reef Resort.**
UT 24, near park entrance; 435-425-3761 or 888-610-9400  **$$$**
One of the area's newer facilities. A pool is open in the summer.

▭ **Days Inn.** 675 E. UT 24, Torrey; 435-425-3111 or 800-329-7466  **$-$$$**
The complimentary breakfast and indoor pool and hot tub that are included in the price make this one of the more desirable off-season locations near Capitol Reef National Park.

▭ **Skyridge.** P.O. Box 750220, at Hwys. 12 and 24 in Torrey; 435-425-3222  **$$$-$$$$**
All rooms have views of the canyon country outside Capitol Reef National Park. Several have private decks, some hot tubs. Evening hors d'oeuvres and breakfast are included.

✕ **Cafe Diablo.** 599 W. Main St., Torrey; 435-425-3070  **$$-$$$**
Colorfully presented, Santa Fe-style gourmet fare, using fresh herbs grown in the flower garden just outside the restaurant.

✕ **Capitol Reef Inn & Cafe.** 360 W. Main St., Torrey; 435-425-3271  **$ - $$**
Healthy food dominates the menu here. Fresh vegetables and bread, several vegetarian entrees, and juices made on the premises. Good espresso.

✕ **Sunglow Cafe.** Bicknell, about 10 mi. west of the park on UT 24; 435-425-3701 **$**
This tiny roadside cafe is known for its unusual pie selection. How does pickle, pinto bean, or oatmeal sound?

## Cedar City *map page 305, E-1/2*

▭ **Abbey Inn.** 940 W. 200 North; 435-586-9966 or 800-325-5411  **$$$**
One of southern Utah's modern hotels. The indoor swimming pool and hot tub make it a year-round favorite.

▭ **Best Western Town & Country Inn.** 200 N. Main; 435-586-9900 or 800-493-4089  **$$-$$$$**
One of the larger and more centrally located motels in Cedar City, this inn features a popular gift shop inside an old train station.

▭ **Cedar City Holiday Inn.** 1575 W. 200 North; 435-586-8888 or 800-432-8828  **$$**
A fairly typical Holiday Inn, but this one has an exercise room, an outdoor pool, and indoor hot tub. Close to I-15.

T **Paxman Summer House B&B.** 170 N. 400 West; 435-586-3755 $$-$$$
This 1900s Victorian home with period decor stands within walking distance of the Utah Shakespearean Festival venues.

X **Milt's Stage Stop.** Cedar Canyon, 5 mi. east of Cedar City in Cedar Canyon; 435-586-9344 $$-$$$
A charming steak and seafood house in a quiet canyon setting. Steaks and prime rib here are among Utah's best.

X **Pizza Factory.** 124 S. Main St.; 435-586-3900
Good pizza, salads, sandwiches, and pasta. An excellent place to take the family. $

X **Sullivan's Cafe.** 301 S. Main St.; 435-586-6761 $-$$
Typical small-town southern Utah restaurant. Try the prime rib sandwich, potato bar, and the huge salad bar.

### Ephraim
*map page 305, D-3*

*EPHRAIM HOMESTEAD B & B*

T **Ephraim Homestead Bed & Breakfast** 135 West 100 North 43-2; 435-283-6367 $$-$$$

Visitors who want to feel as though they are staying in a museum or simply turning back the clock can spend the night in either a refinished 1860s log cabin granary or a barn made from old materials and decorated with antiques. Ask to tour the proprietor's house, a Victorian gothic showpiece.

### Flaming Gorge Nat'l Rec. Area   *map page 305, B-4*

T **Flaming Gorge Lodge** US 191, Dutch John; 435-889-3773 $$-$$$
The only lodging in the area is also the jumping off point for river trips and fishing expeditions. The rustic setting has hiking trails, and there's a good restaurant right in the lodge. *fglodge.com.*

### La Sal
*map page 305, E-5*

T **La Sal Mountain Guest Ranch.** Hwy 46; 435-686-2223 or 888-870-1088 $-$$$
This bed-and-breakfast is located south of Moab on what is still an active cattle ranch. Restored log cabins and ranch houses dating to the 1890s make this unspoiled treasure ideal for family reunions or folks looking for an off-the-beaten-track experience.

T **Mt. Peale Country Inn.** Hwy. 46, milepost 14, Box 366, Old La Sal; 435-686-2284 or 888-687-3253 $$-$$$
Wonderful food, outdoor hot tub, and large stone fireplace add to the charm of this inn at the foot of Mt. Peale. A perfect base for for exploring the mountain on bicycles in the summer and fall, and cross-country skis or snowshoes in the winter.

## Logan
*map page 305, A-3*

☂ **Anniversary Inn.** 169 E. Center St.; 435-752-3443 or 800-324-4152 **$$$$**
This B&B comprises a mansion (built over a century ago by Logan's first doctor) as well as four other houses. Theme rooms from the inexpensive to the very expensive include a honeymoon suite with a heart-shaped hot tub and an "Arabian Nights Suite."

☂ **Comfort Inn.** 447 N. Main St.; 435-752-9141 or 800-228-5150  **$$**
Nice indoor pool and hot tub; overall, a good family hotel.

☂ **University Inn.** Utah State University Campus; 435-797-0016  **$$**
Used primarily by university conference attendees, but open to the public. Basic motel rooms, but with a college atmosphere.

✗ **Bluebird Restaurant.** 19 N. Main; 435-752-3155  **$-$$**
The "Main Street" address fits the wooden booths, 1920s decor, and steak dinners you'll find at this cafe. A chocolate factory adds to the classic American ambience.

✗ **Gia's.** 119 S. Main; 435-752-8384  **$-$$**
Fine service and a high-quality Italian menu. For a less expensive dining experience, head to the basement "Factory" for an Italian sandwich or pizza.

✗ **Grapevine.** 129 N. 100 East; 435-752-1977  **$$$**
Elegant dining in a lovely old home. Choose from an eclectic menu of game, seafood, and beef dishes prepared in a range of international styles.

## Manti
*map page 305, D-3*

☂ **Legacy Inn Bed & Breakfast.** 337 N. 100 E.; 435-835-8352  **$$$**
A newer house designed in Victorian style. A half block from the Mormon Temple.

☂ **Manti House Inn.** 401 N. Main St.; 435-835-0161  **$$-$$$**
First built in 1880 by the Manti Mormon Temple builders. There's a wedding suite with balcony, an in-house spa, ice cream parlor, and free summer evening concerts on the gazebo.*mantihouse.com.*

☂ **Yardley Bed & Breakfast Inn.** 190 S. 200 West; 435-835-1863 or 800-858-6634 **$$-$$$**
Like an old English country inn. Two bedrooms have fireplaces. Indulge in a candlelight dinner in the honeymoon suite, which also has its own jacuzzi and private balcony.

## Marysvale
*map page 305, E-2*

☂ **Big Rock Candy Mountain.** 7 miles from Marysvale on UT 89; 435-326-2000 or 888-560-7625  **$-$$**
Newly refurbished cabins on a grassy clearing next to a river and across from a hiking area. Nice restaurant. River running and ATV rides.

☂ **Moore's Old Pine Inn Bed & Breakfast.** 60 South State, P.O. Box 70; 435-326-4565 or 800-887-4565  **$$-$$$**
An old hotel with a colorful history, lovingly recreated by its owners. Five rooms have private bath. Guests in the other four can

luxuriate in the large claw foot tub down the hall. *marysvale.org\pine-inn.html*

*MOORE'S OLD PINE INN B&B*

## Moab
*map page 305, D/E-4/5*

☗ **Best Western Canyonlands Inn.** 16 S. Main St.; 435-259-2300 or 800-WESTERN **$$$**
One of the newer and certainly among the nicest of the many typical franchise-type motels found in southeastern Utah.

*CASTLE VALLEY INN*

☗ **Castle Valley Inn.** Castle Valley/Moab, off Hwy. 128; 435-259-6012 **$$$-$$$$**
One of the state's quietest bed-and-breakfasts.

An orchard, small cottages with kitchenettes, and a hot tub with views of Castle Valley's sandstone spires, Fisher Towers, add up to a serene experience. *castlevalleyinn.com*

☗ **Lazy Lizard International Hostel.** 1213 S. US 191; 435-259-6057 **$**
A dorm-type hostel with a hot tub. With the most expensive stay about $25 a person, this is the best choice for young travelers on a budget. *gj.net\~lazylzrd\*

☗ **Moab Valley Inn.** 711 S. Main St.; 435-259-4419 or 800-831-6622 **$$$**
This spot offers a few more amenities than most motels: Visitors can enjoy the hot tub, partially enclosed swimming pool, and private park with picnic tables and barbecue grills.

☗ **Pack Creek Ranch.** 15 miles SE of Moab; 435-259-5505 **$$$-$$$$**
A traditional dude ranch offering individual homes and cabins full of interesting decor and books. The food in the dining room is terrific and the views of the nearby La Sal Mountains memorable. Rate includes three meals a day. One of southern Utah's few first-class lodgings. *packcreekranch.com*

*PACK CREEK RANCH*

FOOD & LODGING

## Moab *(continued)*

🛏 **Sunflower Hill Bed & Breakfast.**
185 N. 300 East; 435-259-2974   $$$$
Each elegantly furnished room in this old house offers visitors a private bath, color television, and different decor. Homemade pastries. *sunflowerhill.com*

✕ **Buck's Grill House.** 1393 N. US 191;
435-259-5201  $$
Looks like an old fort with original Western oil paintings on the walls. Chef Tim Buckingham serves a good selction of gourmet vegetarian dishes in addition to excellent chicken, steak, and wild game .

✕ **Center Cafe.** 92 E. Center St.;
435-259-4295  $$-$$$
The kind of dining experience not often found in a small town. With fresh fish, fine vegetarian dishes, gourmet pizzas, and espresso served in a simple but elegant atmosphere, this rates among Utah's finest restaurants.

✕ **Fat City Smoke House.** 36 S. 100
West; 435-259-4302  $
Texas-style barbecue and vegetarian dishes that are both delicious and inexpensive.

✕ **Pack Creek Ranch.** 435-259-5505  $$$
You don't need to stay at the ranch *(see above)* to enjoy an elegant dinner in a quiet mountain setting. Entrees include American specialties from quail to barbecue to seafood.

✕ **Slickrock Cafe.** 5 N. Main St.; 435-259-8004  $-$$$
With an eclectic mix of pastas and Mexican food, this restaurant is in the middle of Moab. The historic sandstone building houses one of the best eateries in town.

✕ **Sunset Grill.** 900 N. US 191; 435-259-7146  $$$
Built by a colorful old uranium miner, the converted mansion affords views of the red rock country and Colorado Plateau. Menu of standard steak, fish, and pasta dishes.

## Monticello
*map page 305, E-5*

🛏 **The Grist Mill Inn.** 64 S. 300 East;
435-587-2597 or 800-645-3762
$ $-$$$
Built as a flour mill in 1933, this building now houses a unique B&B. The original mill equipment has been restored and left in place, but the six rooms are modern. Hot tub.

## Mt. Pleasant
*map page 305, C-3*

🛏 **Larsen House Bed & Breakfast Inn.**
298 S. State St.; 435-462-9337
$$-$$$$
Built in the 1890s, this pleasant B&B features stained glass windows and a scrolled oak staircase.

*LARSEN HOUSE BED & BREAKFAST INN*

## Ogden
*map page 305, B-2/3*

☉ **Historic Ben Lomond Suite Hotel.**
2510 Washington Blvd.;
801-627-1900 $$$$
A large downtown property close to major restaurants and museums.

☉ **Ogden Marriott.** 247 24th St.;
801-627-1190 or 800-421-7599 $$$
Downtown's major conference hotel, near Union Station. Kids love the indoor pool and hot tub.

✗ **Bistro 258.** 258 Historic 25th St.;
801-394-1595 $$$
Fine dining on Ogden's historic 25th Street reminscent of a French bistro. Outdoor seating in the back.

✗ **Roosters.** 253 Historic 25th St.; 801-627-6171 $-$$$
This microbrewery across the street from the bistro, is the gathering place for Ogdenites. It features special brews and an extensive menu ranging from sandwiches to pizzas to an ectlectic mix of fresh nouveau cuicine entrees.

✗ **Union Grill.** 2501 Wall Ave.;
801-621-2830 $-$-$$$
In historic Union Station, run by owners of Roosters. Try their exotic pastas and fresh fish specials.

✗ **Temari.** 350 Washington Blvd.;
801-399-9536 $-$$$
The Japanese owners do all the cooking themselves. Take your time and enyoy their authentic Japanese dishes. Closed Mondays.

## Orem
*map page 305, C-3*

✗ **Los Hermanos.** 395 N. State;
801-785-1715 $
Traditional Mexican fare in a pioneer house in nearby Lindon.

✗ **Restaurant Roy.** 2005 S. State;
801-235-9111 $$-$$$
From its setting in the foothills, this old-world style restaurant gives diners a view of Utah Lake. The upscale fare features pasta dishes, fresh seafood, and steaks.

## Park City
*map page 305, B-3*

☉ **Best Western Landmark Inn.**
6560 N. Landmark Dr.; 435-649-7300 or 800-548-8824 $$$-$$$$
Just off I-80, near all the factory outlet stores. Nice indoor pool, recreation area, and lower rates make this a good stopover for families.

☉ **Goldener Hirsch Inn.**
7570 Royal St. East; 435-649-7770 or 800-252-3373 $$$-$$$$
Located in exclusive Deer Valley and one of Utah's most elegant—and expensive— lodges. Few amenities have been spared at this Austrian-style inn. Hot tubs, saunas, views, and a wonderful restaurant *(see page 315)*.

☉ **The Old Miners' Lodge.**
615 Woodside; 435-645-8068 or 800-648-8068 $$$-$$$$
Built in 1889 and located in Park City's Historic District, this lodge offers a hot tub and complimentary drinks in the evening. A fun ski vacation spot *(see picture next page)*.

## Park City *(continued)*

*THE OLD MINER'S LODGE*

⊤ **Stein Eriksen Lodge.** 7700 Stein Way; 435-649-3700 or 800-453-1302  **$$$$**
Among the best "ski town" lodges in the country, this Deer Valley hostelry spoils its guests with kitchens, pools. Excellent restaurant *(see* Glitretind *below). steinlodge.com*

*STEIN ERIKSEN LODGE*

⊤ **Treasure Mountain Inn.** 255 Main St.; 435-649-7334 or 800-344-2460  **$$-$$$$**
One of the few places to stay on historic Main Street, with its many turn-of-the-century buildings, charming shops, and restaurants. Close to the top, where the Town Lift whisks skiers to the Park City ski area.

✗ **Adolf's.** 1500 Kearns Blvd.; 435-649-7177 **$$$-$$$$**
A Park City institution where diners can choose among veal, spinach pasta, venison, steak, and roast lamb.

✗ **Alex's Bistro.** 442 Main St.; 435-649-5252  **$$$-$$$$**
Exquisite food cooked in the classic French style.

✗ **The Eating Establishment.** 317 Main St.; 435-649-8284  **$-$$**
A less expensive but not necessarily lower quality dining experience near the top of Main Street. Delightful patio in the summer. Food ranges from full dinners to pasta, burgers, sandwiches, and salads. Try the mud pie.

✗ **Glitretind.** Stein Eriksen Lodge, 7700 Stein Way; 435-649-3700 or 800-453-1302  **$$$-$$$$**
Austrian country decor, with exposed beams and stone fireplaces. European cuisine: wonderful seafood, and homemade breads and pastries. *steinlodge.com*

✕ **Goldener Hirsch Inn.** 7570 Royal St.; East; 435-649-7770 or 800-252-3373 $$$-$$$$
Come to this Alpine retreat for a special occasion dinner: entrees include delights such as venison, caribou, and sea bass.

✕ **Grub Steak at Prospector Square.** 2200 Sidewinder Dr.; 435-649-8060 $$
A Park City tradition: famous for its steaks, ribs, and prime rib.

✕ **Main Street Pizza and Noodle.** 530 Main St.; 435-645-8878 $
Sandwiches, pizzas, calzone, and stir fries. One of the city's best family restaurants.

### Price
*map page 305, C-3/4*

▥ **Holiday Inn and Suites.** 8388 Westwood Blvd.; 435-637-8880 or 800-HOLIDAY $$-$$$$
Indoor pool and restaurant .

▥ **Greenwell Inn.** 655 E. Main St.; 435-637-3520 or 800-666-3520 $
A full-service inn with 125 newly-remodeled rooms, a convention center, tropical indoor pool and spa, exercise facilities, free continental breakfast, and a good Mexican family-run restaurant *(see Ricardo's below)* .

✕ **China City Cafe.** 350 E. Main St.; 435-637-8211 $-$$
Huge portions of reasonably priced Chinese and American dishes. Cantonese-style chow mein is excellent; the prime rib's good too.

✕ **Cowboy's Kitchen.** 31 E. Main St., Wellington; 435-637-4223 $$
For a touch of cowboy, drive into Wellington and stop at the Cowboy's Kitchen. A poem by a local, and one of Butch Cassidy's gang, Matt Warner, graces the back of the menu. Lamb specialities harken back to the days of sheep and cattle ranching. Country western bands and dancing weekend nights.

✕ **Pinnacle Brewing Company Grogg .** 1653 Carbonville Rd., Helper;; 435-637-2924 $
A local microbrewery that features generous portions of pizza, burgers, and gourmet sandwiches.

✕ **Ricardo's.** 655 E. Main St.; 435-637-2020 $-$$
Solid Mexican and American dishes; open breakfast, lunch, and dinner.

### Provo
*map page 305, C-3*

▥ **Hotel Roberts.** 192 S. University Ave.; 801-373-3400 $
Interesting old hotel with low rates.

▥ **Provo Marriott** 101 W. 100 North, 801-377-4700 or 800-777-7144 $$-$$$$
The city's best full-service hotel, complete with conference facility, pool, and hot tub. Located downtown, this relatively new hotel is a convenient place to stay.

✕ **Bombay House.** 463 N. University Ave.; 801-373-6677 $$
Brigham Young University's emphasis on foreign countries because of its missionary program has developed an affinity for foreign food. This Indian restaurant is an example.

## Provo *(continued)*

✕ **Brick Oven.** 111 E. 800 North; 801-374-8800 $

Adjacent to the BYU campus, this cafe is a popular place for students to pick up pasta, pizza, and sandwiches.

✕ **Magleby's.** 1675 N. 200 W.; 801-374-6249 $$-$$$

This is a popular gathering place for parents of BYU students. Try the pies.

✕ **Sundance Tree Room.** Provo Canyon; 801-225-4107 $$$-$$$$

Located at Robert Redford's ski resort, and a bit of a drive from downtown: take US 189 north, then UT 92 for 2.5 miles. The atmosphere here is sophisticated, and the food consistently good. The Sunday brunch tops all the competition.

## Roosevelt
*map page 305, C-4*

✕ **Frontier Grill.** 75 South 200 East; 435-722-3669 $-$$

Family-style restaurant with traditional American food; breakfast, lunch, and dinner.

## Salina
*map page 305, D-3*

✕ **Mom's Cafe.** Corner of State and Main; 435-529-3921 $-$$

A central Utah classic. Located at the main crossroads in town, Mom's serves pies and meat and potatoes just like Mom used to fix. Large portions and reasonable prices.

## St. George
*map page 305, F-1*

☷ **Best Western Abbey Inn.** 1129 S. Bluff St.; 435-652-1234 or 888-222-3946 $$$

Next to the St. George Convention Center. Complimentary full breakfast.

☷ **Greene Gate Village Bed & Breakfast.** 76 West Tabernacle St.; 435-628-6999 or 800-350-6999 $$$

Nine restored pioneer homes with modern conveniences are the bed and breakfast part of the complex in the historic part of St. George. Any visitor can make reservations at the Bentley House for a five-course, excellently prepared dinner. Swimming pool and hot tub, too. greenegate.com

☷ **An Olde Penny Farthing Inn.** 278 N. 100 West; 435-673-7755 or 800-943-2920 $$-$$$

Built in the 1860s and fully restored. Rooms have an English decor; there's a Jacuzzi for honeymooners in the Bridal Suite.

☷ **Ranch Inn.** 1040 S. Main; 435-628-8000 or 800-332-0400 $-$$$

A clean, reasonable alternative to the more expensive hotels in town. There's a heated pool and jacuzzi, and some rooms have microwaves and refrigerators.

☷ **Seven Wives Inn.** 217 N. 100 W.; 435-628-3737 or 800-600-3737 $$$

The inn's twelve rooms are each named after a wife of polygamist neighbor Benjamin F. Johnson, an ancestor of the innkeeper. Each room is decorated with antiques, including a jacuzzi in an old car. *sevenwivesinn.com*

✕ **Scaldoni's.** 929 W. Sunset Blvd.; 435-674-1300 **$$**
The great food makes up for this Italian Grocer and Grill's location in a strip mall. Try the cranberry and gorgonzola salad.

## Salt Lake City
*map page 305, B-2/3*

**Anniversary Inn at Kahn Mansion.**
*Two locations:* 460 South 1000 East St.; 678 E. South Temple;
*dial* 801-363-4900 or 800-324-4152 *for either location* **$$$$**
Probably the most elegant place to stay in the Salt Lake area. Built in the 1890s, the Victorian mansion has been remodeled into 13 theme suites, each of which has large-screen television and VCR, Jacuzzi, and triple-sheeted beds.

**Brigham Street Inn.** 1135 E. South Temple; 801-364-4461 or 800-417-4461 **$$$$**
A different designer remodeled each of the nine guest rooms as a benefit for the Utah Heritage Foundation. Fireplaces, cross-country ski trails.
*brighamstreetinn.citysearch.com*

**Hilton.** 255 S. West Temple; 801-328-2000 or 800-HILTONS **$$$-$$$$**
With 499 rooms, this is one of the larger full-service hotels in Salt Lake City. Its location is convenient to the Salt Palace Convention Center and the city's restaurant and brewpub district.

**The Inn at Temple Square.** 71 W. South Temple; 801-531-1000 or 800-843-4668 **$$$-$$$$**
The answer for those craving quiet elegance but tired of upscale chain hotels. Close to Temple Square and Symphony Hall; pool and health club privileges. 100% non-smoking.

**Marriott Hotel.** 75 S. West Temple; 801-531-0800 **$$$-$$$$**
Outstanding among Utah's full-service facilities. Located across the street from the Salt Palace and adjacent to Temple Square, this 500-room hotel features balconies, indoor/outdoor pool, exercise room, and large suites.

**Saltair Bed & Breakfast.** 164 South 900 East; 801-533-8184 or 800-733-8184 **$$**
Utah's oldest continuously operated bed-and-breakfast. Guests sleep in antique brass or oak beds, and there's a hot tub on the redwood deck. Full breakfast.

*SALTAIR BED & BREAKFAST*

## Salt Lake City
### (continued)

🛏 **Wyndam Hotel.** 215 West. South Temple; 801-531-7500 or 800-553-0075  $$$-$$$$
New among the city's hotels, and very convenient to the Salt Palace convention center and the Delta Center. Swimming pool; good restaurant.

✕ **The Absolute Restaurant and Brasserie.** 52 West 200 South; 801-359-0899  $$$
Close to the Capitol Theatre, this elegant restaurant features small but exquisite portions. The glassed-in portion of the restaurant along 200 and the great food makes it feel and taste like Paris.

✕ **Baba Afghan.** 55 East 400 South; 801-596-0786  $-$$
Though some meat is served, this is a good place for vegetarians. One of the city's best luncheon buffets and some fine Afghan curry dishes.

✕ **Baci's Trattoria.** 134 W. Pierpont Ave.; 801-328-1500  $$ - $$$$
Gourmet Italian cuisine, outstanding antipasti. Lively atmosphere; sit indoors in the pleasant dining room, or out on the patio.

✕ **Cafe Trang.** 818 S. Main St.; 801-539-1638  $-$$
A large menu lists some of Utah's best Vietnamese food. Chinese dishes are available as well.

✕ **The Cinegrill.** 344 S. 300 East; 801-328-4900  $-$$
Famous for its salad, a delightful creation heavy on garlic. Good, inexpensive Italian.

✕ **Five-Alls.** 1458 S. Foothill Dr.; 801-582-1400  $$$
A quiet atmosphere, consistently good service, and sophisticated cuisine. Filet Oscar is a filet mignon with asparagus tips, crabmeat, and bearnaise sauce.

✕ **Incantation.** 159 S. Main; 801-533-2722  $-$$
Authentic Peruvian food at modest prices.

✕ **La Caille at Quail Run.** 9565 S. Wasatch Blvd.; 801-942-1751  $$$$
This might be Utah's most elegant and expensive dining experience. Lush gardens, a flowing creek. and wonderful service make this the place to visit for a special event.

✕ **Lamb's Restaurant.** 169 S. Main St.; 801-364-7166  $-$$-$$$
The city's oldest restaurant, where the town's movers and shakers often meet for lunch. Try the Greek bread for a real treat.

✕ **Log Haven.** E. Millcreek Canyon; 801-272-8255  $$$-$$$$
Enjoy the beautiful canyon setting from a table indoors or on the patio. Some of the best fusion cuisine in Salt Lake.

✕ **Martine.** 22 East 100 South; 801-363-9328  $$-$$$$
Spanish tapas (appetizers) are offered at dinner. The food served at lunch or dinner is a work of art, as well as delicious.

✗ **The Metropolitan.** 173 W. Broadway; 801-364-3472 $$$$
Modern decor with small, elegant portions.

✗ **Oceans Restaurant and Oyster Cafe.** 4760 South 900 East; 801-261-0115 $$-$$$
Ranks among the area's best seafood restaurants, with fresh fish flown in daily from the Atlantic, Pacific, and the Gulf Coast. The Oyster Cafe offers lighter and less expensive dishes. On Big Cottonwood Creek.

✗ **Red Iguana.** 736 W. North Temple; 801-322-1489 $ - $$
Not much on atmosphere, but features Utah's best Mexican food. Instead of ordering traditional Mexican fare like tacos and enchiladas (which *are* good here), be adventurous and savor a molé dish.

✗ **Rodizio Grill.** 600S. 700 East, 2nd Fl.; 801-220-0500 $$
Waiters dressed as Argentine gauchos bring skewers of various grilled meats, chicken, vegetables, and sausage. The full meal includes a salad bar with the staples and some great specialities. Bring a big appetite!.

✗ **The Roof Restaurant.** 15 E. South Temple; 801-539-1911 $$$-$$$$
At the top of what was once the elegant Hotel Utah, but today is an office building for the Mormon Church, the Roof boasts a gourmet dinner buffet with imported cheeses, fresh fruit, and seafood. Nice views of Temple Square, too.

✗ **Ruth's Diner.** 2100 Emigration Canyon; 801-582-5807 $$
Though lunch and dinner are also served here, this is a favorite Salt Lake gathering place for breakast. Dining outside in the spring, summer, and fall is delightful.

✗ **Wagonmaster Steak House.** 5485 S. Vine, Murray (south of town); 801-269-1100 $$-$$$
Sit in a covered wagon and eat expertly prepared cowboy-style steak and chicken. Watch for the occasional gunfight.

## Vernal
*map page 305, B-4/5*

▦ **Antlers Best Western.** 423 W. Main St.; 435-789-1202 $$$
Modern hotel with indoor hot tub, exercise room, playground, and pool.

✗ **Casa Rios.** 2015 W. US 40; 435-789-0103 $
South-of-the-border cooking for lunch and dinner. Try the chicken fajitas.

✗ **Curry Manor.** 189 S. Vernal Ave.; 435-789-2289 $$-$$$
An old Victorian home restored for dining. Antique elegance and excellent food is a treat in this part of the world.

FOOD & LODGING

## Zion National Park
*map page 305, F-1 & 2*

Flanigan's Inn. 428 Zion Park Blvd., Springdale; 435-772-3244 or 800-765-7787 $$$
A step above the franchise motels and restaurants in the area. Both modern and older units, a nice pool area, and a very good restaurant *(see below)*. *flanigans.com*

Harvest House Bed & Breakfast. 29 Canyon View Dr., Springdale; 435-772-3880 $$$
Just off the main drive through town is this classic, two-story Western ranch house. Request the rooms with private decks that sit beneath the Watchman Formation at nearby Zion National Park. *harvesthouse.net*

O'Toole's Under the Eaves Guest House. 980 Zion Park Blvd., Springdale; 435-772-3457 $$-$$$
Beautiful views of Zion National Park with a garden Jacuzzi. *otooles.com*

Zion Lodge. Zion National Park; 303-297-2757 $-$$$$
The only lodging in the park, this historic lodge is open year-round. The old cabins, with individual fireplaces, are popular, as are the more modern motel suites, so make reservations well in advance.

✕ Flanigan's Inn. 428 Zion Park Blvd., Springdale; 435-772-3234 or 800-765-7787 $$-$$$
Southwestern-style cuisine, especially variations on salmon and pasta. Open for breakfast, lunch, and dinner. *flanigans.com*

✕ Bit and Spur Saloon and Mexican Restaurant. 1212 Zion Park Blvd., Springdale; 435-772-3498 $$
Interesting Mexican dishes make this restaurant rank among the best south-of-the-border-style spots in the state. Music some weekends.

✕ Switchback Grill. 1149 Zion Park Blvd., Springdale; 435-772-3777 $$
Large picture windows overlooking Zion National Park. Indian rugs add to the Southwestern decor. The wonderful menu features the freshest ingredients in its list of thoughtfully prepared vegetarian dishes, pizzas (fired in a wood-burning oven), and specialty fruit juice drinks.

✕ Zion Lodge. Zion National Park; 435-722-3213 $$-$$$
Historic lodge offering traditional fare such as trout and ribeye, as well as good pastas. Great views of the park. Picnics can be ordered in advance.

✕ Zion Pizza and Noodle Company. 868 Zion Park Blvd., Springdale; 435-772-3815 $
In an old church. It's strictly serve-yourself, but the pizza and pasta are the best in the area.

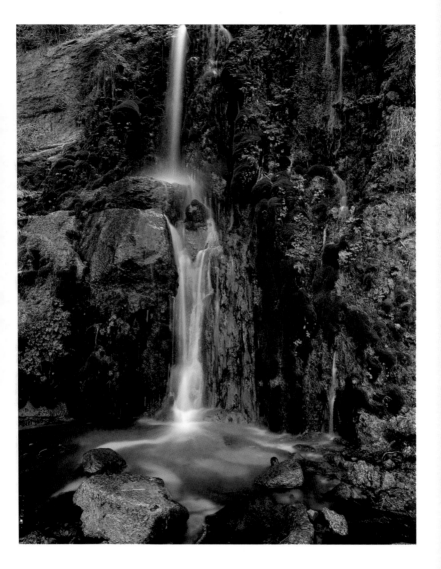

*A spring and grotto in Zion National Park.*

# ■ FESTIVALS & EVENTS

## January

**Park City: Sundance Film Festival.** Premiers the works of independent filmmakers in Park City and at Sundance. 435-328-FILM

## April

**Ogden: Fort Buenaventura State Park. Mountain Man Rendezvous.** 801-621-4808

**Utah County: National Art Exhibit at the Springville Museum of Art.** One-month-long show of major contemporary artists. 801-489-2727

## May

**Brigham City: Bear River Bird Festival.** Held at the Bear River Migratory Bird Refuge. *rb.fws.gov/bearriver*, 435-723-5887 ext. 18.

**Ephraim: Scandinavian Festival.** Food, crafts, dancing. 435-283-4231

**Salt Lake City: Living Traditions Festival.** Celebration of folk and ethnic arts, food, music, and dancing. 801-596-5000

**Springdale: Summer Concert Series.** Symphonies, jazz, ethnic dancing. O. C. Tanner Amphitheater, just outside entrance to Zion National Park. Mid-May to early September. 435-652-7994

## June

**Cedar City: Utah Shakespearean Festival.** Held at Southern Utah State University campus. June to September. 800-752-9849

**American Fork: Pageant of the Arts.** Actors portray famous paintings. 435-756-5110

**Cedar City: Utah Summer Games.** 435-865-8421 or 800-439-1521

**Ft. Duchesne: Ute Pow Wow.** On the Uintah and Ouray Indian Reservation. 435-722-5141

**Logan: Summerfest Art Faire.** Jazz concerts on Tabernacle Square. Artisans, and street performers add to the lively atmosphere.

**Salt Lake City: Utah Arts Festival.** Outdoor performances and art exhibits. 801-322-2428

**Tooele: Arts Festival.** 435-882-8282

**Vernal: Outlaw Trail Festival.** Folk art festival, outdoor musicals, target rifle contest, and a July 4th Festival Day. Continues throughout summer. 435-782-6932 or 800-477-5558.

**Manti: Mormon Miracle Pageant.** Utah's biggest outdoor pageant: Morman history told in musical drama. 435-835-3000.

## July

**Logan: Great West Music Festival.** Classical music performances. 800-882-4433.

**Logan: Utah Festival of the American West.** Recreated Frontier Street and Native American village, craft demonstrations and fair, cowboy poetry, World Championship Dutch Oven Cook-off, Western-style entertainment. 435-797-1143

**Nephi: Ute Stampede.** Rodeo. 435-623-1735

**Ogden: Pioneer Days.** Street festival and rodeo. 801-629-8214

**Provo: America's Freedom Festival.** 385-370-8019.

**Salt Lake City: Days of '47 Festivities.** Month-long celebration honoring the 1847 arrival of the Mormon Pioneers in Salt Lake Valley. Rodeo, pops concert, Western heritage art show, and old-fashioned picnics. Also features one of the largest parades in the country. 801-250-3890

## August

**Bonneville Salt Flats: Speed Week.** Land speed racing. 801-583-2338.

**Garden City: Raspberry Days.** Enjoy Bear Lake's famous fruit; first weekend of August. 800-448-BEAR

**Park City: Arts Festival.** Art exhibits and entertainment on Historic Main Street. 435-649-8882.

**Park City: Bluegrass Festival.** At the Deer Valley Resort. 435-649-1000

**Promontory Point: Railroader's Festival.** Golden Spike National Historic Site. 435-471-2209

## September

**Brigham City: Peach Days.** 435-734-2634.

**Green River: Melon Days.** 435-564-3526

**Midway: Swiss Days.** Celebrates the Swiss heritage and customs of Heber Valley. 435-654-1576

**Ogden: Mountain Man Rendezvous.** Fort Buenaventura State Park. 801-621-4808

**Salt Lake City: Greek Festival.** 801-328-9681

**Salt Lake City: Utah State Fair.** Ten-day festival including rodeo. 801-538-FAIR

**Springdale: Southern Utah Folklife and Music Festival.** 435-772-3434

**Torrey: Capitol Reef Harvest Homecoming Days.** 435-425-3791

## October

**Moab: Canyonlands Fat Tire Festival.** Bicycle rides, events for all ages. 435-259-8825

**St. George: Southwest Symphony.** Concert season begins and continues through May. 435-673-0700 or 652-7994

**St. George: World Senior Games.** 435-674-0550 or 800-562-1268.

## November

**Park City: America's Opening.** Ski racing and exhibitions. 435-649-8111

**Salt Lake City: Festival of Trees.** 801-588-3684

**Salt Lake City: Temple Square Christmas Lighting.** 801-240-1000

## December

**Ogden: Hof Winter Carnival.** Ogden celebrates German traditions with its sister city Hof. 801-629-8242

# ■ UTAH'S PUBLIC LANDS

Utah almost literally belongs to the nation. Nearly 80 percent of its land is controlled by government agencies for public uses such as recreation, timber, and wildlife management, mineral leasing, and livestock grazing.

Before venturing into Utah's thousands of miles of backcountry roads and trails, check with the administering agency about fire restrictions and other regulations. Permits are required in some BLM primitive areas. Travel maps listing places open to off-highway vehicle use are available from local U.S. Forest Service and BLM offices. Backpackers going into National Park Service-administered lands are required to pick up a free permit from a ranger station or visitor center. Camping in most national forests, national parks, recreation areas, and BLM lands is on a first-come, first-served basis. Large group sites, however, can be reserved in advance.

## ◆ BOATING AND RIVER RAFTING

Although Utah is a dry state, it ranks sixth in the nation in surface acres of boatable waters. Power boats and sail craft must meet both Utah and Coast Guard regulations on reservoirs, lakes, and rivers. Some areas restrict the use of motors. For information, contact the Division of Parks and Recreation, the agency charged with managing boating in Utah. *parks.state.ut.us/, 801-538-7220.*

Utah is world-famous for its rafting opportunities. More than 25 outfitters are eager to show visitors the state's whitewater rapids and calm scenic waters. There are more than 400 miles of raftable rivers in the state. For more detailed information, contact the Utah Travel Council and request their free *Utah Travel Guide.* (See page 332.)

## ◆ WILDLIFE VIEWING

While Utahns can enjoy watching wildlife in most parts of the state, few places in the world offer the diversity of the marshes that surround the east side of the Great Salt Lake. The huge federal Bear River Migratory Bird Refuge west of Brigham City combined with state-managed refuges such as Farmington Bay, Ogden Bay, Salt Creek and Locomotive Springs hosts thousands of birds each year including swans, stilts, avocets, waterfowl, eagles, hawks, peregrine falcons and grebes. In the middle of the winter, for example, visitors to Willard Bay State Park can see dozens of bald eagles in the trees or working the water for fish. Add to this mix Antelope Island State Park with its herd of 800 bison coupled with large mule deer, antelope, coyote and bighorn sheep and it is easy to find large numbers of wildlife to view within an hour's drive of the Wasatch Front.

In Northern Utah, a popular winter activity for many is to visit the Hardware Ranch near Hyrum where the Division of Wildlife Resources feeds elk in the winter. Visitors take a sleigh pulled by Clydesdale horses into the midst of the elk.

The federal Fish Springs refuge on the Pony Express Trail in western Utah and the federal Ouray refuge in eastern Utah each offer excellent bird watching opportunities. The Beaver Dam Wash area in the extreme southwestern part of Utah, operated by Brigham Young University and the Nature Conservancy, provides a look at desert bird life, especially in the winter months. This is a zone where the Great Basin, Colorado Plateau and Mojave Desert meet, creating great diversity.

The state contains an extremely diverse selection of wildflowers. Many different ecosystems and microclimates produce showy displays at all times of year. Spring, April and May, is the best time to get the biggest show. The Great Basin is carpeted with brilliant orange globemallow. The Canyonlands explode with ephemeral wildflower shows, especially in wet years. Spring comes at different times at different altitudes, however. The Cottonwood canyons of the Wasatch Front host wildflower enthusiasts in the hundreds in June and early July after the snow melts and flowers bloom. The illusive state flower, the sego lily, blooms in the foothills of Utah in early June. Ubiquitous rabbitbrush covers the desert of the Uintah Basin and Canyonlands with yellow flowers in September. Visit the Red Butte Gardens hotline online for specific flowering dates in each region: *redbutte.utah.edu.*

### ◆ FISHING AND HUNTING

Utah's fishing season—with a few exceptions—is year-round. The sport is regulated by the Utah Division of Wildlife Resources. Licenses can be purchased at their offices in Salt Lake City, Ogden, Springville, Vernal, Price, and Cedar City, on the internet, as well as at most sporting goods stores. Pick up a free fishing update for details on special regulations, limits, and license fees. Anglers can catch trout, bass, walleye, bluegill, whitefish, Bonneville cisco, yellow perch, crappie, and catfish. Hunting seasons are set for deer, elk, antelope, pheasant, duck, geese, sage grouse, forest grouse, chukar partridge, mourning dove, wild turkey, cottontail rabbit, and snowshoe hare. Special permits may be purchased to hunt bear, mountain lion, and bobcat. Once-in-a-lifetime permits for buffalo, desert bighorn sheep, moose, and Rocky Mountain goat are also available via special lottery drawings. Antelope and some deer and elk hunts are on a lottery basis only. Specific hunting regulations are issued annually by the Utah Division of Wildlife Resources. To hunt or fish in Utah, purchase a license at any Utah Division of Wildlife Resources office *(see page 329)* or in most sporting goods stores.

## ◆ NATIONAL PARKS, MONUMENTS, HISTORIC SITES, AND RECREATION AREAS

Utah's national parks, monuments, recreation areas, and historic site are all open year-round. The road into Cedar Breaks National Monument does close in the winter months, but the monument can still be seen by skiers and snowmobilers. Some of the most popular parks are crowded in the summer, but there is always lodging and camping available in private facilities nearby. If you want to camp in Arches, Bryce, Capitol Reef, or Zion National Parks in summer, arrive early in the day to assure yourself a space.

The **Golden Eagle Passport,** for persons over 62, and the **Golden Access Passport,** for the blind and permanently disabled, provide free or discounted entry to the national parks. These passports can be obtained at the parks or agency offices and provide a discount on campsites and other features where a use fee is charged.

**Arches National Park.**
*nps.gov/arch,* PO 125 W. 200 South, Moab, UT 84532; 435-259-8161.

**Bryce Canyon National Park.**
*nps.gov/brea,* Bryce Canyon, UT 85717; 435-834-5322.

**Canyonlands National Park.**
*nps.gov/cany,* Moab, UT 84532; 435-259-7164.

**Capitol Reef National Park.**
*nps.gov/care,* P.O. Box 15 Torrey, UT 84775; 435-425-3791.

**Cedar Breaks National Monument.**
*nps.gov/cebr,* 2390 W. Hwy. 56 #11, Cedar City, UT 84720; 435-586-9451.

**Dinosaur National Monument.**
*nps.gov/dino,* PO Box 4545 Hwy. 40, Dinosaur, CO 81610; 303-374-2216, Quarry Visitor Center; 435-789-2115.

**Flaming Gorge National Recreation Area.**
*fs.fed.us/r4/ashley,* PO Box 279, Manila, UT 84046; 435-784-3445.

**Glen Canyon National Recreation Area.**
*nps.gov/glca,* PO Box 1507, Page, AZ 86040; 520-608-6404.

**Golden Spike National Historic Site.**
*nps.gov/gosp/,* PO Box W, Brigham City, UT 84302; 435-471-2209.

**Grand Staircase-Escalante National Monument.**
*ut.blm.gov/monument,* Escalante Interagency Visitor Center, 755 W. Main, Escalante; 435-826-5499.

**Hovenweep National Monument.**
*nps.gov/hove/,* McElmo Route, Cortez, CO 81321; 970-562-4282.

**Natural Bridges National Monument.**
*nps.gov/nabr,* PO Box 1, Lake Powell, UT 84533; 435-692-1234.

**Timpanogos Cave National Monument.**
*nps.gov/tica/,* RR 3, Box 300, American Fork, UT 84003; 801-756-5238.

**Zion National Park.**
*nps.gov/zion,* PO Box 1099, Springdale, UT 84767; 435-772-3256.

## ◆ NATIONAL FORESTS

Utah's six national forests—all nine-plus million acres of them— range from alpine peaks covered with aspen, pine, and fir to red-rock mountains rich with juniper, piñon, and ponderosa pine. Maps designating roads and areas open to off-highway motorized travel are available at ranger districts and supervisor offices throughout the state. *Campground reservations: Reserve USA, reserveusa.com; 800-284-CAMP (2267).*

**U.S. FOREST SERVICE VISITOR CENTER.**
Union Station, 2501 Wall Ave., Ogden, UT 84401; 801-625-5306

ASHLEY NATIONAL FOREST
**Supervisor; Vernal Ranger District.**
355 N. Vernal, Vernal, UT 84078; 435-789-1181

**Duchesne Ranger District.**
85 W. Main, Duchesne, UT 84021; 435-738-2482

**Flaming Gorge Ranger District Hdqtrs.**
P.O. Box 279, Manila, UT 84046; 435-784-3445

**Roosevelt Ranger District.**
244 W. Hwy. 40, Box 333-6, Roosevelt, UT 84066; 435-722-5018

DIXIE NATIONAL FOREST
**Supervisor; Cedar City Ranger District.**
82 N. 100 East, Cedar City, UT 84720; 435-865-3700

**Escalante Ranger District.**
Escalante Interagency Visitor Center, 755 W. Main, Escalante; 435-826-5499.

**Pine Valley Ranger District.**
Arizona Strip Interagency Association, 345 E. Riverside, St. George, UT 84790; 435-688-3246.

**Powell Ranger District.**
225 E. Center, Panguitch, UT 84759; 435-676-8815

**Teasdale Ranger District.**
138 E. Main, Teasdale, UT 84773; 435-425-3435

FISHLAKE NATIONAL FOREST
**Supervisor; Richfield Ranger District.**
115 E. 900 North, Richfield, UT 84701; 435-896-9233

**Beaver Ranger District.**
575 S. Main, Beaver, UT 84713; 435-438-2436

**Fillmore Ranger District.** 390 S. Main, Fillmore, UT 84631; 435-743-5721

**Loa Ranger District.**
138 S. Main, Loa, UT 84747; 435-836-2811

MANTI-LASAL NATIONAL FOREST
**Supervisor; Price Ranger District.**
599 W. Price River Dr., Price, UT 84501; 435-637-2817

**Ferron Ranger District.**
115 W. Canyon Rd., Ferron, UT 84523; 435-384-2372

**Moab Ranger District.**
Information Center, Main at Center St.; 435-259-8825 or 800-635-6622.

**Monticello Ranger District.**
496 E. Central, Monticello, UT 84535; 435-587-2041.

**Sanpete Ranger District.**
540 N. Main St., Ephraim, UT 84627; 435-283-4151

UINTA NATIONAL FOREST

**Supervisor.**
88 W. 100 North, Provo, UT 84601;
801-377-5780.

**Heber Ranger District.**
2460 S. Hwy. 40, PO Box 190, Heber
City, UT 84032; 435-654-0470.

**Pleasant Grove Ranger District.**
390 N. 100 East, Pleasant Grove, UT
84062; 801-785-3563.

**Spanish Fork Ranger District.**
44 W. 400 North, Spanish Fork, UT
84660; 801-798-3571.

WASATCH-CACHE NATIONAL FOREST

**Supervisor.**
8226 Federal Bldg., 125 South St., Salt
Lake City, UT 84138; 801-524-5030.

**Kamas Ranger District.**
50 E. Center St., PO Box 68, Kamas,
UT 84036; 435-783-4338.

**Logan Ranger District.**
1500 E. Hwy. 89 Logan, UT 84321;
435-753-2772.

**Ogden Ranger District.**
507 25th St., Ogden, UT 84401;
801-625-5112.

**Salt Lake City District.**
6944 S. 3000 East, Salt Lake City,
UT 84121; 801-943-1794.

*The primrose in bloom in the Henry Mountains, BLM land near Hanksville.*

# ◆ Bureau of Land Management

The Bureau of Land Management (BLM) administers 43 percent of the land in Utah, including Grand Staircase–Escalante National Monument. Off-road vehicle use, hiking, and camping are popular in most of these areas. The BLM administers river rafting in both Desolation and Westwater canyons on the Green and Colorado rivers, as well as in a number of primitive areas. Several million acres of BLM land are under consideration for national wilderness area designation. When driving through Utah, BLM offices located throughout the state often provide a good source for topographical maps and advice on hiking and camping conditions. Popular developed BLM recreation sites, like the Little Sahara Sand Dunes near Delta, the Dixie Red Cliffs near St. George, and the Calf Creek area near Escalante, give campers a chance to get away from the more crowded conditions often found in nearby national and state parks. *blm.gov/utah*

**Utah State Office.**
324 S. State St., Salt Lake City, UT 84111; 801-539-4001.

**Cedar City District Office.**
176 East D.L. Sargent Dr., Cedar City, UT 84720; 435-586-2401.

**Fillmore Field Office.**
35 E. 500 North, Fillmore, UT 84631; 435-743-3100.

**Grand Staircase-Escalante National Monument, Interagency Office.**
755 W. Main St., Escalante, UT 84726; 435-826-5600. (also Cannonville Visitor Center. 10 Center St., Cannonville, UT 84718; 435-679-8980).

**Henry Mountains Field Station.**
406 S. First West, Hanksville, UT 84734; 435-542-3461.

**Moab Field Office.**
82 E. Dogwood, P.O. Box 970 Moab, UT 84532; 435-259-6111.

**Monticello Field Office.**
435 N. Main St., Monticello, UT 84535; 435-587-1500.

**Price Field Office.**
125 S. 600 West, Price, UT 84501; 435-636-3600.

Richfield Field Office.
150 E. 900 North, Richfield, UT 84701; 435-896-1500.

**Salt Lake Field Office. (Bear River & Pony Express Resource Area ).**
2370 S. 2300 West, Salt Lake City, UT 84119; 801-977-4300.

**St. George Field Office.**
**Arizona Strip Interagency Association.**
345 E. Riverside Dr., St. George, UT 84790; 435-688-3246

**Vernal District Office. (Diamond Mountain/Book Cliffs Resource Area).**
170 S. 500 East, Vernal, UT 84078; 435-781-4400.

PROFESSIONAL SPORTS

◆ UTAH DIVISION OF PARKS AND RECREATION

The Utah Division of Parks and Recreation administers 45 developed state parks encompassing over 94,000 acres of land and over a million surface acres of water. Its state parks contain individual or group campsites and facilities for boating, hiking, off-highway vehicle use, and other outdoor sports. In addition, several parks contain cultural and natural history museums. *parks.state.ut.us/, 801-538-7220 or camping reservations; 800-322-3770.*

◆ UTAH DIVISION OF WILDLIFE RESOURCES

*nr.state.ut.us/dwr/dwr.htm,* recorded information; 877-592-5169

**Salt Lake Office.**
1594 W. North Temple, Suite 2110; Salt Lake City, UT 84114; 801-538-4700.

**Northern Region.**
515 E. 5300 South, Ogden, UT 84405; 801-476-2740.

**Northeastern Region.**
152 E. 100 North, Vernal, UT 84078; 435-789-3103.

**Central Region.**
1115 N. Main St., Springville, UT 84663; 801-489-5678.

**Southeastern Region.**
475 W. Price River Dr., Suite C, Price, UT 84501; 435-636-0260.

**Southern Region.**
1470 N. Airport Rd., Cedar City, UT 84720; 435-865-6100

■ PROFESSIONAL SPORTS

**Utah Jazz and Utah Starzz**
The NBA's Utah Jazz and the WNBA's Starzz play in the Delta Center. *301 W. South Temple, Salt Lake City; 801-325-7328.*

**Salt Lake Buzz**
Salt Lake City's Franklin Covey Field is the home of the AAA Pacific Coast League's Salt Lake Buzz. An affiliate of the Minnesota Twins, the Buzz sets PCL attendance records. *77 W. 1300 South; 801-485-3800 or SMITHTIX 800-888-TIXX*

**Utah Grizzlies and Utah Freezz**
The Utah Grizzlies, a professional hockey team in the International Hockey League, and the Utah Freezz, a member of the world indoor soccer league, play in the E Center. *3200 S. Decker Lake Dr., West Valley City; 801-988-8888.*

**Utah Blitzz**
This United Soccer League team will play in a new stadium in West Valley City. *21st South at I-215; 801-401-8000.*

**Zion Pioneerzz**
The Western Baseball League's Zion Pionerzz play in St. George. *zionpioneerzz.com*; 435-656-9990 or 887-239-TEAM.

**Ogden Raptors**
The Pioneer League's Ogden Raptors play at Lindquist Field in Ogden. *2330 Lincoln; 801-393-2400*

# ■ GENERAL INFORMATION RESOURCES

**Salt Lake Area Chamber of Commerce.**
400 S. Second East, Salt Lake City;
801-364-3631
*(Cities and large towns also have their own chambers of commerce.)*

**Utah Arts Council.**
617 E. South Temple, Salt Lake City;
801-533-5895
General information and publications on Utah arts organizations.

**Utah Campground Owners Association.**
1370 W. North Temple, Salt Lake City;
801-521-2682
Manages private campgrounds throughout the state, most of which offer more amenities (swimming pools, hookups, showers) than those found in public facilities. Ask for their free brochure.

**Utah Convention and Visitors Bureau.**
180 S. West Temple, Salt Lake City;
801-521-2822.

**Utah Department of Transportation.**
4501 S. 2700 West, Salt Lake City.
**Road report:** 801-964-6000 or
800-752-7600 (toll free within Utah).
**Utah Highway Map.** Road conditions, construction sites.

**Utah Heritage Foundation.**
355 Quince St., Salt Lake City;
801-533-0858
Nonprofit organization. Historic Salt Lake City tours. Publications.

**Utah Hotel Association.**
9 Exchange Pl., Ste. 812, Salt Lake City;
801-359-0104

**Utah State Historical Society.**
300 Rio Grande, Salt Lake City;
801-533-5755
**Library:** Utah, Mormons, the West.
**Photo collections:** Mormons, Utah. Also historical publications and information on historical preservation.

**Utah Travel Council.**
Council Hall/Capitol Hill, Salt Lake City;
801-538-1030 or 800-200-1160
fax 801-538-1399
The Council's free *Utah Travel Guide* includes listings of airlines, taxis, ground tours, guides and outfitters, aerial tours, bicycle tours, backcountry tours, four-wheel-drive tours, hunting and fishing guides, dude ranches, marinas, cabins, river-running, boat tours, Salt Lake City tours, and a tour operator index. Also try the **Tourism and Recreation Information Center** at 801-538-1467.

**Winter Snow Report.**
801-521-8102.

*(following pages) Goblin Valley in Winter.*

# RECOMMENDED READING

■ DESCRIPTION AND TRAVEL

Bannon, Jan. *Utah State Parks.* The Mountaineers, 1995. A comprehensive look at things to do in Utah's state parks.

Carr, Stephen L. *The Historical Guide to Utah Ghost Towns.* Salt Lake City: Western Epics, 1986. Maps, historical photos, and many details.

De Courten, Frank. *Dinosaurs of Utah.* University of Utah Press, 1998. The newest information on Utah's favorite fertile dionsaur grounds. Includes drawings, photos, and color illustrations.

Hirsch, Bob. *Houseboating on Lake Powell.* Phoenix: Primer Press, 1988. A good guide about a great way to see Lake Powell.

Hirsch, Bob and Stan Jones. *Fishin' Lake Powell.* Sun Country Publications. Helpful advice on where and how to catch the lake's gamefish.

Jones, Stan. *Boating and Exploring Map: Lake Powell and Its 96 Canyons.* Sun Country Publications, 1985. This map points out natural features, marinas, Indian sites, hiking trails and four-wheel-drive tracks, points of interest, navigation, history, fishing, and wildlife.

Scholl, Barry and Frances Cannon. *Utah: A Guide to the State.* Gibbs Smith Publisher, 1998. An update to the Utah Writers' Program and the Works Projects Administration.

Sorenson, Ella. *Seductive Beauty of the Great Salt Lake.* Gibbs Smith Publisher, 1997. Artistic photography and essays of the Great Salt Lake.

Smart, William and John Telford. *Utah: A Portrait.* University of Utah Press, 1995. Photos and essays that describe the state's geography.

Thompson, George A. *Some Dreams Die: Utah's Ghost Towns and Lost Treasures.* Salt Lake City: Dream Garden Press, 1982. With his fascinating tales, Thompson encourages readers to seek the lost treasures of the ghost towns.

Till, Tom. *Utah: Magnificent Wilderness.* Newport Beach: Westcliffe Publishers, Inc., 1989. A photographic essay by Tom Till. The foreword was written by Pulitzer Prize winner Wallace Stegner.

Trimble, Stephen. *Blessed By The Light.* Layton: Gibbs M. Smith, Inc., 1986. An anthology of great writing and photography about the Colorado Plateau.

Utah Division of Wildlife Resources. *Lakes of High Uintas.* A series of 10 booklets, 1981-1985, available from Utah Division of Wildlife Resources (1596 West North Temple, Salt Lake City, UT 84116). $1 plus postage. A good practical guide for hikers, fishermen, campers, and packhorse enthusiasts.

Van Cott, John W. *Utah Place Names.* Salt Lake City: University of Utah Press, 1990. How Utah towns and geographic locations got their names.

Wharton, Tom. *Utah! A Family Travel Guide.* Salt Lake City: Wasatch Publishers, Inc., 1987. How to enjoy Utah's outdoors in a way families and older travelers find relaxing

Wharton, Tom, with Craig Hansell and Brett Prettyman. *One Day in Utah.* Salt Lake City: Salt Lake Tribune, 1995. Over 175 write-ups on things to do, local culture and history of Utah cities, national parks and monuments, ski areas, and universities.

## ■ HISTORY

Fradkin, Philip L. *A River No More.* New York: Alfred A. Knopf, 1981. Historical account of water usage in Utah.

May, Dean L. *Utah: A People's History.* Salt Lake City: University of Utah Press, 1987. A look at the history of people living and working in Utah.

*Harry Longbaugh a.k.a. the Sundance Kid and Etta Place (Utah State Historical Society).*

Morgan, Dale L. *The Great Salt Lake.* Albuquerque: University of New Mexico Press, 1947. A history of the lake before late twentieth-century developments.

Powell, John Wesley. *The Exploration of the Colorado River and Its Canyons.* New York: Dover Publications, 1961. First published in 1895, Powell's descriptions are a must for all river lovers.

Schindler, Harold. *In Another Time/ Sketches of Utah History.* Utah State University Press, 1998. First published in the Salt Lake Tribune.

Wallace, Irving. *The Twenty-seventh Wife.* New York: E.P. Dutton, 1962. An account of the private life of Brigham Young, particularly in relation to his twenty-seventh wife. Includes comments from Young's contemporaries and from other historians and students of Mormonism.

Wharton, Tom & Gayen. *It Happened in Utah.* Falcon Publishing, 1998. Twenty-six events that shaped the state.

## ■ HIKING, BICYCLING, SKIING, AND CLIMBING

Barnes, F. A. *Canyon Country Hiking and Natural History.* Salt Lake City: Wasatch Publishers, Inc., 1977. Hiking the canyons and mountains of southeastern Utah.

Hall, David. *The Hiker's Guide to Utah.* Helena: Falcon Press Publishing Co., Inc., 1982. Day and overnight hikes all over Utah, ranging in difficulty.

Kelner, Alexis. *Skiing in Utah: A History.* Self-published, 1980. Full of anecdotes as well as facts.

Kelner, Alexis and David Hanscom. *Wasatch Tours Vols. I and II.* Salt Lake City: Wasatch Publishers, Inc., 1993 & 1995. A comprehensive look at ski touring in the Wasatch Mountains with maps, trails, and avalanche information.

Kelsey, Michael R. *Canyon Country Hiking Guide to the Colorado Plateau.* Provo: Kelsey Publishing, 1986. A good guide with maps to hikes in the Utah, Colorado, and New Mexico areas of the Colorado Plateau. Also by Kelsey, *Hiking Utah's San Rafael Swell* (Provo: Kelsey Publishing, 1986) provides historical information and maps of the Swell's hidden canyons.

Lambrechtse, Rudi. *Hiking the Escalante*. Salt Lake City: Wasatch Publishers, Inc., 1985. Descriptions and maps for 42 hikes of varying difficulty.

Ringholz, Raye Carleson. *Park City Trails*. Salt Lake City: Wasatch Publishers, Inc., 1984. Tour descriptions of hikes and cross-country treks in the mountains and canyons surrounding this historical mining town.

Veranth, John. *Hiking the Wasatch*. Salt Lake City: Wasatch Publishers, Inc., 1988. Hiking trails of varying difficulty through the Wasatch Mountains east of Salt Lake City.

Wharton, Tom and Gayen. *An Outdoor Family Guide to the Southwest*. Four Corners: The Mountaineers, 1995. Descriptions of hikes under 3 miles and other tourist information for the Four Corners region.

Wood, John. *Cache Trails*. Salt Lake City: Wasatch Publishers, Inc., 1987. Hiking trails in the mountains of northern Utah near Logan.

## ■ RIVER-RUNNING

Abbey, Edward. *Down the River*. New York: E.P. Dutton, 1982. Abbey's descriptions of travels along rivers through deserts of the West. River-runners like to quote from this book. Also by Abbey is *Desert Solitaire*. Tucson: University of Arizona Press, 1988 (reprint). Originally published in 1971, and one of Abbey's most prized essay collections. Much of the book describes Arches National Monument.

Zwinger, Ann. *Run, River, Run: A Naturalist's Journey Down One of the Great Rivers of the American West*. New York: Harper and Row, 1975. The author's experiences along the Green and Colorado rivers mixed with her knowledge of geology, Indian ruins, plants, and wildlife.

## ■ ARCHAEOLOGY

LeBlanc, Steven A.. *Prehistoric War in the American Southwest*. University of Utah Press, 1999. Controversial new information and theories on the prehistoric Basketmakers and Pueblo Indians.

# ■ NATURAL SCIENCES

Barnes, F.A. *Canyon Country Geology for the Layman and Rockhound.* Salt Lake City: Wasatch Publishers, Inc., 1978. Geologic history; rockhounding guide.

Fiero, Bill. *Geology of the Great Basin.* Reno: University of Nevada Press, 1986. Comprehensive and fairly easy for the non-geologist to understand.

Shaw, Richard J. *Utah Wildflowers.* Logan: Utah State University Press, 1995. A guide to the state's wildflowers, complete with color photographs.

Sigler, William F. and Robert Rush Miller. *Fishes of Utah.* Salt Lake City: Utah Division of Wildlife Resources, 1963. Descriptions, illustrations, and life histories of Utah's fish.

Welsh, Stanley L. and Bill Ratcliffe. *Flowers of the Canyon Country.* Moab: Canyonlands Natural History Association, 1986.

# ■ REFERENCE

*Utah Atlas & Gazetteer: Topo Maps of the Entire State.* Freeport, ME: DeLorme Mapping, 1993. A book full of detailed topographical maps of Utah ideal for exploring the state's many backroads.

# ■ MISCELLANEOUS

Grey, Zane. *Riders of the Purple Sage.* New York: Pocket Books, Inc., 1974. Also by Grey is *The Rainbow Trail* (Santa Barbara: Santa Barbara Press, 1985).

Lyon, Thomas and Terry Tempest Williams, ed.. *A Great and Peculiar Beauty/ A Utah Reader.* Gibbs Smith Publisher, 1995. A collection of essays from Utah's diverse inhabitants throughout its history.

Twain, Mark. *Innocents Abroad* and *Roughing It.* New York: Library of America, 1984.

Williams, Terry Tempest. *Refuge.* New York: Vintage, 1991. A personal look at the "dying" of the Great Salt Lake waterfowl refuges, told as the narrator's mother dies.

# I N D E X

**Abajo Mountains** 14, 264;
  *also see Blue Mountains*
Abbey, Edward 207, 256
Abravanel, Maurice 11, 130-132
accommodations 303, 305-320
Adams Memorial Theatre 211
Alpine Loop 142
Alta 279, *280,* 281-282; food & lodging 306
American West Heritage Center 151
Anasazi *see Ancestral Puebloans*
Anasazi State Park 26, 28, 233
Ancestral Puebloans 25-28, 33-36, 42, 43, 232, 23, 266-272
Antelope Island 17, 198, 202
antelope 25, 38
Apache 44
archaeology 25-35, 40, 42, 178, 232, 233, 266-272
Arches National Park 14, 250-252, 326
Arizona 12, 13, 43, 44, 84, 266, 272
art galleries and exhibits ; *also see specific museums*
Ashdown Gorge Wilderness 215
Ashley, William 52, 147
Ashley National Forest 327
Assembly Hall 108
Astor, John Jacob 52
*atlatl* 26
Atwood, Genevieve 201-203

**backpacking** 11, 154, 160, 215, 229, 238, 240, 246, 324, 326-329
Baker, James *58*
Ballet West 129, 131, 132
Barrett, Bob 284
Basin and Range 13, 16-19
Basketmakers 26, 269; *also see Anasazi*
baskets 27
Bassett, Ann
Bear Lake 56, 152-153
Bear River 156
Bear River Migratory Bird Refuge 322, 324
Beaver Mountain 279, 289
Beaver 210
Beaver Dam Wash 222
Beckwourth, Jim 147
Beehive House 73, 109
Bernstein, Leonard 131
Bicknell 239
Big Cottonwood Canyon *283,* 284
Big Rock Candy Mountain 17
Bingham Canyon 188, 190
Bingham Copper Mine 17, 188
birdwatching 193, 222, 324-325
Black Hawk War 41, 192
Blackfoot 50
Blacksmith Fork Canyon 152
Blanding 28, 40, 42, 244, 266, 268, 269; food & lodging 306
Blue Mountain 264

Bluff 28, 40, 42, 269
boating 153, 163, 243-244, 324
Bonneville Salt Flats 12, 199, 200
Bonneville Speedway 199-201
*Book of Mormon* 63, 64, 67, 91, 146
boomtowns 81, 188-192
Boulder 233; food & lodging 307
Boulder Mountains 233
Bountiful 139
Braithwaite, Wilbur 145-146
Brannan, Sam 66
Breedlove, Craig 199
Brian Head 16, 213, 215, 279, 290
Bridger, Jim 50, 52, 80
Brigham City 62, 149, 187, 188, ; food & lodging 307
Brigham Young University 98, 99, 140-142
Brighton, William S. 284
Brighton 279, 284
brine shrimp 196
bristlecone pine 215, 225
Brown's Park 165-166
Brown, Baptiste 165
Browne Lake 159
Bryce Canyon National Park 16, 224-225, *226-227, 325;* food & lodging 307-308
Buchanan, James 75, 79
buffalo or bison 38, 193, 246, 324, 325

Bureau of Land Management 22, 28, 182, 184, 193, 329
Burr Trail 238
Burton, Sir Richard 76-78
*Butch Cassidy and the Sundance Kid* 134, 212-213, 222-223
Butler Wash 266

**Cache County** 149-153
California 44-46, 54, 66, 72, 84, 182, 185
California Trail 180
Camp Floyd 184
Campbell, Sir Malcolm 199
camping 324, 326-330
Cannonville 229
Canyons, The 279, 287
Canyonlands Field Institute 42
Canyonlands National Park 13, 30-31, 60, 249, 256-263, 325
Capitol, Utah State 100, 111
Capitol Reef National Park 13, 19, 236-239, 325; food & lodging 308; map 237
Capitol Theatre 129, 133
Carnegie, Andrew 22
Cascade Springs 142
Cassidy, Butch 166, 213; *also see* Parker, Robert LeRoy
Cataract Canyon 11, 12
Cathedral of the Madeleine 100, 110
Catholics 10, 109, 110, 139
caves 144
Cedar Breaks National Monument 213-215, 325

Cedar City 42, 210; food & lodging 308-309
Cedars State Park 32
Central Pacific 185, 196
Chaco Canyon 28, 266
Chief Kanosh 40, 210
Chief Ouray 41
Chief Posey 41
Chief Sowiette 40
China Meadows 158
Chinese 187
Chinle Wash 34
Christensen, William 132
Christmas 92, 103, 323
Cleveland, Grover 89
Cleveland-Lloyd Quarry 20, 22, 176
cliff dwellings 266, 269, 272
climate 12, 303
Clinton, Bill 229, 230
College of Eastern Utah 42
Colorado 13, 28, 84, 266, 272
Colorado Plateau 13-16, 17-22, 24, 45, 52, 61, 222, 263, 325
Colorado River 13, *14*, 16, 25, 49, 56, 58, 61, 79, 84, 95-96, 209, 232-233, 240, 241, 244, 247, 249, 256
Columbia River 52, 54
Comanches 48, 56
Comb Ridge *14*
Comb Wash 41
Comstock Lode 73
Connor, Patrick Edward 80, 137
continental drift 13
Coral Pink Sand Dunes State Park 223-224

Corinne 187
Corn Creek Canyon 210
Coronado, Francesco Vasquez de 44
Cortez, Hernán 44
cotton 220
Cottonwood Canyon 229
Council Hall 113
Council of the Twelve 65
cross-country skiing 263, 292-294

**dance** 146, 148-150, 322-323
Dance Hall Rock 85, 232-233
Davis, Mel 293
Days of '47 103, 323
Dead Horse Point State Park 258
Deer Valley 131, 279, 286
Deering, John 144
Delta 192
Delta Center 11, 98, 103
Deseret, State of 67, *69*, 71, 73, 75, 80
*Deseret News* 87, 89, 111
Deseret Peak 180
desert 12, 25, 38, 55, 180, 184, 192, 229
DeVries, William 120
dining out 304-320; *also see* restaurants
Dinosaur National Monument 20-22, 166-175, 325
dinosaurs 20-22, 148, 166-175, 176
Dirty Devil River 246
Dixie National Forest 233, 327
Dominguez, Francisco Atanasio 38, 45, 46, 48

Dominguez-Escalante Journal 45

Donner party 180

drought 25, 33, 220

Duchesne 161

Duchesne River 156, 159

Dugway Proving Grounds 55

Duncan, Clifford 36

**earthquakes** 17, 18, 19, 201-203

Eccles Dinosaur Park 148

Edge of the Cedars State Historical Park 266

Elk Meadows 279, 290

Emigration Canyon 139, 146

Ephraim 145, 322; food & lodging 309

erosion 12-14, 16, 165, 241

Escalante Canyon 229

Escalante Interagency Visitors Center 232, 327, 329

Escalante Petrified Forest State Park 22, 232

Escalante River 230

Escalante, Silvestre Velez de 38, 44, 46, 49

Eureka 188, 191

explorers 44-61

**Farmington** 196

fauna 192, 193, 217, 324-325

festivals and events 322-323

Festival of the American West 152, 322

Fiery Furnace 14

Fillmore 209

Fish Springs Nat'l Wildlife Refuge 193

fishing and hunting 137, 144, 148, 153, 158, 159, 160-161, 163, 164, 210, 232, 233, 243-244, 324, 325, 329

Fishlake National Forest 210, 239, 327

Flaming Gorge 52, 56, *162*, 163-165, 325; food & lodging 309

flora 225, 229, 325

food & lodging 305-320; map 305

Fort Buenaventura State Park 50, 322

Fort Deseret 192

Fort Douglas 80, 123, 187

Fort Duchesne 43

Fort Panguitch 36

fossils 12, 20, 22, 166-175, 192

Four Corners 266, 272

Fradkin, Philip L. 95

Frémont, John C. 66

Fremont Indian State Park 27

Fremont Indians 25-27, 33-34, 36, 42, 178, 238

Fremont River 238

Frisco 188

Fruita 236

**Gabelich, Gary** 199

Garden City 153

general information resources 331

geology 12-22, 165, 166, 201-203, 236, 252

Glen Canyon Dam 243

Glen Canyon National Recreation Area 243, 326

Goblin Valley 241-243, *332-333*

Golden Spike National Historic Site 184-187, 326

Gold Hill 184, 188, 191

gold rush 99, 182

Goodyear, Miles 147

Goshute Indians 35, 36, 38, 43, 180

Grafton 222-223

Grand Canyon 12, 223

Grand Circle 26, 266-272

Grand Gulch Primitive Area 269

Grand Staircase–Escalante National Monument 229-23, 326

Grant, Ulysses S. 86

Grantsville 180

Great Basin 16- 22, 27, 54, 179-205, 222, 325

Great Basin National Park 54, 192

Great Salt Lake 10, 12, 16, 17, 43, 45, 48, 50, 54-55, 59, 179, 180, 196

Great Salt Lake Desert 55, 179

Great Salt Lake Valley 67, 71, 75, 79, 80, 92

Greeley, Horace 78, 184

Green River 15, 49, 56, 58, *172-173*, 174, 240-241

Green River State Park 241

Grey, Zane 244, 262

Gunnison Massacre Monument 192

**Haight, Isaac** 79

Hanksville 243

Hansen Planetarium 113

Hardware Ranch 152, 325

Heber City 62, 175

Utah Museum of Natural History   21, 122
Utah Opera Company   129, 131
Utah State University   150-151
Utah Symphony   130-132
Utah Territory   75, 86, 89, 187
Utah Travel Council   113, 332
Ute Indians   25, 33, 35, 36, 38, 41, 40, 43, 50, 52, 60139, 180

Vernal   163, 175; food & lodging   319
Virgin River   25, 59, 217
volcanoes   17

Wahweap   49
Walker War   36, 40, 192
Wasatch Fault   17-19
Wasatch Front   11, 17, 18, 136-153, 180; map   138
Wasatch Mountain State Park   293, 294, 330
Wasatch -Cache National Forest   292

water   95-96
watermelon   240
Wayne, John   248
Weber River   149, 156
Weber State University   147-148
Wellsville Mountains   137, 149, *150*
Wendover, Nevada   200
Wheeler Farm   126
White Mesa Indian Reservation   41
Wild Bunch   213
wilderness areas   137, 139, 192, 215, 229, 264
wildlife   152, 217, 246, 325
wildlife refuges   149, 152, 156, 193-194, 325
Wilson, Woodrow   174
Winter Olympics (2002)   123, 176, 296-301; map   301
Wolfe Ranch   252
Woodruff, Wilford
Wyoming   84, 178

'Young, Brigham   10, 11, 40, 65-67, 69, 71, 72, 73, 75, 76-81, 87, 98, 103, 127, 146, 147, 149, 151, 188, 220, *221*
Young, John   196

Zion   69
Zion National Park   12, 13, 42, 215-217, *218-219,* 326; food & lodging   320
Zion's Cooperative Mercantile   81, 100, 114
Zuni Plateau   34

# COMPASS
# AMERICAN
# GUIDES

*Compass American Guides are available in general and travel bookstores, or may be ordered directly by calling (800) 733-3000. Please provide title and ISBN when ordering.*

**Alaska**
(2nd edition)
$19.95 ($27.95 Can)
0-679-00230-8

**Arizona**
(5th edition)
$19.95 ($29.95 Can)
0-679-00432-7

**Boston**
(2nd edition)
$19.95 ($27.95 Can)
0-679-00284-7

**Chicago**
(2nd edition)
$18.95 ($26.50 Can)
1-878-86780-6

**Coastal California**
(2nd edition)
$21.00 ($32.00 Can)
0-679-00439-4

**Colorado**
(5th edition)
$19.95 ($29.95 Can)
0-679-00435-1

**Florida**
(1st edition)
$19.95 ($27.95 Can)
0-679-03392-0

**Georgia**
(1st edition)
$19.95 ($29.95 Can)
0-679-00245-6

**Gulf South**
(1st edition)
$21.00 ($32.00 Can)
0-679-00533-1

**Hawaii**
(4th edition)
$19.95 ($27.95 Can)
0-679-00226-X

**Idaho**
(1st edition)
$18.95 ($26.50 Can)
1-878-86778-4

**Las Vegas**
(6th edition)
$19.95 ($29.95 Can)
0-679-00370-3

**Maine**
(3rd edition)
$19.95 ($29.95 Can)
0-679-00436-X

**Manhattan**
(3rd edition)
$19.95 ($29.95 Can)
0-679-00228-6

**Minnesota**
(2nd edition)
$19.95 ($29.95 Can)
0-679-00437-8

**Montana**
(4th edition)
$19.95 ($29.95 Can)
0-679-00281-2

**Nevada**
(1st edition)
$21.00 ($32.00 Can)
0-679-00535-8

**New Mexico**
(4th edition)
$21.00 ($32.00 Can)
0-679-00438-6

| **New Orleans** (4th edition) $21.00 ($32.00 Can) 0-679-00647-8 | **North Carolina** (2nd edition) $19.95 ($29.95 Can) 0-679-00508-0 | **Oregon** (3rd edition) $19.95 ($27.95 Can) 0-679-00033-X | **Pacific Northwest** (2nd edition) $19.95 ($27.95 Can) 0-679-00283-9 | **Pennsylvania** (1st edition) $19.95 ($29.95 Can) 0-679-00182-4 |

| **San Francisco** (5th edition) $19.95 ($29.95 Can) 0-679 -00229-4 | **Santa Fe** (3rd edition) $19.95 ($29.95 Can) 0-679-00286-3 | **South Carolina** (3rd edition) $19.95 ($29.95 Can) 0-679-00509-9 | **South Dakota** (2nd edition) $18.95 ($26.50 Can) 1-878-86747-4 | **Southern New England** (1st ed) $19.95 ($29.95 Can) 0-679-00184-0 |

| **Southwest** (3rd edition) $21.00 ($32.00 Can) 0-679-00646-X | **Texas** (2nd edition) $18.95 ($26.50 Can) 1-878-86798-9 | **Underwater Wonders of the National Parks** $19.95 ($27.95 Can) 0-679-03386-6 | **Utah** (4th edition) $18.95 ($26.50 Can) 0-679-00030-5 | **Vermont** (1st edition) $19.95 ($27.95 Can) 0-679-00183-2 |

| **Virginia** (3rd edition) $19.95 ($29.95 Can) 0-679-00282-0 | **Washington** (2nd edition) $19.95 ($27.95 Can) 1-878-86799-7 | **Wine Country** (3rd edition) $21.00 ($32.00 Can) 0-679-00434-3 | **Wisconsin** (2nd edition) $18.95 ($26.50 Can) 1-878-86749-0 | **Wyoming** (3rd edition) $19.95 ($27.95 Can) 0-679-00034-8 |

# ■ ABOUT THE AUTHORS

Tom and Gayen Wharton are natives of Utah who have spent much of their lives exploring and enjoying the many cultural and recreational opportunities found in their state.

The Whartons both graduated with honors from the University of Utah, where Gayen earned her degree in education and Tom studied journalism.

Tom has been a sports writer and outdoor editor for the *Salt Lake Tribune* since 1970. His first book, *Utah! A Family Travel Guide,* appeared in 1987. His work has been published in many magazines, including *Field and Stream* and *Outdoor Life.* A member of the Outdoor Writers Association of America, he has captured numerous national and local awards for his journalism. He is listed in *Who's Who in the West.*

Gayen has taught elementary school for eight years, and has been active in a number of community service projects. She served as vice-chairman of her local community council, a member of the Board of Directors of the Salt Lake City YWCA, and as a member of the Utah League of Women Voters.

Tom and Gayen, with their four children, love to spend as much time as possible in Utah's great outdoors, camping, hiking, backpacking, fishing, and skiing.

# ■ ABOUT THE PHOTOGRAPHER

Tom Till is one of the premier American Landscape photographers in the United States. His work has appeared in a number of books on the American West and Southwest, including *Colorado, Images from Above,* an aerial portrait of the state, which he also authored. His photography frequently appears in magazines such as *Audubon, Wilderness, Sierra* and *Omni,* as well as in calendars for both the National-al Geographic Society and the Audubon Society.

When not on the road capturing images for his photo stock library, Tom makes his home in Moab, Utah, where he enjoys the beauty of Utah's magnificence with his wife Marcy and their two children.